ontinued from front flap)

ie studies in this collection do not
etend to offer any single key to un-
erstanding the totality of the Shake-
ean achievement; rather each il-
es a significant area of knowledge.
sources of modern

the
enon

TWENTIETH CENTURY VIEWS

The aim of this series is to present the best in contemporary critical opinion on major authors, providing a twentieth century perspective on their changing status in an era of profound revaluation.

Maynard Mack, *Series Editor*
Yale University

SHAKESPEARE
THE TRAGEDIES

SHAKESPEARE
THE TRAGEDIES

A COLLECTION OF CRITICAL ESSAYS

Edited by

Alfred Harbage

DELTA COLLEGE LIBRARY

A SPECTRUM BOOK

Prentice-Hall, Inc., *Englewood Cliffs, N. J.*

PR 2983 .H27 1964

Harbage, Alfred, 1901-

Shakespeare : the tragedies

© 1964 BY PRENTICE-HALL, INC.

ENGLEWOOD CLIFFS, N. J.

All rights reserved. No part of this book may be reproduced in any form, by mimeograph or any other means, without permission in writing from the publishers.

LIBRARY OF CONGRESS CATALOG CARD NO.: 64-23068

Printed in the United States of America

C
P80773
C80774

Table of Contents

Introduction

by Alfred Harbage

I have tried, in this collection, to choose essays which express the present without repudiating the past. Although controversy, and perhaps even bustling novelty, have a place in the dialogue we call Criticism, that place must of necessity be limited in so small a sampling as is offered here. Hence the absence of quick-acting stimulants and splenetic ripostes. My ideal has been to display twentieth century criticism of Shakespeare's tragedies as a necessary supplement to that of A. C. Bradley and his predecessors and to let the individual essays work together in suggesting the nature of that supplement. Perhaps the essay most dogmatic in tone is my own, included in exercise of the inalienable right of anthologists, but this only illustrates the difficulty of practicing what one preaches. In general I have wished to exclude dogmatism, as well as manifestoes or testimonials of faith in particular critical "schools."

My chief regret is that I have provided so few samplings of the whole books devoted to Shakespearean tragedy or to individual tragedies. The reason is that the book-length studies resist excerption. The excerpt is apt either to misrepresent the book or to seem dilute. The reader is strongly recommended to explore for himself the items in the appended bibliography. So far as the pieces included are concerned, the principle of selection has been simple. Is the critic saying something revealing, saying it well, and in a manner that proves he is truly concerned? Further than that, does what he is saying bear up under objective examination? The question of whether an essay provides, in sufficient measure, a "twentieth century" view is less difficult than might be supposed. One need only ask if it could have been written as it stands in Bradley's time or before.

Most pre-twentieth century criticism placed the main emphasis upon characters and their psychological truth to life, and upon the specific moral lessons taught by the plays. Thus, the first recorded word of praise for *King Lear* mentioned the distinction adroitly maintained between Lear's "real" and Edgar's "pretended" madness. The distinction is there —and it deserves praise. We should not lose sight of it even though we are no doubt right in viewing it as less important in the total scheme of

1

the play than our ancestors seem to have done. It may be unfair to cite
the oldest *Lear* criticism in illustrating the hazards of the narrowly mor-
alistic approach, but the fact remains that the play was damned so long
as it was assumed to be a preachment against "filial ingratitude." Cordelia should not have been allowed to suffer. Although the criticism
rather than the play was defective, we must not forget that the play does
indeed condemn "filial ingratitude." The critical gain lies in the recognition not that the play does something different but that it does something more.

The nineteenth century put us on the right road in our estimate of
King Lear. Although nineteenth century criticism may seem to us to have
been too prone to view *Hamlet* as a homily against sloth, *Othello* as a
homily against jealousy, *Macbeth* as a homily against ambition, it is
absurd to pretend that such criticism persistently mistook dramatic characters for "real" people or was impervious to larger ethical and philosophical issues, to the poetic quality of the plays, or even to the significance of their historical background. The older critics were more concerned than we with the more obvious things, principally because there
was still much to be said about them. We should be grateful that they
left us something to do.

What distinguishes twentieth century criticism is its attempt to broaden
the base of inquiry with respect to both form and content. The German
romantics and Coleridge spoke of "organic form," but critics still found
it difficult to discuss the structure of the plays except in terms of such
things as "exposition" or "climax" or the presumed function of each of
the presumed "acts." Ideas of structure are now less limited, and although
there is danger that the word "structure" may become a meaningless
counter if its plasticity increases indefinitely, there is surely value in our
present recognition that the nature and arrangement of verbal components must be stressed in the discussion of anything so inclusive as "structure." Many things are subsumed under the heading of "organic form."

In the search for meaning, there is now less concern with practical
moral instruction than with philosophical vistas. The criticism of the
past tended to seek in the plays, by no means fruitlessly, confirmation of
its own moral and religious orthodoxy. The criticism of the present tends
to seek, again not fruitlessly, systems sufficiently hospitable or ill-defined
to accommodate its heterodoxy. At the same time the present is conscious
of the dangers of anachronism. We inform ourselves about "Elizabethan"
attitudes and beliefs in order, ideally, to determine the extent of Shakespeare's conformity or nonconformity with them; or else we bypass these
attitudes and beliefs by· viewing his works in the context of universal
myths, symbols, and rituals.

Since we are now committed to "frames of reference" ranging in size
from the ideal generic form of tragedy to the all-embracing tragic "pre-

dicament," perhaps the most useful thing I can do in the present introduction is to suggest the nature of Shakespeare's tragic inheritance, especially since I have been able to find no essay on the subject that is sufficiently brief. Such a sketch must deal with the substance and purpose of tragedy rather than its form, because popular Elizabethan Tragedy inherited no form, Senecan or other, which distinguishes it from History or Comedy. It adopted no formal conventions such as the Chorus or the "Unities," or even simplicity of design. A Tragedy might be as *episodic* as a History or as *complicated* as a Comedy. It was defined not by its structure, in the obvious sense of that term, but by its subject matter and informing spirit. It had to end in the meaningful death of its single or dual protagonist—just as popular Comedy had to end in meaningful marriage.

Poets of the Middle Ages and the emerging Renaissance told sad stories of the deaths of kings and called the stories "Tragedies." They were not great works of art, were not even plays, but the playwrights of Shakespeare's generation derived their notions of the substance and purpose of Tragedy mainly from this proliferating body of mortuary verse. The stories, if viewed singly, seem only lugubrious biography, pieced out with laments about the bitch-goddess Fortune and the iniquities of men. But they should not be viewed singly. Always presented in clusters, or in relation to existing clusters, each conforms to a pattern which each helps to create, and the pattern itself is *Tragedy*.

The pattern is single yet multiple, a basic concept with overlays. The basic concept is old and may be said to express either pagan pessimism or Christian resignation, according to the point of view. In the words of Aelius Donatus of the fourth century, who viewed Tragedy as the reverse image of Comedy: "The moral of tragedy is that life should be rejected." The idea of terrestrial justice is excluded. Since virtue confers no immunity to death, and death is the nub, virtue must be seen as conferring no immunity to death's preliminary pangs in worldly reversal. Suffering and death are not avoidable accidents in a rational world of cause and effect but inevitable curses in an idiot universe where all are at the mercy of chance as symbolized by Fortune's wheel. Or, in religious terms, where all are sojourners in a sublunary world of evil, a "vale of tears" where innocent and guilty writhe alike as they sink to the final horror—to that *death* which is meted out as punishment not to wicked men but to sinful Man.

This might almost be called "*ur*-tragedy," since pure examples are rare. The best in English is Chaucer's *Monk's Tale*. The Monk tells seventeen of the hundred "tragedies" he has garnered in his cell, and in most of them the victim is morally blameless. Vicious Nero perishes miserably, but so also does virtuous Zenobia. There is the point—the good and bad share the same earthly fate. Chaucer's definition of Tragedy, several times repeated, is that of Donatus—and, surprisingly enough, so also is that of Shakespeare's contemporary Thomas Heywood, even in so ebullient a work as his *Apology for Actors*. In spite of the social eminence of the typical protagonist (lending itself to the exciting movement of steep rise and steep fall), the mood of this kind of Tragedy is egalitarian, with Death the "leveler" as in James Shirley's famous dirge—

> Sceptre and crown
> Must tumble down,
> And in the dust be equal made
> With the poor humble scythe and spade.

Since the dirge appears in *The Contention of Ajax and Ulysses,* 1658, which rings down the final curtain on Renaissance drama, we have witness of the persistence of an idea.

This *"contemptus mundi* tragedy," as it may be conveniently called, is no glozing stuff. It treats the greatest thing happening to the great, and invites all men to face up to mortality. But though big and honest, it is monolithic and inscrutable, and it daunts artistry by saying what it has to say once and for all, inviting no refinement of its message. If a great dramatist were to write once in this mode—let us say on the fate of the Monk's Zenobia—he would never have to write another tragedy, but simply append an affidavit as to his pagan or Christian orthodoxy. It tends to divest human actions of meaning, since rejection of life is the only significant choice available to humanity. It could not survive unmodified in an age of enterprise.

The impulse to give Tragedy greater moral utility and artistic viability was operating before Chaucer's Monk bored the Canterbury Pilgrims. It is evident in Boccaccio's *De Casibus Virorum Illustrium* of the 1360's, more evident in Lydgate's expansive redaction of the French version in *The Fall of Princes* of the 1430's, and overwhelmingly evident in the continuation of the latter between 1559 and 1610, when Baldwin and Higgins, with sundry aides and interlopers, begat the monumental *Mirror for Magistrates*. In this vast accretion of tragic tales we see biblical, classical, and medieval history and legend ransacked for suffering princes who deserved all they got. Seneca's stories (to call them his) were incorporated before Seneca's plays were widely read. The fifteenth century supplied the cursed dynasties of York and Lancaster, and the sixteenth its home-grown Jasons and next-door Clytemnestras. Queen Elizabeth's nearest kinsmen were tactfully omitted from the fatal roll, but the memory of their lives provided the right atmosphere. Since the object was moral and political admonition, the power of Fortune appears decreasingly decisive: "It is not she that pryncis gaff the fall," said Lydgate, "but viscious lyvyng." Even though Fortune is still constantly arraigned, the typical protagonist is a tyrant, or one who aspires to tyranny, or one who feeds on tyranny's nauseous fruits, often as a "remorseless, treacherous, lecherous, kindless villain." With some consternation, we observe human action becoming significant by being reprehensible, and the mystery of evil boxed up as the willful wickedness of particular men.

This "*de casibus* tragedy" in its modification of the original concept has the dubious merit of being easily understood, easily defensible against Philistine attacks upon the triviality of poetry, and easily, indeed explosively, adaptable to the theater. At its best it converts Tragedy into a juridical display of trespass, arrest, and execution; at its worst, into a spectacle of lust and bloodshed, exploiting the fascination of sin while preaching that sin does not pay. Revenge became a favorite motif because the agent of retribution is himself subject to retribution and can be sent to slaughter along with his victim. Sometimes the protagonist is a mere master of intrigue, while death loses its cosmic dignity and becomes a sensational toy. It is interesting to observe that the overt preoccupation with death, as evidenced in the *danse macabre* and similar fashions, was a fairly late medieval manifestation, appearing concurrently with the increased value placed upon life. It is as if, with the waning of resignation, the idea of death had become so horrible that it had to be reduced to familiarity—domesticated, so to speak—with the ubiquitous graveyard tokens functioning as a kind of *contemptus mori*. Shakespeare himself was no heir to morbidity. With him, death remained meaningful.

Abuse of the retributive theme helps explain why Elizabethan tragedies are so often fine theater and so seldom fine Tragedy; why the age produced no succession of great tragic poets like ancient Greece but really only one. The *de casibus* development in tragic tales, and now on the stage as well, is reflected in critical writing. Puttenham makes an unclassical distinction between the substance of epic and of tragic poetry and says that "poets, finding in men generally much to reprove and litle to praise, made . . . three kinds of poems reprehensive, to wit the Satyre, the Comedie, and the Tragedie." Philip Sidney drew all his examples of virtuous action from epic poetry and of vicious action from dramatic poetry, especially tragedies, but his definition of Tragedy is a composite: ". . . high and excellent Tragedy, that openeth the greatest wounds, and sheweth forth the Ulcers that are covered with Tissue; that maketh Kinges feare to be Tyrants, and Tyrants manifest their tirranicial humors"—thus far the currently dominant idea of tragedy as *reprehensive,* but Sidney continues—"that, with sturring the effects of admiration [*i.e.,* wonder] and commisseration, teacheth the uncertainety of this world, and upon how weake foundations guilden roofes are builded. . . ." This is the *contemptus mundi* concept, recessive but persistent, tinctured with distorted rumors from Aristotle. Like all Elizabethan definitions, it is utilitarian but non-Aristotelian, embracing what Aristotle had specifically rejected—the idea of the protagonist as villain, and the psychological effect as dissuasion from crime. It is not the *Poetics* but the Donatan formula that provides it with its second, more spiritual dimension.

At this point the tragic poet is in the odd position of having made guilt meaningful but leaving innocence meaningless. The fate of the wicked is rationalized, but the fate of the innocent victim of wickedness must be referred to the residual *contemptus mundi* concept where innocence is meaningful, if at all, only as it establishes credentials for existence in a better world to come. Virtuous princes make poor protagonists. In the *de casibus* version of the Lear story, Cordelia must be the protagonist, since her father died a natural death. After leading an exemplary life, she is imprisoned by evil nephews and is impelled to hang herself in despair. This gives Higgins a chance to moralize upon her damnation. Cordelia's shining career is meaningless since it is cancelled out by her final act. Obviously, virtue has become superfluous in Tragedy, indeed a positive embarrassment.

But we have another modification to record. *De casibus* Tragedy could not maintain complete isolation from heroic and commemorative poetry, especially in those instances where virtuous actions led to immediate death. Great men had died defending their country and loved ones, great women in defending their honor. Their stories importuned the compilers of the admonitory tomes, so that a few unblemished heads rise stubbornly in the guilty throng, such as that of Alcibiades in Boccaccio and Lydgate, that of Nennius in Baldwin and Higgins. Lydgate restored the supreme power of the goddess Fortune long enough to absolve Alcibiades, whom he dispatched to the House of Fame. After 1559 a step toward dramatic form was taken by letting the complaining ghosts of the afflicted tell their own stories. The line against good ghosts was pretty firmly held until 1587, when the *Mirror for Magistrates* was supposedly completed, but ghosts continued to rise, especially good ones, and these now voiced the supplementary complaint that they had been excluded from the *Mirror:* the bad ones had been enjoying all the publicity.

Its form and concluding emphasis prevent Shakespeare's *Lucrece* from providing a good illustration of this trend, but illustrations are provided by the narrative verse of another popular playwright, Michael Drayton, in his tragic tale of *Matilda* (1594)—"All things decay, yet Vertue shall not dye"—and his *Robert Duke of Normandy* (1596). Matilda joined the chaste paragons of antiquity, Virginia, Lucrece, Sophonisba; her story, like theirs, was given form on the stage as well as in "mirror" or "complaint" narratives. In 1601 John Weever offered the example of Sir John Oldcastle in verses titled *Mirror for Martyrs*. In 1610 Richard Niccols rearranged the *Mirror for Magistrates* and tried to correct its imbalance by adding "worthie mirrours."

No age hath bin, since nature first began
To work Iove's wonders, but hath left behind
Some deeds of praise for Mirrours unto man.

Most of these tragic tales of the virtuous had their theatrical counter-
parts, usually in texts never printed. Like other forms of Elizabethan
idealism, the taste for self-sacrificing heroism was popular, even humble,
and the poets who catered to it are often listed with the literary disrepu-
tables. However, we must be careful not to disregard them, since Shakespeare has the distracting habit of mingling his voice with theirs. Nicolls,
in his valedictory addition to *de casibus* tragedy of the narrative sort,
lets "memory" preside and usher in the good ghosts with the trump of
Fame: their deeds have defeated death by keeping their names alive as
an enduring inspiration to mankind. A few definitions of stage Tragedy,
like Chapman's of 1611, include the note that it provides "elegant and
sententious excitation to virtue" as well as "deflection from her contrary."
    The suffering and death of the good might have seemed significant to
Shakespeare's audience also in less obvious but more significant ways.
The playwrights were forbidden by royal proclamation of 1559 to meddle
with "matters of religion" and by Parliamentary action of 1606 even to
use the name of God. Theirs was perforce a secular activity, but they
lived in a Christian society, and their minds were habituated to ideas of
redemption and atonement. Stage plays stood in direct descent from the
Moralities and Moral Interludes, and although the latter had also taken
the "reprehensive" turn in Elizabeth's reign, converting God into an off-
stage beadle, the idea of redemption was central to the Morality tradition, which remained pervasive in Elizabethan popular drama, helping
to give romantic Comedy its distinctively nonsatirical and hopeful cast.
Unlike the idea of redemption, the idea of atonement is both heroic and
tragic. The sixteenth century produced a vast literature of martyrdom,
Protestant and Catholic, with Foxe's *Acts and Monuments* rivaling the
Mirror for Magistrates in bulk and popularity. The popular drama celebrated a few religious martyrs—Oldcastle, More, Cromwell—but naturally dealt more often with patriots or with others who had died in non-
religious causes. The idea of martyrdom was transferable to secular contexts, and the excessive suffering of the righteous might well suggest
atonement.
    A virtuous protagonist in this variation upon traditional Tragedy
might be either of two things: a theme of praise whose fame would in-
spire others to imitation, or a symbol of sacrificial cleansing. In Shakespeare's *I Henry VI*, which would have been viewed as a "tragedy," the
patriot Talbot dies on the field of battle, holding in his arms the body
of his son. In the welter of evil self-interest in the action, these alone have

been true to England. This stage emblem of grieving parent and dead child suggests a *pietà* and might well be remembered in discussions of *King Lear*. Nashe speaks of the tears of ten thousand spectators when Talbot triumphed again on the stage, and anyone "defining" Shakespearean Tragedy must ponder the nature of the limbeck in which these tears were distilled. In the Prologue and conclusion of *Romeo and Juliet* we have again the suggestion of "Sacrificial Tragedy":

> From forth the fatal loins of these two foes
>   A pair of star-crossed lovers take their life
> Whose misadventured piteous overthrows
>   Doth with their death bury their parents' strife.

At the end the lovers are called "poor sacrifices of our enmity" who are to be commemorated in statues of gold. Here is the old concept of Tragedy as a product of inevitable mutability and the whims of Fortune—as suggested by the words "fatal," "star-crossed," "misadventured," and by much of the action—but the concept is modified by ideas of atonement: these lovers are also scapegoats, human sacrifices, whose death has cleansed Verona of senseless rage.

Of course, whatever its medieval heritage, Elizabethan Tragedy was not "medieval," and whatever his status as an Elizabethan dramatist, Shakespeare was not a typical "Elizabethan." His creative faculties were such that he cannot be considered typical of anything. The danger of approaching his Tragedy by the route just traversed is that we may over-estimate its didacticism. In some measure he shared in a general tendency among the playwrights of his time to view life with a new objectivity and to "report" remarkable things for their intellectual interest and with a determination never to bore. A full discussion of his Tragedy would have to take into consideration the distinction so habitually ignored between his fables like *Romeo and Juliet, Hamlet, Othello, Macbeth,* and *King Lear* and his histories like *Julius Caesar, Antony and Cleopatra,* and *Coriolanus,* which lie somewhere between his English chronicle plays, after they had separated themselves from the tragic genre, and his "pure" Tragedies. Where to put *Titus Andronicus* and *Timon of Athens,* not to speak of *Troilus and Cressida,* remains a problem to keep us humble.

Still, there is some value in formulations. If I were asked to symbolize Tragedy in Shakespeare's time, I would design three escutcheons: the first black, emblazoned with a skull or with Fortune's Wheel (*memento mori* or *contemptus mundi* tragedy); the second red, total gules, emblazoned with a scourge (*de casibus* tragedy); the third white, emblazoned with a golden trumpet which at fitful intervals tends to reshape itself as a cross (inspirational or sacrificial tragedy). Shakespeare's contemporaries are more apt to give us pure examples of each variety, especially the second, than is Shakespeare himself. In the case of his greatest tragedies the escutcheons, to be properly symbolic, must be translucent and superimposed, so that in seeing one we see all. However much eclecticism they show, they came into the theater of their day fully accredited as Tragedy upon traditional grounds. Romeo and Juliet were not princes, but the tradition was not rigid in this regard. Some among the learned, Ben Jonson for instance, might have cavilled that some of Shakespeare's tragedies were no "right" tragedies because they mingled two stories or admitted a clown, but no one, including Jonson, would have objected that Shakespeare should have made more precise calculations about the percentage of defect in the protagonists so that "poetic justice" would be served, or about the psychology of the spectators so that their emotions might be properly "purged."

Neoclassical ideas about unity, decorum, and historical truth in Tragedy were current (though popularly disregarded), but those about *hamartia* and *catharsis* were not. Even among the more learned writers, Aristotle's definition of the tragic hero and the tragic effect was not known, or not understood, or not deemed interesting. Like Aeschylus, Sophocles, and Euripides, Shakespeare proceeded without Aristotle's aid. His tragedies resemble theirs in certain ways, defying the definition, which tends to eliminate their mystery. Even if the doctrine of the *Poetics* had been fully valid, lucid, and accessible, the fact would remain that a fine rational discourse can derive from great Tragedy, but great Tragedy cannot derive from a fine rational discourse. It can derive from, or at least relate to, something so irrational as the shimmering concept emblemized by my three-plied escutcheon—when the synthesizing agent is a great poetic mind.

Humanism and Mystery

by H. B. Charlton

Tragedy ends in death; but its fatal ending must not appear as an exhibition arbitrarily contrived by the dramatist. The tragic author must exonerate himself completely from all complicity in his hero's death: the hero's fate is not at the author's choice; it springs irresistibly from the ultimate nature of things, from the final compulsion, from ἀνάγκη, the last all-powerful Necessity. The dramatist is not devising a spectacle. His imaginative vision has caught glimpses of the ways of destiny; he simply reveals his hero's death as the inevitable outcome of primary universal law. That is, indeed, the fundamental note of tragedy, a sense conjured in us by the miracle of poetry, convincing us that the action we are watching must sweep irresistibly to its inevitable end. The inevitability is primarily impressed on us, not precisely, and not purely, as an intellectual conviction. It arises from a state of induced feeling in which intellectual satisfaction is only one element, often, too, an element which afterthought alone makes conscious to us. Indeed, intellectual acquiescence is all that is immediately required; one is aroused to feel that the action is inevitable, but reason cannot formulate the ultimate principles which make it inevitable. The riddle of the universe remains; and mystery is still one of the major threads in the web of human destiny. But the tragic dramatist has a larger awareness than ours, and the profit of it to us is not so much that he diminishes the ultimate mystery, but that he enables us to grasp the knowable and the mysterious as elements in a potential universe, a cosmic system whose laws in the end are inscrutable, but indisputably are laws. In the greater Shakespeare tragedies, man enthrals the attention more than does his universe, for Shakespeare's world is moral rather than metaphysical; humanism and humanity hold him far more passionately than theology and religion, men more than angels, earth more than heaven. The philosophic pattern implicitly adumbrated in his imaginative presentation of life is that of morality in emergence. In the earlier

"Humanism and Mystery." From the Introduction and Conclusion to *Shakespearian Tragedy* (Cambridge University Press, 1948), by H. B. Charlton, pp. 8-14, 230-38. Copyright 1948 by Cambridge University Press. Reprinted by permission of Cambridge University Press.

tragedies, man accepts morality easily and conventionally as the law of God. Then, in later ones, he begins to discover it in nature. In the end, Shakespeare watches nature-in-man, or human nature, visibly making morality, shaping it in the creative mind by some ultimate and mysterious impulse in him for which the name may well be God.

This is the ground-tone of Shakespeare's greatest tragedies. But as its heroes wring out of life its meaning, they succumb, and inevitably succumb, to its strain. They die, but the inevitability of their death is itself the mightiest force by which the truth which their life has revealed is driven home in us with absolute conviction. In some sort, then, the most direct and the simplest way in which to begin appraising the tragic value of a tragedy is to ask, "Why does the hero die?" From great tragedy the only answer is, "Because, such being the nature of things, he inevitably must": and part, but part only, of the grounds for this conviction of his inevitable end, will it be possible to state in reasoned form. The scope within which such ratiocinative sanction contributes to the necessary absoluteness of final conviction is very different in modern tragedy from what it was in Greek tragedy. All turns on the extent and the nature of a common religious belief. Broadly speaking, the Greek conception of Nemesis as the ultimate Necessity, in the last resort the arbiter of the universe and all that is therein, gods and men alike, is a magnificent philosophic back-cloth for the tragic scene. The inherent force of the moral order of the cosmos exerts itself to redress distortions of its nature, and to restore the stability by which it endures. Hence purely personal problems of individual motive are insignificant compared with the outcome of the deed done. Man, trusting to his own judgment, may determine to dispense himself from one obligation in order to fulfil what he regards as a higher good. Prometheus, for the benefit of mankind, steals fire from heaven. But, despite the motive, his act is an infraction of the highest good; his conscious motive was worthy, but his unconscious motive was *hubris*, pride. So he suffers the tragic doom. Or Oedipus also sins, but in sheer ignorance. Still, the offence has come, and woe even to the unwitting offender through whom it comes. Here, then, is the inevitability of Greek tragedy. This doom must follow this act, because all religiously believe that such is the course of destiny.

But when modern tragedy started in the sixteenth century there was no such universal agreement about the ways of God with man; and above all, the one common and dominant element in Europe's religion was apparently far less apt to the idea of tragedy. Christianity seemed to remove the foundations of the whole tragic scheme. Seeing life on earth as a mere moment in eternal immortality, it took finality from death; and it made sin mainly a matter of personal responsibility. The doctrine of redemption promised salvation for all except the worst of the wicked; and death on earth, for all but these, was but a gateway to everlasting bliss. So, a really tragic doom is reserved alone for the entirely reprobate: the evil man is destroyed by his iniquity. But is this really tragic? On the contrary, is it not a gratifying assurance of the Christian hope?

Whether these speculations on the apparent incompatibility between the traditional groundwork of tragedy and the tenets of Christianity are sound or not, one thing is certain: the tragedians of the new tragedy, Shakespeare and his fellows, seem to have thrust the Christian articles of current belief far into the background of consciousness. There is, for instance, in all Shakespeare's greater tragedies no admission of the Christian conception of immortality. In *Richard III* (I, iv, 255), a murderer, gruesomely consoling the man whom he is about to murder, tells him that death is a deliverance "from this world's thraldom, to the joys of heaven"; but the occasion of the utterance and the substance of it are part of that quality in the play which makes it inferior to the greater tragedies. In them as in *Hamlet*, after death "the rest is silence." Perhaps it is the sheer imaginative potency of the artist which stirs instincts buried more deeply in us than the feelings grafted on to a comparatively new faith; maybe he liberates primitive sensations of the early man which we all inherit from the time when death was a final extinction. However that may be, the result is that, in essence, whereas the foundation of Greek tragedy was religious, that of Shakespeare's tragedy is not. Elizabethan tragedy had perforce to explore other sources of the indispensable inevitability, the ultimate Necessity. The most effective one that it found was in the newly discovered wonder of human personality. What a piece of work is a man! Here, in the hidden resources of will, the unmeasurable strength of passion, the uncountable vagaries of impulse were the powers which patently participated in the shaping of destiny, though, of course, they did not finally determine it. So in Elizabethan drama, character becomes the smith of fortune, if not entirely of fate: and tragic drama finds its *ultima ratio*, its spring of inevitability, in the interplay of man and the world, in which the subtle though elusive link of psychological cause and effect gives to events sufficient appearance of a cosmic order. The mind of the reader is moved to acquiescence, his imagination sweeps him into the total acceptance which is for the moment absolute conviction.

For this reason, most inquirers into Shakespeare's tragic genius have occupied themselves with his instinct for characterisation, and expositions of his tragedies have been largely given to an analysis of the character of his tragic hero.

But our argument is passing well beyond its immediate purpose. It started merely to put forward a few assumptions which seemed commonplace enough to be axiomatic, and has led itself into propositions more fitted for a concluding estimate, to follow only when the tragedies have been duly surveyed. One advantage, however, such perfunctory anticipation may have had. It may have made clear the structure which it is proposed to give to the treatment of the theme.

Summarily these are its main principles and its main lines. On the whole Shakespeare is taken to mean what he seems to mean. His meaning is public for all sorts of men. His plays are plays: as other plays, they show human beings engaged in human action in a world which is the world of all of us. His tragedies depict men and women struggling with life and brought by it to death. In the dramatic execution of such a momentous action, the death of a great human being, a "hero," the dramatist must evoke from the stuff of his play the force of powers sensibly compelling the course of incident to its inevitable ending. The source of these powers in Shakespeare is his intuitive sense of personality and his intuitive vision of the ways of mortal destiny, the cosmic arbiters and universal laws of human life. To be admitted to such imaginative insight into truth and reality is for the spectator itself a pleasure. But a more intimate and personal gratification alleviates the painful sense of destruction: there emerges through the grief a growing sense of the immeasurable spiritual potentiality within man. Pessimism is banished by the revelation of desperate trial and loss as the main circumstance which brings forth and even creates deeper and deeper spiritual resources. The nobility of man triumphs over tragedy through tragedy. For Shakespeare, tragedy becomes the stern, awful but exalting picture of mankind's heroic struggle towards a goodness which enlarges and enriches itself as human experience grows longer and wider through the ages. Shakespearian tragedy is the apotheosis of the spirit of man.

It is generally agreed that the most consummate expressions of Shakespeare's tragic art are to be found in the four great tragedies, *Hamlet, Othello, Macbeth* and *King Lear*. In them the conflict between man and that which is hostile to his well-being in most intense. It is of profounder significance because, on the one hand, the man in them embodies richer or more fundamental or more vivid or more universal traits of permanent human character, and, on the other hand, the powers in them alien to man's good are in their turn more intimate or more elemental or more universal or more ultimate. Between them these four tragedies exhibit the depredations of the tragic fact at receding levels of human evolution, in different spiritual epochs; they seem like pictures of human life at great stages in the past history of its spiritual progress. With *Hamlet,* we are in the complex, elaborate, even sophisticated civilisation and culture of to-day's moral world, just as in Hamlet himself there are the full development of mind and the completed articulation of those multitudinous elements of spiritual sensibility which make man what he now is. In *Othello,* two worlds clash. The drawing-rooms of the delicate and refined children of an exquisite modern culture open their doors to one in whose blood runs the more primitive traditions of African tribal warrior-princes. But the ultimate tragic fact is lurking no less certainly in Othello's character than in Hamlet's. Man has not always had in his nature that capacity for intellectual subtleties which is part of Hamlet's native endowment; indeed, mankind which had not yet grown to the possession of it, must have been immune from the particular strokes of tragedy which destroy Hamlet. But passion is older than thought, nearer to the animal: and it is even more liable to stir tragic consequences when, lacking a restraining counterpoise in intellect, it finds itself moving in a more intellectual world. Even in its setting, *Macbeth* reflects nothing peculiar to the modern world. Its hero is in some ways even more primitive than Othello, for in Macbeth it is the moral sense which is but dimly beginning to recognise the faintly articulated imperatives of the still small voice; in his guilt, Macbeth manifests not so much the awakening of conscience as a stage in the process of its emergence. In *King Lear* the wheel comes full circle. The world of it is shorn of all its acquired circumstance and most of its cultural trappings. The tragic situation, though it enmeshes a king, is not the outcome of a social order even so far developed as to have organised a simple monarchical system. The tragedy of it springs from the simplest and the primary social entity, the family, and from the human relationship which is the absolute beginning of all and every human society, parenthood, the relation of father to child and of child to father. Like the setting and the circumstance, the people of *King Lear* mark the backward reaches of symbolic human time. Man is near indeed to the animal, sometimes in sheer simplicity of innocence, but more often in worse than animal bestiality, his intellectual sense serving only as craft to add a finer edge to his cruelty. With such people as its persons, and parentage as its sole plot, *King Lear* bares the tragedy of human life to absolute simplicity and to almost absolute universality. . . .

Shakespearian tragedy is profoundly spiritual, and yet in no real sense is it at all religious. To say that it is entirely humanist is to invite a misunderstanding of its scope. It is almost completely confined to life as the human experience of living. In its whole ambit, it takes life as a manifestation of the phenomena which are the substance of morality. But it is occupied with life as life is lived in a universe wherein mightier forces than those of man are perpetually exerting their powers in shaping the lot of mankind. These are the vast circumambient mysteries. In their ways, they are too inscrutable to be resolved into any but the simplest and vaguest theological formulary, and their complicity in making man's destiny is so indirect and so remote that, as divinities, they have no assessable or definable rôle in the overt plan of Shakespeare's tragedies. Nor does that plan presuppose or promise ampler and more gratifying revelation of the nature of God or of the gods. At farthest, it vaguely apprehends that the ultimate arbiters cannot be hostile to man's search for goodness, though they leave to man himself the immense rigour of the strife. Shakespeare's abiding interest is in the absorbing spectacle of this effort. His preoccupation is moral, and not religious.* In his normal day-to-day existence, there is no reason to suspect that Shakespeare was not a good Elizabethan Anglican: but the ideal world in which he moved when he was imaginatively excited was the world of man and of morality, not that of the gods and of theology.

Yet Shakespeare's moral world is not inconsistent with a universe capable of being apprehended religiously. At all events, and without distorting its outlines, hosts of men have fitted it into their own sectarian dogmas. Predominantly, however, Shakespeare's major concern is that of the humanist. But it is that of a humanist whose imaginative grasp is wider than his rational comprehension, and who therefore is always too conscious of the elusive mystery of things ever to be a consistent rationalist or even to be professedly an agnostic. For he has an unswerving faith. It is faith in the mysterious spirit of man.

In Shakespeare there is no hard and fast dichotomy between body and soul. He appears to find the spirit of man as the characteristic functioning of the complex organism of flesh, blood, nerve, heart, and brain, as in each man it manifests itself distinctively through a form of conduct which is the outcome of that particular man's instinct, passion, reason, and will. In his tragedies, physical death involves a cessation of the spirit within the body. But bodily death is only tragic when it entails, or follows, or occasions mutilation of the individual and, thereby, of the general spirit. The death of the human spirit is the extermination of man. Hence the note which marks the final depth of tragedy is often the voice which cries that no longer is there anything serious in mortality, that life is no longer worth the living. For this annihilates the spiritual universe into which mankind seems to be arduously ascending. . . .

The mainspring is Shakespeare's sense of what life is. Life begins in mystery, both in beast and in man. But all living creatures have one capacity which is godlike in its nature: they have the power to create their own kind as out of nothing, to bring something new into the world. Procreation, however, is the prerogative both of beast and of man. On the one hand, it is this common and magic creative gift which perpetually reminds Shakespeare of the close and primary link between the human and the animal kingdom. Yet on the other hand, it is in the differences subsequent to the production of their offspring that Shakespeare sees the essential differentiation between man and beast. The reproductive impulse in beasts may impel them for a brief moment to instinctive protection of their offspring. But the human animal has the added gift of self-consciousness. His paternal protective instinct becomes an emotion, and his recognition of mere kind begins to emerge as the sentiment of kindness. Once the sentiment is familiarly and consciously experienced, it takes on far-reaching implications. It impels behaviour which will come to be recognised as obligatory. The idea of duty is beginning, and as it slowly grows, man is becoming more and more of a moral being, more and more distinct from the animal. Kindness will grow to human kindliness, as the sense of obligation extends itself beyond the ties of immediate paternity. Yet the initiatory impulse is the nuclear and peculiar instinct which is specific to the human kind. The first great stage of this discovery is lived through in *King Lear,* and the second in *Macbeth.* In *Othello* and in *Hamlet,* man has travelled much farther along the way by which he is moralising his nature. He has become more and more aware of a larger and a still larger good. In a merely human relationship, through instinct and emotion, Othello and Desdemona are discovering for themselves and for us a way in which man may shape a higher good in life than he has hitherto dreamed of as possible. In *Hamlet,* the mind of man has a sense that it is almost able to make goodness itself. At moments it would appear, and in no cynical mood, that "there's nothing either good or bad, but thinking makes it so."

It is in this moral creative power of man when his instinctive nature has grown to the disciplined awareness of his spiritual consciousness that Shakespeare sees the sanctity of human life. It is the developed expression of the impulse which is the primary activity by which man becomes man and by which he is distinct from all other forms of life. No achievement of the spirit is beyond its reach. There is high significance in the fact that the chronological order of Shakespeare's greater tragedies is from *Hamlet* to *King Lear.* The wonder of man and the marvel of his spiritual potentiality is unmistakable in the first: but in the last, the miracle has been traced back to its very rudiments, and is discovered in the primary nucleus or gene of the human species. Hence Shakespeare's faith in mankind; for man's essential nature and his distinctive property is a specific something or other which makes predominantly and progressively for good; and when he sets himself against his own kindness, he fordoes himself.

Yet throughout his existence, he remains, as man, a part of the animal kingdom. Moreover, physically, he is subject to a material universe. The beast is always within himself; and often the universe about him appears like an un-moral power which stimulates the beast more than the man in him, and which, even when less apparently hostile, shows no obvious preference to assist the higher as against the lower of his efforts. Happiness is seldom apportioned to degrees of worthiness for it. Suffering is more certain than joy. Yet somehow or other, the bad and the good, each in their way, are extending and deepening the sense of goodness. Though the progress involves immense pain and irreparable loss, and the process is heartbreakingly slow, the things of the spirit are gradually gaining on the inheritance of the beast. Mankind is realising more and more the nature of human kindness. The individual passes, aware of the destructiveness of his evil; or, on the other hand, though painfully failing to reach the good for which he strove, he manifests, in his ripeness to accept his fate, his own fellowship in the human kind, for whom the common or general good is the highest good. It is this faith in the nature of man which permeates Shakespeare's poetry. Even in its agonies, human life is worthwhile; for the instinctive sense of human kindness not only impels man to live, it impels him no less certainly to suffer and to die for the spiritual enrichment of this kind. Ultimately therefore it is no longer merely a question of personal happiness. It is a matter of spiritual progress in the well-being of humanity at large. To Shakespeare evil is inhumanity, not only in the sense that evil is the source of the cruelty which man inflicts on other men, but in the deeper sense that evil is a distortion of the essential nature of man. For to Shakespeare, man is the human kind, and the vitalising element of the human kind is human kindness, and human kindness is fellowship, and fellowship is love, and love is the means by which man perceives or makes the goodness on which the happiness of his kind depends.

But all these assertions, of course, are not obviously an intellectual transmission of the immediate response which our whole sentient nature makes to Shakespeare's tragic plays. They are merely attempts to see the plays dispassionately when they have receded, as do all other facts of our experience, into that body of awareness which cumulatively is for each one of us what he means by his life. We endeavour to build this mass of material into some sort of shape which will satisfy the mind's thirst for order. But what we are really handling are not direct and immediate perceptions, they are afterthoughts succeeding those perceptions. Yet there would appear to be some sort of evidence that Shakespeare's own afterthoughts tended in the same direction. . . .

The Tragic Qualm

by Willard Farnham

We are justified in saying that the greatest Greek tragedy and the greatest Gothic tragedy never make tragic justice an entirely open book, and that they are in a certain sense unmoral, because they are concerned with much deeper ethical difficulties than those of squaring life with some simple and well-accepted moral code. When Shakespeare thus allies himself in profundity with the classic dramatists of Greece, however, he does so without any apparent benefit from Greek models and with essential distinction from them in manner. He is true to the Gothic spirit, even when he most transforms its less subtle ways of presenting the circumstances leading to human catastrophe.

Frequently we feel that Greek tragedy—and we are apt to feel it most in those plays which have been counted most memorable—is built not upon the violation of some law which the universe has plainly established for man's guidance, but upon violation of some law not plainly established, or even upon man's inability to reconcile apparent contradictions in ethical laws. This is peculiarly a feeling of that tragic qualm which rises when accepted foundations of human action are unsettled by exploration.[1] The qualm is strong when we see Antigone confronted by two antagonistic duties, both powerfully sanctioned; but it is strongest perhaps when we find that divine forces having sway over mankind are in dire conflict concerning the path which an Orestes should follow. Both divinity and humanity, though they may have good and just intentions, are then only struggling in darkness for guiding light, and tragedy seems inevitable for man, whichever course he pursues. His very gods have disagreed, each giving injunctions most plausibly justified, and the one

"The Tragic Qualm." From the Conclusion of *The Medieval Heritage of Elizabethan Tragedy* (Berkeley: University of California Press, 1936), by Willard Farnham, pp. 438-46. Copyright 1936 by the University of California Press. Reprinted by permission of the University of California Press.

[1] Here I am indebted to P. H. Frye, *Romance and Tragedy*, Boston, 1922. The curious reader may discover differences as well as agreements in our views, however. The expression "tragic qualm," which I use more than once in this chapter, I borrow gratefully from Professor Frye (pp. 146 ff.).

god will punish him for following the other. Even the gods themselves may suffer tragedy for their lack of ability to reconcile the conflicting demands of goodness. It is good for Prometheus to benefit mankind in the way he does, but he must nevertheless undergo torture after his beneficial act because it is also good to obey the Zeus against whom that act is rebellion. When these things are presented to us without pessimism and with an implied hope of ultimate reconciliation, as notably in Aeschylus, we feel that the struggle is of the highest ethical importance, even though a clear and final tragic justice cannot be shown. We feel that we are witnesses at the first stages of painful birth for some more catholic ethical principle than has before been operative in our universe and found expression in human ideas of morality. Emphatically we are not uplifted here by any exposure of perfection in universal laws or their enforcement, but by an exposure of imperfection (so far as mortal eyes are concerned) working dynamically toward perfection with the accompaniment of agony.

In Shakespeare there is a comparable revelation of what one may call grandeur in the imperfection of good. As in Aeschylus or Sophocles, a distinction between good and evil is taken for granted, and at times we may even see acts which are very simply evil according to traditional moral judgment gaining apparent retribution for their authors. But of the series of major tragedies beginning with *Hamlet,* only one—namely, *Macbeth*—may in any way be thought of as given over to the taking of downright evil toward exemplary punishment. Even so, *Macbeth* is far from being a *Richard III* and has a certain kinship of unmoral subtlety with other tragedies of the later group. At other times in Shakespeare we may see acts that rise from faults, or taints, or flaws, in character—qualities which would never be called good though they might not be called evil—leading their possessors inevitably to suffering. The later Shakespearean tragedies make much of these flaws, and hence tempt us strongly to explain the catastrophes by actions of the characters that are "wrong." Even while catastrophes have these aspects of retribution, however, they are apt to have another aspect as results of imperfection in human character. Here the imperfection is placed before us not as a taint in or falling away from goodness or nobility so much as a lack of balance, even a civil war of goods, in man's noblest nature. Under this aspect a catastrophe may seem to be partly produced by good itself—ironically, if one has what usually passes as the moral view of things. It is thus that Shakespearean tragedy joins Greek tragedy in the dramatic exploration of imperfection in good. It can raise in us a similar qualm, or moral vertigo, though it inclines to search and question not the good that lies in laws and principles under which man lives, but the good that lies in man's inner qualities.

One need not labor the well-known examples of this. In *Hamlet* we discover a protagonist who is at war with himself in all that we should call his noblest being. We are forced to make the conclusion that he might have escaped catastrophe if he had had narrower nobility, or if he had not been embarrassed, so to speak, with multiple nobility. Hamlet the man of fine intellectual perception is inimical to Hamlet the man of courageous instinctive action at points most crucial for his general success, though not, to make the irony more delicate, upon occasions like his boarding of the pirate ship. A man such as Fortinbras, admirable merely as a courageous doer, finally gets the kingdom and might well have had thorough success in Hamlet's place as an avenger of a murdered father. It deserves all possible emphasis that Shakespeare does not make Hamlet struggle with the inconsistency between a barbaric tribal code and the Christian code of morals in the matter of revenge, as a Christian Aeschylus might have made him struggle. There is never a sign that Hamlet or anyone else in the play recognizes this inconsistency, however much we may recognize it and be tempted to read the tragedy accordingly, or however much an Elizabethan auditor may have recognized it in the light of the current condemnation of revenge. Shakespeare is dramatically about other business.

Macbeth is quite unlike Hamlet in that he progressively degrades his nobility by embracing what he recognizes to be evil:

> For Banquo's issue have I fil'd my mind;
> . . . and mine eternal jewel
> Given to the common enemy of man,
> To make them kings, the seed of Banquo kings!
>
> [III. i. 65-70]

Nevertheless, his ruin has more than a little of the causation just noticed for Hamlet's downfall. Ill-assorted qualities separately admirable seem to unfit Macbeth for rough and ready rule as a warrior king. He has real kinship with Hamlet as a man called to forthright action and bringing with him a delicacy of imaginative perception with regard to consequences which cramps direct action upon the more momentous occasions and even makes him appear superficially a coward. His imaginative perception is visionary and prophetic instead of intellectual, and it works against him with all possible force when stimulated by rising conscience through an evil course of action.

Shakespeare searches and questions the goodness of man's noblest nature by different but no less effective means in *Othello* and *King Lear*. The search does not expose inimical divisions in good, but it does expose the ways by which a disproportionate quality of good may help to make catastrophe inevitable. Faults Othello certainly has, but it is often difficult not to feel that his tragedy springs most deeply from his very magnanimity, with which he is so embarrassingly endowed that he trusts Iago. To say merely that Othello by this trust earns his suffering through a flaw in wisdom is not to take necessary account of that "intolerable" character which so many have attributed to the play. In Lear and in Gloucester there are also faults, but again the suffering which follows faulty action is intolerable according to any normal human sense of proportion. Throughout *King Lear* one can never forget that one is seeing the fate of parental love preyed upon and tortured the more readily by evil because it is expansively trustful.

By a course of its own, then, Shakespearean tragic drama attains delicate balance between an overwhelming assault upon man's proud but imperfect moral security and a stimulating challenge to his faith in moral existence. The result, especially in the assault upon human pride, is one which fulfills rather than departs from the earlier impulses of Gothic tragedy. Even the impulse to expose inherent imperfection in the mortal world which dominated Gothic tragedy in its beginnings has some share of fulfillment.

For the tragic world must here be looked at under two distinct guises. So far as the *individual* is concerned, the world of later Shakespearean tragedy is assuredly not to be embraced hopefully or to be regarded as achieving, or even struggling toward, a gratifying show of decorum and of poetic justice through natural law. The basest indignity and injustice for the individual seem to be shockingly natural accompaniments of life in the flesh. The grossnesses of flesh and of fleshly death, as we have found, are never far from the poet's mind. Moreover, the nobility of man's spirit, which contrasts so strongly with ignobleness in his flesh, and to which we look for a saving quality, is only human nobility after all, divided against itself or unbalanced, and able to command no just consideration from the forces of mundane life. It seems even to turn these forces against the protagonist ironically. All this is obviously reminiscent of Contempt of the World. The disgusting odor of mortality is strong. Pride is dashed for the good as well as for the evil. Fortune, with her wheel, and the stars, with their emanations, no longer are appealed to simply and seriously, but they are still talked about poetically, and man's mortal being appears to be by no means truly free from some such power, often whimsical. With reference to the individual alone, the world is even more fiendishly unworthy of trust than it is in ascetic *De Casibus* tragedy, for it deceives us with infinite subtlety, toys with us, gives high intimations of law and order only to withdraw them, instead of wearing a thoroughly disordered look upon its face. It tempts us to find a neatly working key to Shakespearean tragedy in the moral responsibility which is there allotted to man without question: in the willful evil committed by Macbeth which so definitely works against him, in a sort of deadly sin of sloth for Hamlet, in courses of folly responsibly chosen by Othello and Lear.

Or it tempts us to find such a key in some scientific principle. And it deserts us after we have done so.

But so far as *mortal life* without reference to the individual is concerned, the world of later Shakespearean tragedy has a quality which ascetic Contempt must of necessity not admit. It is here that Shakespeare embraces life for a show of beauty in dependability and is so little inclined to deny general goodness to the mortal scheme of things that he makes life magnificently heroic in its intolerance of evil. As Professor Bradley says, it is a very important fact that in the Shakespearean tragedy "villainy never remains victorious and prosperous at the last." [2] As he says further, in a discussion now classic, the life presented in Shakespeare's major tragedies is one which contends against evil as it would against a poison, struggles against it in agony, and eventually casts it forth, though it must rend itself in so doing and must tear out much good along with the evil. The good individual in the body politic must often suffer as much as, or more than, the evil individual through this agonized convulsion; or the good in an individual must be destroyed, and even help to destroy itself, because of the evil in him which is also to be destroyed. The process is quite other than one of weighing good and evil, determining relative merits, and administering rewards and punishments in due proportion. It is, indeed, a frightfully wasteful process, involving both order and disorder. After it has run its course, "what remains is a family, a city, a country, exhausted, pale, and feeble, but alive through the principle of good which animates it; and, within it, individuals who, if they have not the brilliance or greatness of the tragic character, still have won our respect and confidence." [3] The working force has had to lose "a part of its own substance—a part more dangerous and unquiet, but far more valuable and nearer to its heart than that which remains—a Fortinbras, a Malcolm, an Octavius. There is no tragedy in its expulsion of evil: the tragedy is that this involves the waste of good." [4] And life produces refined tragedy because "—at any rate for the eye of sight—the evil against which it asserts itself, and the persons whom this evil inhabits, are not really something outside the order, so that they can attack it or fail to conform to it; they are within it and a part of it. It itself produces them —produces Iago as well as Desdemona, Iago's cruelty as well as Iago's courage. It is not poisoned, it poisons itself." [5]

Thus Shakespeare allays the tragic qualm which, by unsettling the very foundations of our moral conceptions, he raises in us. He purges our emotions of pity and fear by making us acquiesce without bitterness in catastrophe which at first sight may seem the result of goodness turning false to itself and aiding evil in the production of suffering with cruelly refined

[2] A. C. Bradley, *Shakespearean Tragedy* (ed. 2), London, 1920, p. 32.
[3] *Ibid.*, p. 35.   [4] *Ibid.*, p. 37.
[5] *Ibid.*, pp. 36-37.

irony. It is not an easy reconciliation that he offers, any more than the reconciliation provided by Aeschylus, and perhaps somewhat less. It cannot even spare the life of a Hamlet as Greek reconciliation can spare the life of an Orestes. Death is a sure part of the tragedy because the tragedy is Gothic. All that Shakespeare alone will permit us to say is that the yoke of life is hard but supremely worth the bearing in the interest of general good. Ultimate reasons for its being hard are not brought to our perception.

Construction in *Titus Andronicus*

by H. T. Price

. . . The best "parallel" by which we can test authorship is construction. Phrases may be borrowed here and there, but construction refers to the planning of the work as a whole. It is the most intimate expression of the author's meaning. Lyly, indeed, taught Shakespeare certain details of balance. But the pupil soon outstripped his teacher, and the masterly use Shakespeare made of what he learned gives him a place apart among Elizabethan dramatists. The carriage of the plot and the weaving together of many motifs to form unity require a particular kind of skill without which all outside aid is futile.

The closest parallel to *Titus* is the plot of *Lear*. Here as there we have two parties, whom we may crudely call the good and the bad. In both there are different kinds of good men opposed to different kinds of bad. Some critics find that the plot of *Titus* is weakened because the leadership of the "bad" party varies. It is now in the hands of Tamora, now with Aaron. I do not think this criticism has any force, since this variation does nothing to impede the sweep and rush of the play. In any case there is the same thing in *Lear*. Sometimes it is Goneril, sometimes it is Edmund, who takes the lead against Lear. In both plays the effect is the same. The forces of evil, no matter who embodies them, work with unabated intensity until the climax is reached.

If then one is looking for parallels, the only parallel to the plot of *Titus* is to be found in the other works of Shakespeare. Greene and Peele are so loose and episodic, so naïf in construction that it is incredible that they should have achieved anything so good as *Titus*. Nor is there any plot of Marlowe's so intricate, so varied or so well sustained. *Titus* is the expression of a conflict intenser than anything the Elizabethan stage had as yet known. Shakespeare applies in *Titus* those principles of balance and contrast which he had learned from Lyly and had already tested in comedy. He sets up against one another two parties, each led by formidable characters. It is the play of fence between the high incensed points of these

"Construction in *Titus Andronicus*." From "The Authorship of *Titus Andronicus*" by H. T. Price (Urbana, Ill.: University of Illinois Press), *Journal of English and Germanic Philology*, XLVII (1943), 55-81. Reprinted by permission of H. T. Price.

mighty opposites that makes the drama. There is nothing like this in Marlowe, whose super-men dominate his plays and dwarf everybody else in them. There is nothing like it in Greene and Peele, who indeed lacked the personality to create a drama of tense conflict.

Titus then resembles Shakespeare's other work, both comedy and tragedy, in that it is built upon the principle of contrast. We have the contrasting pairs or groups: Titus-Aaron, Lavinia-Tamora, Saturninus-Bassianus, the sons of Titus—the sons of Tamora. Not only are members of the opposite party contrasted, there are also contrasts within the same party. Marcus, as we shall see, by his mildness throws into higher relief the sterner traits of Titus. Contrast dominates the play and informs every scene of it. As we have already noted, whatever is fine in the Romans appears finer still in comparison with the vices of their opposites. On the one hand we have courage, stern probity, honor, but also stubbornness, hardness, and stupidity, on the other hand, slipperiness, trickiness, intrigue, the lie, foulness of every sort. None of the dramatists who are supposed to have had a hand in the play, could conceive a plan so intricate or adhere to it so closely, once it was conceived. But Shakespeare goes farther. He uses contrast to heighten incident and situation as well as character. Act ii.ii. and iii. are admirable examples of Shakespeare's technique. The delightful freshness of dawn and the beauty of the woods are not described for their own sake, still less are they, as some critics assert, a homesick reminiscence of Stratford. They are written in cold blood with the deliberate purpose of accentuating by contrast the horrors that follow. Shakespeare is again borrowing from the technique of Seneca. . . .

The plot is superior to anything that Greene, Peele, Marlowe, or Kyd could achieve, by its quick succession of closely knit incidents, enlivened by many sudden turns and surprises, by its intricacy, in that the fates of so many persons are involved in it and yet the thread is never lost, and by the skill with which all the different threads are bound up into one knot and untied at once in the fifth act. Intricacy with clearness, a firm hand on the story, a swift succession of effective situations logically leading out of what precedes and on to what follows, these are qualities lacking in the dramatists who are supposed to have shared in the composition of Titus.

It must be admitted that the plot hinges on several Elizabethan conventions that are now strange to us. For instance the ruse, no matter how transparent, always succeeds, first when Titus is tricked, later when Titus himself takes to deception. Aaron eavesdrops in ii.i.—the Elizabethans took in this trick a childish delight which we cannot recapture. Quite suddenly Saturninus falls head over heels in love with Tamora—the Elizabethan believed in these swift and overwhelming effects of passion. Shakespeare is full of them. Every dramatist must work according to the rules of the game as it is understood in his time. The play is not less likely

to be by Shakespeare because it is so full of the conventions of the
theatre.

We come to an important aspect of the plot which scholars tend to
overlook. *Titus* is a political play, and Shakespeare is the most political
of all dramatists. His work excited the admiration of statesmen like Glad-
stone and Bismarck, who both wondered how he managed to penetrate
so many secrets of their profession. Shakespeare's political interest shows
itself in various ways. He likes to connect his heroes with an action involving the fortunes of the state, he is skilful in tracing the course of
political intrigue, and he delights in exposing those kinks of character or
intellect which unfit even men of action for public life. The real hero of
his political plays is the state. In some plays it is England, in others it is
Rome. Now *Titus* centres round an affair of state, and its hero is no particular person but it is Rome herself. All the characters are viewed in
their relation to Rome and they are set against Rome as a background.
This theme is sustained throughout the play; it dominates the fifth act as
the first. No member of that writers' syndicate—large as it is—which the
revisionists credit with *Titus* has Shakespeare's deep love of the state or
his understanding of the criss-cross currents of politics. The intense political interest of Titus points to the man who wrote Shakespeare's historical and Roman plays, and it points to no one else.

But even if we grant that *Titus* could not have been written by any-
body but Shakespeare, its horrible cruelty still leaves us profoundly dis-
satisfied. It is not only that Titus is cruel; it is more, he is cruel to the
end. He is not a Lear who grows in stature as the play proceeds and whose
sufferings purge his character of its baser elements until he emerges a
man entirely good. Titus alone of Shakespeare's tragic heroes never arrives at healing self-knowledge. At the beginning of the play we hope
that Titus will succeed against his enemies; at the end we wish that he
had not. But we must not forget the task that Shakespeare has set himself.
He is writing a Senecan play according to the rules, that is to say, a play
in which the hero is a man who inexorably pursues revenge and who dies
in the act of taking it. Such a plan leaves no room for change of character.
Shakespeare, therefore, has been obliged to split what he had to say between Titus and Marcus. Roughly speaking, Lear is a Titus who becomes
a Marcus, but a revenge-play necessarily precluded this type of development. Shakespeare has not been deluded into thinking revenge is a fine
thing. He sets up Marcus to show us the better way. The great fault of
the drama from our point of view is that Titus never finds that way. But
his stern pursuit of revenge is inherent in the revenge-play and Shakespeare could only have got round it by making his hero a kind of Hamlet. . . .

If we could acquit Shakespeare of being an accomplice in *Titus,* we
should all be glad to do so. But it is attributed to him by close colleagues

who presumably knew Shakespeare well enough to be aware of what they were doing. At any rate they knew him much better than we do. All the tests of affinities, parallels, resemblances, and methods of technique point definitely to Shakespeare. No convincing evidence has been brought forward which would connect *Titus* with any other dramatist. The horrors of the play are undeniable. But if scholars would refrain from still harping upon these horrors and would instead consider the play on its merits as an excellent piece of stagecraft, they might see in it something not unworthy of the young Shakespeare.

The School of Love: *Romeo and Juliet*

by Donald A. Stauffer

Among the enemies that beset the course of true love, Shakespeare in *A Midsummer Night's Dream* realizes momentarily, with a poignancy that almost destroys the dream itself, that the most dangerous enemy is Time. Seeking some source of belief that will not alter, Shakespeare has settled upon love, which he often equates with faith or loyalty. Yet how can its truth be sealed unalterably, if the moving finger of Time has the power to mar, to alter, or to destroy? Shakespeare had already given to the wronged Lucrece a long diatribe against "Misshapen Time," whose artistic irrelevance only emphasized Shakespeare's preoccupation. "Injurious, shifting Time," the "ceaseless lackey to Eternity," has as its servant "Opportunity"—that is, chance, or accident—which sets life-as-it-is in place of life-as-it-ought-to-be.[1] The quality of Time that Shakespeare feels most piercingly is its power, helped by its servants Opportunity and Oblivion, to blot and spoil and change whatever is noble and dignified. If brevity is the soul of wit, it is also the foe of worth. The ideal good can be changed only for the worse by Time, if Time has power at all. This cosmic pathos Shakespeare most frequently presents in wide symbols of the world's decay:

> To ruinate proud buildings with thy hours . . .
> And waste huge stones with little waterdrops.
>
> [*The Rape of Lucrece,* 944, 959]

"The School of Love: *Romeo and Juliet*." From *Shakespeare's World of Images* (New York: W. W. Norton & Company, Inc. 1949), by Donald A. Stauffer, pp. 53-59. Copyright 1949 by W. W. Norton & Company, Inc. Reprinted by permission of W. W. Norton & Company, Inc.

[1] Time is vilified in ingenious epithets and conceits in *The Rape of Lucrece* (925-96); it is the carrier of grisly care, the eater of youth, the false slave to false delight, sin's packhorse, virtue's snare, the universal murderer. Characteristic of Shakespeare's thought, Time is dual and may act as an avenger. It is "tutor both to good and bad," one of whose functions is "To wrong the wronger till he render right."

In Lysander's lines in *A Midsummer Night's Dream,* Time the quick murderer is etched in stiletto strokes as the destroyer of true love:

> War, death, or sickness did lay siege to it,
> Making it momentary as a sound,
> Swift as a shadow, short as any dream,
> Brief as the lightning in the collied night,
> That, in a spleen, unfolds both heaven and earth,
> And ere a man hath power to say "Behold!"
> The jaws of darkness do devour it up:
> So quick bright things come to confusion.

Such a tragic thunderclap startles the moonlit landscapes and fantastic laughter of the midsummer night. To convey his vivid intuition of the place and duration of love in the dark world of time, Shakespeare finds the lightning-in-the-night adequate as the germinating and organizing symbol for *Romeo and Juliet.* The theme of love, which he expands in other keys in plays before and after, remains central, though now it is to be idealized in all seriousness. Yet since the dark shades of hate are here little more than the touches of an artist designed to set off the brilliant lightning flash of passion, *Romeo and Juliet* shows less the tragedy than the pathos of pure love: "So quick bright things come to confusion!"

The school of love is still in session. The hero is still fickle, the heroine constant. Romeo's moonstruck calf-love for Rosaline must be laughed out of him by his friends Benvolio and Mercutio, by his guide Friar Laurence, and by his own true love. But since Rosaline is so cool that beauty itself is "starved with her severity," she is easily forgotten. She is no more than a name that proves Romeo an apt pupil from the start, a young man who can mint conceits, imagine the tears of fickle love as "transparent heretics," and cope with the best of witlings in defining his fashionable passion in a rain of paradoxes: "Feather of lead, bright smoke, cold fire, sick health!" Once "Romeo is belov'd, and loves again," the mutual attraction is so strong that any further twitting of his fickleness is wasted.

Even more obvious, in this play love becomes the teacher of society. Shakespeare was never more patently the schoolmaster than in his repeated moralizing that love must destroy hate: The prologue tells us that the misadventured piteous overthrows of the two lovers bury their parents' strife. Nothing could remove the continuance of their parents' rage except their children's end. The moral lesson is so shaped formally that it becomes the main theme of the drama: the opening scene stops the bitter feud temporarily; the middle act results in two deaths and the separation of the lovers when murderous quarreling breaks out again; the closing scene offers the sacrifice of innocents to wipe out in blood the cursed strife of the old partisans. Church and state combine at the end to

arraign the hate-filled families. The Friar presents himself "both to im-
peach and purge." And the Prince of Verona speaks the ironic moral:

> Capulet, Montague,
> See what a scourge is laid upon your hate,
> That heaven finds means to kill your joys with love!

"All are punish'd." Yet the houses are reconciled in clasped hands, and
golden statues shall rise as memorials to these "Poor sacrifices of our
enmity!" The universe is guided by "the rigour of severest law"; and
Time works inevitably "to wrong the wronger till he render right." In-
sofar as this play is a tragedy of fate—and Shakespeare sets up dozens of
signposts pointing toward the foregone moral conclusion—all accidents
and events work toward the final sacrifice. Romeo and Juliet are puppets,
since the moral punishment of the raging clans becomes more powerful
in proportion to the innocence and helplessness of the sacrifices. In no
other play does Shakespeare envisage a general moral order operating
with such inhuman, mechanical severity.

On the surface, social evil is castigated and purged by "Fate," which is
an extra-human moral order. Yet in contrast to this often declared thesis,
and by no means reconciled with it, Shakespeare intrudes a line of thinking which was to become central in his serious philosophy: that the causes
of tragedy lie in the sufferers themselves. The doctrines of individual
responsibility and of fate as a social Nemesis offer divergent motivations:
this play may fail as serious tragedy because Shakespeare blurs the focus
and never makes up his mind entirely as to who is being punished, and for
what reason. Later he learned to carry differing hypotheses simultaneously,
to suggest complex contradictory interactions convincingly; but that is not
the effect of the double moral motivations in *Romeo and Juliet*.

The dangerous fault of the two lovers is their extreme rashness. The
Friar chides his protégé's sudden haste: "Wisely, and slow. They stumble
that run fast." He has rebuked him earlier "for doting, not for loving."
And even in a love affair which he approves he will counsel Romeo to

> Love moderately: long love doth so;
> Too swift arrives as tardy as too slow.

The explosive force of pure passion throughout the play he casts in its
characteristic imagery:

> These violent delights have violent ends
> And in their triumph die, like fire and powder,
> Which, as they kiss, consume.

Juliet, too, is uneasily aware of what may be their fault:

> I have no joy of this contract to-night.
> It is too rash, too unadvis'd, too sudden;
> Too like the lightning, which doth cease to be
> Ere one can say "It lightens."

If the theme of personal responsibility were not drowned out by the theme of fate, it might be argued that the lovers' deaths in the tomb are caused by Romeo's sudden decision to buy poison, and again by his immediate suicide when he mistakes Juliet's sleep for death. But this is quibbling with destiny.

It is not quibbling to point out Shakespeare's emphasis on their surging wrong-headed impulses midway in the drama, so much more cunningly wrought and convincing than the moral tags. Juliet, when she hears that her husband has killed her cousin Tybalt, at once breaks out in a para-doxical curse twelve times illustrated: "O serpent heart, hid with a flow'ring face!" True, she soon veers back to her loyalty, but fast running has led to stumbling at the start. In the preceding scene, Romeo has banished "respective lenity" to heaven and has embraced "fire-ey'd fury" to kill Tybalt. And in the succeeding scene, Romeo's passion turns him hysterical. He has become a "fond mad man," who grovels on the floor of the Friar's cell, weeping and blubbering, who is drawn to his feet by the nurse's words—"Stand up, stand up! Stand, an you be a man"—only to unsheathe his dagger to kill himself, and who is finally restored to his senses by the Friar's bitterest as well as his most powerful adjurations. He has shown "the unreasonable fury of a beast"; he has betrayed the form of man; his spirit

> Like powder in a skilless soldier's flask,
> Is set afire by thine own ignorance.

No less than in the hatred of brawling houses, then, "unreasonable fury" may be shown in love. And Shakespeare's own sounder moral sense answers the philosophy of this so-called "tragedy of fate" in the Friar's direct statement:

> Why railest thou on thy birth, the heaven, and earth?
> Since birth and heaven and earth, all three do meet
> In thee at once; which thou at once wouldst lose.

Man cannot evade his pilotage by proclaiming himself "fortune's fool."
Such are the moralizings in this play. They protest too much in words,

attest too little in experience. The actual ethical energy of the drama resides in its realization of the purity and intensity of ideal love. Here there is no swerving. Both Romeo and Juliet are wholly devoted to their overpowering discovery: from the religious imagery of the wooing to the feasting imagery of the Capulet vault, when Romeo's wit plays its "lightning before death," the power of love is idealized; and true love, as though it were a hyphenated compound, echoes through the play.[2]

Shakespeare has found skill adequate to his ambition. Nothing but the finest part of pure love inhabits his scenes of romantic enchantment—the courtship at the ball, the moonlit wooing, the bridal night. He has intensified its purity by contrasting it with Romeo's first posings, with Capulet's bargainings and tantrums, with Mercutio's bawdry, with the Friar's benign philosophizing, and with the nurse's loose opportunism. He has shown that love makes lovers fearless. He sings its hymn in Juliet's epithalamium, and consecrates it as rising above life, in the successive draughts, of sleep and of death, which each lover drinks to the other. His favorite theme of Death the Bridegroom he has introduced when the lean abhorred monster, in Romeo's imaginings, keeps Juliet "in dark to be his paramour."

Above all, he has brought out the pathos of love by violent contrasts. Time hurries all things away, and in the lightning imagery the kiss and the consummation are as fire and powder. Frail love, surrounded by disasters, becomes a thing of light in blackness, itself "like a rich jewel in an Ethiop's ear." All is loneliness: Juliet is deserted by her father, then by her mother, then by her nurse, until she is left only with the power to die, or to consign herself to the horrible vault. Romeo is exiled—and indeed through the middle scenes "banished! banished!" beats like a pulse.[3] Desperate and exiled, love knows only enemies, ranging from the vulgar nurse to "love-devouring death" itself.

The secret of the play is that the deaths of the lovers are *not* the result of the hatred between the houses, nor of any other cause except love itself, which seeks in death its own restoring cordial. Love conquers death even more surely than it conquers hate. It sweeps aside all accidents, so that fate itself seems powerless. Time is conquered, in that first stirring of a belief that Shakespeare came later to trust completely: that the intensity of an emotion towers above its temporal duration or success. Shakespeare's moral measurements are to be qualitative, not quantitative. Romeo says in the second act:

---

[2] V, iii, 161; II, vi, 33; III, ii, 163—all Juliet's.

[3] "Some word there was . . . That murd'red me," says Juliet (III, ii, 108-09). Variants on "banished" or "exiled" occur 31 times in III, ii and III, iii. Note also "despair" and "death" in the play.

> But come what sorrow can,
> It cannot countervail the exchange of joy
> That one short minute gives me in her sight.

And when he has indeed experienced such sorrow, in exile, at Mantua, he turns to his happy, flattering dream:

> I dreamt my lady came and found me dead
> (Strange dream that gives a dead man leave to think!)
> And breath'd such life with kisses in my lips
> That I reviv'd and was an emperor.

The dream is closer to truth than to dramatic irony. For the intensity of their single-souled impulse has turned their passion into a death-devouring love. Their life is in their kisses, and Juliet turns to Romeo's murdered lips for a restorative. The suicidal weapon is a "happy dagger," wedding the lovers to eternity. Man's deeper instincts play strange juggleries in attaining truth beyond the reach of metaphysics, so that there is a mysterious authenticity in Romeo's phrase "a triumphant grave." From the time he hears of Juliet's death, all his actions in this world are those of "a dead man" until he can reaffirm his marriage to Juliet, this time with no possible separation, by drinking the poison cup. The sense of triumph descends upon the play from a love so straight, so simple, and so certain that its very bravery transforms death and time and hatred—yes, and the accidents of Fate—into insubstantial shadows. The quick bright things remain shining and alive.

"Or Else Were This a Savage Spectacle"
[Ritual in *Julius Caesar*]

by Brents Stirling

Modern readers are prone to find the tragedy of Brutus in his rigid devotion to justice and fair play. Many members of the Globe audience, however, believed that his virtues were complicated by self-deception and doubtful principle. In sixteenth-century views of history the conspiracy against Caesar often represented a flouting of unitary sovereignty, that prime point of Tudor policy, and exemplified the anarchy thought to accompany "democratic" or constitutional checks upon authority. Certain judgments of Elizabethan political writers who refer to Brutus are quite clear upon this point.[1] Although naturally aware of his disinterested honor and liberality, contemporary audiences could thus perceive in him a conflict between questionable goals and honorable action, a contradiction lying in his attempt to redeem morally confused ends by morally clarified means. The Elizabethan tragedy of Brutus, like that of Othello, is marked by an integrity of conduct which leads the protagonist into evil and measures him in his error.

The distinction between modern and Elizabethan views of *Julius Caesar* is not the point of our inquiry, but it is a necessary beginning, for the older view of Brutus determines both the symbolic quality and the structure of the play. I hope to show that a sixteenth-century idea of Brutus is as thoroughly related to Shakespeare's art as it is to his meaning.

" 'Or Else Were This a Savage Spectacle' [Ritual in *Julius Caesar*]." From *Unity in Shakespearian Tragedy* (New York: Columbia University Press, 1956), by Brents Stirling, pp. 40-54. Copyright © 1956 by Columbia University Press. Reprinted by permission of Columbia University Press.

[1] See the discussion in J. E. Phillips's *The State in Shakespeare's Greek and Roman Plays* (New York, 1940), pp. 172ff. Mr. Phillips quotes at length from such typical spokesmen as Sir Thomas Elyot and Thomas Craig. His analysis of *Julius Caesar* on this basis is also illuminating. See also the present author's *The Populace in Shakespeare* (New York, 1949), p. 147, for a condemnation by William Covell of Romans who aroused civil dissension by covering their purposes "with the fine terms of a common good, of the freedom of the people, of justice. . . ." The parallel with Brutus is a very close one, and Covell, moreover, explicitly avows a topical relation of such Roman history to the civil tensions of Elizabethan England.

When a dramatist wishes to present an idea, his traditional method, of course, is to settle upon an episode in which the idea arises naturally but vividly from action and situation. Such an episode in *Julius Caesar* is the one in which Brutus resolves to exalt not only the mission but the tactics of conspiracy: /having accepted republicanism as an honorable end, he sets out to dignify assassination, the means, by lifting it to a level of rite and ceremony.[2] In II.i, as Cassius urges the killing of Antony as a necessary accompaniment to the death of Caesar, Brutus declares that "such a course will seem too bloody . . . ,/ To cut the head off and then hack the limbs." With this thought a sense of purpose comes over him: "Let's be sacrificers, but not butchers, Caius." Here his conflict seems to be resolved, and for the first time he is more than a reluctant presence among the conspirators as he expands the theme which ends his hesitation and frees his moral imagination:

> We all stand up against the spirit of Caesar,
> And in the spirit of men there is no blood;
> Oh, that we then could come by Caesar's spirit,
> And not dismember Caesar! But, alas,
> Caesar must bleed for it! And, gentle friends,
> Let's kill him boldly, but not wrathfully;
> Let's carve him as a dish fit for the gods,
> Not hew him as a carcass fit for hounds.

This proposed conversion of bloodshed to ritual is the manner in which an abstract Brutus will be presented in terms of concrete art. From the suggestion of Plutarch that Brutus' first error lay in sparing Antony, Shakespeare moves to the image of Antony as a limb of Caesar, a limb not to be hacked because hacking is no part of ceremonial sacrifice. From Plutarch's description of Brutus as high-minded, gentle and disinterested, Shakespeare proceeds to the Brutus of symbolic action. Gentleness and disinterestedness become embodied in the act of "unwrathful" blood sacrifice. High-mindedness becomes objectified in ceremonial observance.

A skeptical reader may ask why the episode just described is any more significant than a number of others such as Brutus' scene with Portia or his quarrel with Cassius. If more significant, it is so only because of its relation to a thematic design. I agree, moreover, that Shakespeare gains his effects by variety; as a recognition, in fact, of his complexity I hope to show that the structure of *Julius Caesar* is marked by reference both varied and apt to Brutus' sacrificial rite, and that this process includes

---

[2] My article on the ritual theme in *Julius Caesar* (*PMLA*, LXVI, pp. 765ff.) appeared in 1951 as an early draft of this chapter. Some of my principal observations have been repeated by Ernest Schanzer in a recent essay ("The Tragedy of Shakespeare's Brutus," *ELH* (March, 1955), pp. 1ff.; see pp. 6-8).

expository preparation in earlier scenes, emphasis upon "mock-ceremony" in both earlier and later scenes, and repeated comment by Antony upon butchery under the guise of sacrifice—ironical comment which takes final form in the parley before Philippi.

Derived in large measure from Plutarch, but never mechanically or unselectively, the theme of incantation and ritual is thus prominent throughout *Julius Caesar,* and this is no less true at the beginning than during the crucial episodes of Acts II and III. In the opening scene of the play we are confronted with a Roman populace rebuked by Marullus for ceremonial idolatry of Caesar:

> And do you now put on your best attire?
> And do you now cull out a holiday?
> And do you now strew flowers in his way
> That comes in triumph over Pompey's blood?

For this transgression Marullus prescribes a counter-observance by the citizens in immediate expiation of their folly:

> Run to your houses, fall upon your knees,
> Pray to the gods to intermit this plague
> That needs must light on this ingratitude.

To which Flavius adds:

> Go, go, good countrymen, and for this fault,
> Assemble all the poor men of your sort;
> Draw them to Tiber banks, and weep your tears
> Into the channel, till the lowest stream
> Do kiss the most exalted shores of all.

And after committing the populace to these rites of atonement for their festal celebration of Caesar, the two tribunes themselves leave to remove the devotional symbols set up for his welcoming. "Go you . . . towards the Capitol;/ This way will I. Disrobe the images/ If you do find them decked with ceremonies./ . . . let no images/ Be hung with Caesar's trophies." It is the hope of Flavius that these disenchantments will make Caesar "fly an ordinary pitch,/ Who else would soar above the view of men."

Act I, scene ii is equally unusual in carrying the theme of ritual. It is apparent that Shakespeare had a wide choice of means for staging the entry of Caesar and his retinue; yet he selects an entry based upon Plutarch's description of the "feast Lupercalia" in which the rite of touching or striking barren women by runners of the course is made prominent. Caesar, moreover, after ordering Calpurnia to be so touched by Antony, commands: "Set on; and leave no ceremony out." It can be said, in fact, that the whole of this scene is written with ceremonial observance as a background. Its beginning, already described, is followed by a touch of solemnity in the soothsayer's words; next comes its main expository function, the sounding of Brutus by Cassius, and throughout this interchange come at intervals the shouts and flourishes of a symbolic spectacle. When the scene is again varied by a formal reentry and exit of Caesar's train, Casca remains behind to make a mockery of the rite which has loomed so large from off-stage. Significantly, in Casca's travesty of the ceremonial crown-offering and of the token offering by Caesar of his throat for cutting, Shakespeare has added a satirical note which does not appear in Plutarch.

The process, then, in each of the two opening episodes has been the bringing of serious ritual into great prominence, and of subjecting it to satirical treatment. In the first scene the tribunes denounce the punctilio planned for Caesar's entry, send the idolatrous crowd to rites of purification, and set off themselves to desecrate the devotional images. In the second scene a multiple emphasis of ceremony is capped by Casca's satire which twists the crown ritual into imbecile mummery. At this point, and in conformity with the mood set by Casca, occurs Cassius' mockery in soliloquy of Brutus:

> Well, Brutus, thou art noble; yet I see
> Thy honorable mettle may be wrought
> From that it is dispos'd; therefore it is meet
> That noble minds keep ever with their likes;
> For who is so firm that cannot be seduc'd?

The next scene (I. iii) is packed with omens and supernatural portents, a note which is carried directly into II. i where Brutus, on receiving the mysterious papers which have been left to prompt his action, remarks,

> The exhalations whizzing in the air
> Give so much light that I may read by them.

Appropriately, the letters read under this weird glow evoke his first real commitment to the "cause":

> O Rome, I make thee promise
> . If the redress will follow, thou receivest
> Thy full petition at the hand of Brutus!

Now appear his lines on the interim "between the acting of a dreadful thing/ And the first motion" in which "the state of man/ Like to a little kingdom, suffers then/ The nature of a insurrection." This conventional symbolizing of political convulsion by inward insurrection is followed by the soliloquy on conspiracy:

> O, then by day
> Where wilt thou find a cavern dark enough
> To mask thy monstrous visage? Seek none, Conspiracy!
> Hide it in smiles and affability.

The conflict within Brutus thus becomes clear in this scene. First, the participant in revolution suffers revolution within himself; then the hater of conspiracy and lover of plain dealing must call upon Conspiracy to hide in smiling courtesy.

We have now reached the critical point (II. i. 154ff.) to which attention was first called, an outward presentation of Brutus' crisis through his acceptance of an assassin's role upon condition that the assassins become sacrificers. Already a theme well established in preceding scenes, the idea of ritual is again made prominent. As the soliloquy on conspiracy closes, the plotters gather, and the issue becomes the taking of an oath. Brutus rejects this as an idle ceremony unsuited to men joined in the honesty of a cause and turns now to the prospect of Caesar's death. This time, however, honorable men do need ceremony, ceremony which will purify the violent act of all taint of butchery and raise it to the level of sacrifice. But although Brutus has steadied himself with a formula his conflict is still unresolved, for as he sets his course he "unconsciously" reveals the evasion which Antony later will amplify: to transmute political killing into ritual is to cloak it with appearances. We began with Brutus' passage on carving Caesar as a dish for the gods; these are the lines which complete it:

> And let our hearts, as subtle masters do,
> Stir up their servants to an act of rage,
> And after seem to chide 'em. This shall make
> Our purpose necessary and not envious;
> Which so appearing to the common eyes,
> We shall be called purgers, not murderers.

The contradiction is interesting. In an anticlimax, Brutus has ended his great invocation to ritual with a note on practical politics: our hearts shall stir us and afterward seem to chide us; we shall thus "appear" to the citizenry as purgers, not murderers.

Shakespeare never presents Brutus as a demagogue, but there are ironical traces of the politician in him which suggest Covell's adverse picture of Roman liberators.[3] It is curious, in fact, that although Brutus is commonly thought to be unconcerned over public favor, he expresses clear concern for it in the passage just quoted and in III. i. 244-51, where he sanctions Antony's funeral speech only if Antony agrees to tell the crowd that he speaks by generous permission, and only if he agrees to utter no evil of the conspiracy. Nor is Brutus' speech in the Forum wholly the nonpolitical performance it is supposed to be; certainly Shakespeare's Roman citizens are the best judges of it, and they react tempestuously. Although compressed, it scarcely discloses aloofness or an avoidance of popular emotive themes.

Act II, scene ii now shifts to the house of Caesar, but the emphasis on ritual continues as before. With dramatic irony, in view of Brutus' recent lines on sacrificial murder, Caesar commands, "Go bid the priests do present sacrifice." Calpurnia who has "never stood on ceremonies" (omens) is now terrified by them. News comes that the augurers, plucking the entrails of an offering, have failed to find a heart. Calpurnia has dreamed that smiling Romans have laved their hands in blood running from Caesar's statue, and Decius Brutus gives this its favorable interpretation which sends Caesar to his death.

The vivid assassination scene carries out Brutus' ritual prescription in dramatic detail, for the killing is staged with a formalized approach, ending in kneeling, by one conspirator after another until the victim is surrounded. This is met by a series of retorts from Caesar ending in "Hence! Wilt thou lift up Olympus," and the "sacrifice" is climaxed with his "Et tu Brute!" The conspirators ceremonially bathe their hands in Caesar's blood, and Brutus pronounces upon "this our lofty scene" with the prophecy that it "shall be acted over/ In states unborn and accents yet unknown!"

The mockery in counterritual now begins as a servant of Antony enters (III. i. 121) and confronts Brutus:

> Thus, Brutus, did my master bid me kneel,
> Thus did Mark Antony bid me fall down;
> And being prostrate, thus he bade me say:
> Brutus is noble, wise, valiant, and honest.

Here a threefold repetition, "kneel," "fall down," and "being prostrate," brings the ceremonial irony close to satire. Following this worship of the new idol by his messenger, Antony appears in person and with dramatic timing offers himself as a victim. In one speech he evokes both the holy scene which the conspirators so desired and the savagery which underlay it:

[3] See the reference and quotation in note 1.

> Now, whilst your purpled hands do reek and smoke,
> Fulfill your pleasure. Live a thousand years,
> I shall not find myself so apt to die;
> No place will please me so, no mean of death,
> As here by Caesar, and by you cut off.

The murder scene is thus hallowed by Antony in a manner which quite reverses its sanctification by the conspirators. Brutus, forbearing, attempts to mollify Antony with his cherished theme of purgation:

> Our hearts you see not. They are pitiful,
> And pity to the general wrong of Rome—
> As fire drives out fire, so pity pity—
> Hath done this deed on Caesar.

Antony's response is again one of counterceremony, the shaking of hands in formal sequence which serves to make each conspirator stand alone and unprotected by the rite of blood which had united him with the others. The assassins had agreed as a token of solidarity that each of them should stab Caesar. Antony seems to allude to this:

> Let each man render me his bloody hand.
> First, Marcus Brutus, will I shake with you;
> Now, Caius Cassius, do I take your hand;
> Now, Decius Brutus, yours; now yours, Mettellus;
> Yours, Cinna; and, my valiant Casca, yours;
> Though last, not least in love yours, good Trebonius.
> Gentlemen all—alas what shall I say?

It is then that Antony, addressing the body of Caesar, suddenly delivers his first profanation of the ritual sacrifice:

> Here wast thou bay'd brave hart;
> Here didst thou fall; and here thy hunters stand,
> Sign'd in thy spoil, and crimson'd in thy lethe.

And lest the allusion escape, Shakespeare continues Antony's inversion of Brutus' ceremonial formula: the dish carved for the gods is doubly transformed into the carcass hewn for hounds with further hunting metaphors of Caesar as a hart in the forest and as "a deer strucken by many princes." Brutus agrees to give reasons why Caesar was dangerous, "or else were this a savage spectacle," and the stage is set for what may be called the play's chief counterritual. Only Brutus, who planned the rite of sacrifice, could with such apt irony arrange the "true rites" and "ceremonies" which are to doom the conspiracy.

> I will myself into the pulpit first
> And show the reason of our Caesar's death.
> What Antony shall speak, I will protest
> He speaks by leave and by permission,
> And that we are contented Caesar shall
> Have all true rites and lawful ceremonies.

But exactly after the manner of his speech announcing the ritual sacrifice (II. i) Brutus concludes again on a note of policy: "It shall advantage more than do us wrong."

Next follows Antony *solus* rendering his prophecy of "domestic fury and fierce civil strife" symbolized in Caesar's ghost which will

> Cry "Havoc," and let slip the dogs of war,
> That this foul deed shall smell above the earth.

The passage is similar in utterance, function, and dramatic placement to Carlisle's prophecy on the deposition of Richard II, and for that reason it is to be taken seriously as a choric interpretation of Caesar's death. Significantly, the beginning lines again deride Brutus' erstwhile phrase, "sacrificers but not butchers":

> O, pardon me, thou bleeding piece of earth,
> That I am meek and gentle with these butchers!

It is unnecessary to elaborate upon the Forum scene; Antony's oration follows the speech of Brutus with consequences familiar to all readers. But there is an element in Antony's turning of the tables which is just as remarkable as the well-known irony of his references to "honorable men." If we remember that Shakespeare has emphasized ritual at various planes of seriousness and of derision, the conclusion of Antony's speech to the populace will link itself with the previous theme. For here Antony reenacts the death of Caesar in a ritual of his own, one intended to show that the original "lofty scene" presented a base carnage. Holding Caesar's bloody mantle as a talisman, he reproduces *seriatim* the sacrificial strokes, but he does so in terms of the "rent" Casca made and the "cursed steel" that Brutus plucked away with the blood of Caesar following it. Again, each conspirator had struck individually at Caesar and had symbolically involved himself with the others; for the second time Antony reminds us of this ritual bond by recounting each stroke, and his recreation of the rite becomes a mockery of it. Brutus' transformation of blood into the heady wine of sacrifice is reversed both in substance and in ceremony.

For the "realists" among the conspirators what has occurred can be summed up in the bare action of the play: the killing of Caesar has been accomplished, but the fruits of it have been spoiled by Brutus' insistence that Antony live and that he speak at Caesar's funeral. "The which," as North's Plutarch has it, "marred all." With reference to Brutus, however, something much more significant has been enacted; the "insurrection," the contradiction, within him has taken outward form in his attempt to purify assassination through ceremony. This act, not to be found in Plutarch,[4] symbolizes the "Elizabethan" Brutus compelled by honor to join with conspirators but required by conscience to reject Conspiracy.

We have followed the ritual theme in *Julius Caesar* from early scenes to the point of Antony's oration, at which it is completely defined. There remains, however, a terminal appearance of the theme in the first scene of Act V. The ultimate clash between the idealism of Brutus and Antony's contempt for it comes during the parley on the eve of Philippi, at which Antony again drives home the old issue of ceremonial imposture. Brutus has observed that his enemy wisely threats before he stings; the reply is Antony's last disposition of the sacrificial rite:

[4] A reference at this point to Plutarch will serve both to clarify my meaning and to allay some natural doubts concerning the dramatist's intention. While it is true that the ritual murder of Caesar is Shakespeare's own contribution, the expository preparation for it in Act I comes from an episode in Plutarch in which Antony concludes the Lupercalian rites by offering a laurel crown twice to Caesar, and in which the tribunes are described as desecrating ritual offerings (*Shakespeare's Plutarch*, I, 92-3; see also II, 19-20). Hence we have basic ritual materials for Shakespeare's first two scenes present in one convenient block of his source which also offered a convenient beginning for the play. Does this prevent us from attaching significance to the unusual presence of ritual elements in the exposition scenes? I believe it does not, for two reasons. First, the choice of source material by a dramatist is itself significant; Shakespeare could have started the play with other episodes in Plutarch or with scenes of his own invention. Secondly, it is immaterial whether he began *Julius Caesar* with this episode in his source and, because of its wealth of ritual detail, was led to the theme of ritualized assassination, or whether he began with the theme and chose source materials for exposition which agreed with it. In either case the same remarkable unity between earlier and later parts of the play would have been achieved, and it is this unity which is important. Guesses about its origin in the playwright's composition are profitless. We do know that Shakespeare's Brutus plans the killing of Caesar as ritual, while Plutarch presents it as the very opposite of this. Plutarch's description of the assassination emphazies, in fact, resemblance to the hunting down of an animal, the very effect Brutus seeks explicitly to avoid in the "carcass-hounds" figure, and the one which Antony magnifies in his counteremphasis of imagery drawn from hunting. North notes it thus: "Caesar turned him nowhere but he was stricken at by some . . . and was hacked and mangled among them, as a wild beast taken of hunters." (*Shakespeare's Plutarch*, I, 101-2.)

> Villains, you did not so when your vile daggers
> Hack'd one another in the sides of Caesar,
> You show'd your teeth like apes, and fawn'd like hounds,
> And bow'd like bondmen, kissing Caesar's feet;
> Whilst damned Casca, like a cur, behind
> Struck Caesar on the neck.

Antony invokes the "hacking" which Brutus earlier foreswore, and he again inverts the cherished formula of sacrifice: once more the dish carved for gods becomes the carcass hewn for hounds. Over the body of Caesar he had previously employed the hunting-hound figure ("Here wast thou bay'd, brave hart."); the apes, the hounds, and the cur of these lines complete his vengeful irony of metaphor.

What, finally, is to be inferred from Antony's concluding passage on "the noblest Roman of them all"? Commonly found there is a broad vindication of Brutus which would deny an ironical interpretation. When Antony's elegiac speech is read plainly, however, its meaning is quite limited: it declares simply that Brutus was the only conspirator untouched by envy, and that, in intention, he acted "in a general honest thought/ And common good to all." The Elizabethan view of Brutus as tragically misguided is thus consistent with Anthony's pronouncement that he was the only disinterested member of the conspiracy. But Brutus is not to be summed up in an epitaph; as the impersonal member of a conspiracy motivated largely by personal ends, he sought in a complex way to resolve his contradiction by depersonalizing, ritualizing, the means.

Shakespeare's achievement, however, is not confined to the characterization of a major figure, for we have seen that the ceremonial motive extends beyond the personality of Brutus into the structure of the play. Exposition stressing the idea of ritual observance leads to the episode in which Brutus formulates the "sacrifice," and clear resolution of the idea follows in event and commentary. Structural craftsmanship thus supplements characterization and the two combine, as in *Richard II*, to state the political philosophy implicit in the play.

The World of *Hamlet*

by *Maynard Mack*

My subject is the world of *Hamlet*. I do not of course mean Denmark, except as Denmark is given a body by the play; and I do not mean Elizabethan England, though this is necessarily close behind the scenes. I mean simply the imaginative environment that the play asks us to enter when we read it or go to see it.

Great plays, as we know, do present us with something that can be called a world, a microcosm—a world like our own in being made of people, actions, situations, thoughts, feelings, and much more, but unlike our own in being perfectly, or almost perfectly, significant and coherent. In a play's world, each part implies the other parts, and each lives, each means, with the life and meaning of the rest.

This is the reason, as we also know, that the worlds of great plays greatly differ. Othello in Hamlet's position, we sometimes say, would have no problem; but what we are really saying is that Othello in Hamlet's position would not exist. The conception we have of Othello is a function of the characters who help define him, Desdemona, honest Iago, Cassio, and the rest; of his history of travel and war; of a great storm that divides his ship from Cassio's, and a handkerchief; of a quiet night in Venice broken by cries about an old black ram; of a quiet night in Cyprus broken by swordplay; of a quiet bedroom where a woman goes to bed in her wedding sheets and a man comes in with a light to put out the light; and above all, of a language, a language with many voices in it, gentle, rasping, querulous, or foul, but all counterpointing the one great voice:

Put up your bright swords, for the dew will rust them.

> O thou weed
> Who art so lovely fair and smell'st so sweet
> That the sense aches at thee. . . .

"The World of *Hamlet*" by Maynard Mack. From *The Yale Review*, XLI (1952), 502-23. Copyright 1952 by Yale University Press. Reprinted by permission of Maynard Mack and *The Yale Review*.

> Yet I'll not shed her blood
> Nor scar that whiter skin of hers than snow,
> And smooth as monumental alabaster.
>
> I pray you in your letters,
> When you shall these unlucky deeds relate,
> Speak of me as I am; nothing extenuate,
> Nor set down aught in malice; then must you speak
> Of one that loved not wisely but too well;
> Of one not easily jealous, but being wrought,
> Perplex'd in th' extreme; of one whose hand,
> Like the base Indian, threw a pearl away
> Richer than all his tribe. . . .

Without his particular world of voices, persons, events, the world that both expresses and contains him, Othello is unimaginable. And so, I think, are Antony, King Lear, Macbeth—and Hamlet. We come back then to Hamlet's world, of all the tragic worlds that Shakespeare made, easily the most various and brilliant, the most elusive. It is with no thought of doing justice to it that I have singled out three of its attributes for comment. I know too well, if I may echo a sentiment of Mr. E. M. W. Tillyard's, that no one is likely to accept another man's reading of *Hamlet,* that anyone who tries to throw light on one part of the play usually throws the rest into deeper shadow, and that what I have to say leaves out many problems—to mention only one, the knotty problem of the text. All I would say in defense of the materials I have chosen is that they seem to me interesting, close to the root of the matter even if we continue to differ about what the root of the matter is, and explanatory, in a modest way, of this play's peculiar hold on everyone's imagination, its almost mythic status, one might say, as a paradigm of the life of man.

The first attribute that impresses us, I think, is mysteriousness. We often hear it said, perhaps with truth, that every great work of art has a mystery at the heart; but the mystery of *Hamlet* is something else. We feel its presence in the numberless explanations that have been brought forward for Hamlet's delay, his madness, his ghost, his treatment of Polonius, or Ophelia, or his mother; and in the controversies that still go on about whether the play is "undoubtedly a failure" (Eliot's phrase) or one of the greatest artistic triumphs; whether, if it is a triumph, it belongs to the highest order of tragedy; whether, if it is such a tragedy, its hero is to be taken as a man of exquisite moral sensibility (Bradley's view) or an egomaniac (Madariaga's view).

Doubtless there have been more of these controversies and explanations than the play requires; for in Hamlet, to paraphrase a remark of Falstaff's, we have a character who is not only mad in himself but a

cause that madness is in the rest of us. Still, the very existence of so many
theories and countertheories, many of them formulated by sober heads,
gives food for thought. *Hamlet* seems to lie closer to the illogical logic
of life than Shakespeare's other tragedies. And while the causes of this
situation may be sought by saying that Shakespeare revised the play so
often that eventually the motivations were smudged over, or that the
original old play has been here or there imperfectly digested, or that the
problems of Hamlet lay so close to Shakespeare's heart that he could not
quite distance them in the formal terms of art, we have still as critics to
deal with effects, not causes. If I may quote again from Mr. Tillyard, the
play's very lack of a rigorous type of causal logic seems to be a part of its
point.

Moreover, the matter goes deeper than this. Hamlet's world is pre-
eminently in the interrogative mood. It reverberates with questions,
anguished, meditative, alarmed. There are questions that in this play, to
an extent I think unparalleled in any other, mark the phases and even
the nuances of the action, helping to establish its peculiar baffled tone.
There are other questions whose interrogations, innocent at first glance,
are subsequently seen to have reached beyond their contexts and to
point towards some pervasive inscrutability in Hamlet's world as a
whole. Such is that tense series of challenges with which the tragedy
begins: Bernardo's of Francisco, "Who's there?" Francisco's of Horatio
and Marcellus, "Who is there?" Horatio's of the ghost, "What art thou
. . . ?" And then there are the famous questions. In them the interrogations seem to point not only beyond the context but beyond the play, out
of Hamlet's predicaments into everyone's: "What a piece of work is a
man! . . . And yet to me what is this quintessence of dust?" "To be, or
not to be, that is the question." "Get thee to a nunnery. Why wouldst
thou be a breeder of sinners?" "I am very proud, revengeful, ambitious,
with more offenses at my beck than I have thoughts to put them in,
imagination to give them shape, or time to act them in. What should
such fellows as I do crawling between earth and heaven?" "Dost thou
think Alexander look'd o' this fashion i' th' earth? . . . And smelt so?"

Further, Hamlet's world is a world of riddles. The hero's own language
is often riddling, as the critics have pointed out. When he puns, his puns
have receding depths in them, like the one which constitutes his first
speech: "A little more than kin, and less than kind." His utterances in
madness, even if wild and whirling, are simultaneously, as Polonius discovers, pregnant: "Do you know me, my lord?" "Excellent well. You are
a fishmonger." Even the madness itself is riddling: How much is real?
How much is feigned? What does it mean? Sane or mad, Hamlet's mind
plays restlessly about his world, turning up one riddle upon another.
The riddle of character, for example, and how it is that in a man whose
virtues else are "pure as grace," some vicious mole of nature, some "dram

of eale," can "all the noble substance oft adulter." Or the riddle of the
player's art, and how a man can so project himself into a fiction, a dream
of passion, that he can weep for Hecuba. Or the riddle of action: how
we may think too little—"What to ourselves in passion we propose," says
the player-king, "The passion ending, doth the purpose lose"; and again,
how we may think too much: "Thus conscience does make cowards of
us all, And thus the native hue of resolution Is sicklied o'er with the
pale cast of thought."

There are also more immediate riddles. His mother—how could she
"on this fair mountain leave to feed, And batten on this moor?" The
ghost—which may be a devil, for "the de'il hath power T' assume a
pleasing shape." Ophelia—what does her behavior to him mean? Surprising her in her closet, he falls to such perusal of her face as he would
draw it. Even the king at his prayers is a riddle. Will a revenge that takes
him in the purging of his soul be vengeance, or hire and salary? As for
himself, Hamlet realizes, he is the greatest riddle of all—a mystery, he
warns Rosencrantz and Guildenstern, from which he will not have the
heart plucked out. He cannot tell why he has of late lost all his mirth,
forgone all custom of exercises. Still less can he tell why he delays: "I do
not know Why yet I live to say, 'This thing's to do,' Sith I have cause
and will and strength and means To do't."

Thus the mysteriousness of Hamlet's world is of a piece. It is not simply a matter of missing motivations, to be expunged if only we could
find the perfect clue. It is built in. It is evidently an important part of
what the play wishes to say to us. And it is certainly an element that the
play thrusts upon us from the opening word. Everyone, I think, recalls
the mysteriousness of that first scene. The cold middle of the night on
the castle platform, the muffled sentries, the uneasy atmosphere of apprehension, the challenges leaping out of the dark, the questions that
follow the challenges, feeling out the darkness, searching for identities,
for relations, for assurance. "Bernardo?" "Have you had quiet guard?"
"Who hath reliev'd you?" "What, is Horatio there?" "What, has this
thing appear'd again tonight?" "Looks 'a not like the king?" "How now,
Horatio! . . . Is not this something more than fantasy? What think you
on 't?" "Is it not like the king?" "Why this same strict and most observant
watch . . . ?" "Shall I strike at it with my partisan?" "Do you consent
we shall acquaint [young Hamlet] with it?"

We need not be surprised that critics and playgoers alike have been
tempted to see in this an evocation not simply of Hamlet's world but of
their own. Man in his aspect of bafflement, moving in darkness on a
rampart between two worlds, unable to reject, or quite accept, the one
that, when he faces it, "to-shakes" his disposition with thoughts beyond
the reaches of his soul—comforting himself with hints and guesses. We
hear these hints and guesses whispering through the darkness as the sev-

eral watchers speak. "At least, the whisper goes so," says one. "I think it be no other but e'en so," says another. "I have heard" that on the crowing of the cock "Th' extravagant and erring spirit hies To his confine," says a third. "Some say" at Christmas time "this bird of dawning" sings all night, "And then, they say, no spirit dare stir abroad." "So have I heard," says the first, "and do in part believe it." However we choose to take the scene, it is clear that it creates a world where uncertainties are of the essence.

Meantime, such is Shakespeare's economy, a second attribute of Hamlet's world has been put before us. This is the problematic nature of reality and the relation of reality to appearance. The play begins with an appearance, an "apparition," to use Marcellus's term—the ghost. And the ghost is somehow real, indeed the vehicle of realities. Through its revelation, the glittering surface of Claudius's court is pierced, and Hamlet comes to know, and we do, that the king is not only hateful to him but the murderer of his father, that his mother is guilty of adultery as well as incest. Yet there is a dilemma in the revelation. For possibly the apparition *is* an apparition, a devil who has assumed his father's shape.

This dilemma, once established, recurs on every hand. From the court's point of view, there is Hamlet's madness. Polonius investigates and gets some strange advice about his daughter: "Conception is a blessing, but as your daughter may conceive, friend, look to 't." Rosencrantz and Guildenstern investigate and get the strange confidence that "Man delights not me; no, nor woman neither." Ophelia is "loosed" to Hamlet (Polonius's vulgar word), while Polonius and the king hide behind the arras; and what they hear is a strange indictment of human nature, and a riddling threat: "Those that are married already, all but one, shall live."

On the other hand, from Hamlet's point of view, there is Ophelia. Kneeling here at her prayers, she seems the image of innocence and devotion. Yet she is of the sex for whom he has already found the name Frailty, and she is also, as he seems either madly or sanely to divine, a decoy in a trick. The famous cry—"Get thee to a nunnery"—shows the anguish of his uncertainty. If Ophelia is what she seems, this dirty-minded world of murder, incest, lust, adultery, is no place for her. Were she "as chaste as ice, as pure as snow," she could not escape its calumny. And if she is not what she seems, then a nunnery in its other sense of brothel is relevant to her. In the scene that follows he treats her as if she were indeed an inmate of a brothel.

Likewise, from Hamlet's point of view, there is the enigma of the king. If the ghost is *only* an appearance, then possibly the king's appearance is reality. He must try it further. By means of a second and different kind' of "apparition," the play within the play, he does so. But then, immediately after, he stumbles on the king at prayer. This appearance has a relish of salvation in it. If the king dies now, his soul may yet be saved. Yet actually, as we know, the king's efforts to come to terms with heaven have been unavailing; his words fly up, his thoughts remain below. If Hamlet means the conventional revenger's reasons that he gives for sparing Claudius, it was the perfect moment not to spare him—when the sinner was acknowledging his guilt, yet unrepentant. The perfect moment, but it was hidden, like so much else in the play, behind an arras.

There are two arrases in his mother's room. Hamlet thrusts his sword through one of them. Now at last he has got to the heart of the evil, or so he thinks. But now it is the wrong man; now he himself is a murderer. The other arras he stabs through with his words—like daggers, says the queen. He makes her shrink under the contrast he points between her present husband and his father. But as the play now stands (matters are somewhat clearer in the bad Quarto), it is hard to be sure how far the queen grasps the fact that her second husband is the murderer of her first. And it is hard to say what may be signified by her inability to see the ghost, who now for the last time appears. In one sense at least, the ghost is the supreme reality, representative of the hidden ultimate power, in Bradley's terms—witnessing from beyond the grave against this hollow world. Yet the man who is capable of seeing through to this reality, the queen thinks is mad. "To whom do you speak this?" she cries to her son. "Do you see nothing there?" he asks, incredulous. And she replies: "Nothing at all; yet all that is I see." Here certainly we have the imperturbable self-confidence of the worldly world, its layers on layers of habituation, so that when the reality is before its very eyes it cannot detect its presence.

Like mystery, this problem of reality is central to the play and written deep into its idiom. Shakespeare's favorite terms in *Hamlet* are words of ordinary usage that pose the question of appearances in a fundamental form. "Apparition" I have already mentioned. Another term is "seems." When we say, as Ophelia says of Hamlet leaving her closet, "He seem'd to find his way without his eyes," we mean one thing. When we say, as Hamlet says to his mother in the first court scene, "Seems, Madam! . . . I know not 'seems,' " we mean another. And when we say, as Hamlet says to Horatio before the play within the play, "And after, we will both our judgments join In censure of his seeming," we mean both at once. The ambiguities of "seem" coil and uncoil throughout this play, and over against them is set the idea of "seeing." So Hamlet challenges the king in his triumphant letter announcing his return to Denmark: "To-morrow shall I beg leave to see your kingly eyes." Yet "seeing" itself can be ambiguous, as we recognize from Hamlet's uncertainty about the ghost; or from that statement of his mother's already quoted: "Nothing at all; yet all that is I see."

Another term of like importance is "assume." What we assume may be what we are not: "The de'il hath power T' assume a pleasing shape."

But it may be what we are: "If it assume my noble father's person, I'll
speak to it." And it may be what we are not yet, but would become; thus
Hamlet advises his mother, "Assume a virtue, if you have it not." The
perplexity in the word points to a real perplexity in Hamlet's and our
own experience. We assume our habits—and habits are like costumes, as
the word implies: "My father in his habit as he liv'd!" Yet these habits
become ourselves in time: "That monster, custom, who all sense doth eat
Of habits evil, is angel yet in this, That to the use of actions fair and
good He likewise gives a frock or livery That aptly is put on."

Two other terms I wish to instance are "put on" and "shape." The
shape of something is the form under which we are accustomed to apprehend it: "Do you see yonder cloud that's almost in shape of a camel?"
But a shape may also be a disguise—even, in Shakespeare's time, an actor's costume or an actor's role. This is the meaning when the king says
to Laertes as they lay the plot against Hamlet's life: "Weigh what con-
venience both of time and means May fit us to our shape." "Put on" supplies an analogous ambiguity. Shakespeare's mind seems to worry this
phrase in the play much as Hamlet's mind worries the problem of acting
in a world of surfaces, or the king's mind worries the meaning of Hamlet's transformation. Hamlet has put an antic disposition on, that the
king knows. But what does "put on" mean? A mask, or a frock or livery
—our "habit"? The king is left guessing, and so are we.

What is found in the play's key terms is also found in its imagery.
Miss Spurgeon has called attention to a pattern of disease images in
Hamlet, to which I shall return. But the play has other patterns equally
striking. One of these, as my earlier quotations hint, is based on clothes
In the world of surfaces to which Shakespeare exposes us in Hamlet,
clothes are naturally a factor of importance. "The apparel oft proclaims
the man," Polonius assures Laertes, cataloguing maxims in the young
man's ear as he is about to leave for Paris. Oft, but not always. And so
he sends his man Reynaldo to look into Laertes' life there—even, if need
be, to put a false dress of accusation upon his son ("What forgeries you
please"), the better by indirections to find directions out. On the same
grounds, he takes Hamlet's vows to Ophelia as false apparel. They are
bawds, he tells her—or if we do not like Theobald's emendation, they
are bonds—in masquerade, "Not of that dye which their investments
show, But mere implorators of unholy suits."

This breach between the outer and the inner stirs no special emotion
in Polonius, because he is always either behind an arras or prying into
one, but it shakes Hamlet to the core. Here so recently was his mother
in her widow's weeds, the tears still flushing in her galled eyes; yet now
within a month, a little month, before even her funeral shoes are old,
she has married with his uncle. Her mourning was all clothes. Not so his
own, he bitterly replies, when she asks him to cast his "nighted color off."

"Tis not alone my inky cloak, good mother"—and not alone, he adds, the sighs, the tears, the dejected havior of the visage—"that can denote me truly."

> These indeed seem,
> For they are actions that a man might play;
> But I have that within which passes show;
> These but the trappings and the suits of woe.

What we must not overlook here is Hamlet's visible attire, giving the verbal imagery a theatrical extension. Hamlet's apparel now is his inky cloak, mark of his grief for his father, mark also of his character as a man of melancholy, mark possibly too of his being one in whom appearance and reality are attuned. Later, in his madness, with his mind disordered, he will wear his costume in a corresponding disarray, the disarray that Ophelia describes so vividly to Polonius and that producers of the play rarely give sufficient heed to: "Lord Hamlet with his doublet all unbrac'd, No hat upon his head; his stockings foul'd, Ungarter'd, and down-gyved to his ankle." Here the only question will be, as with the madness itself, how much is studied, how much is real. Still later, by a third costume, the simple traveler's garb in which we find him new come from shipboard, Shakespeare will show us that we have a third aspect of the man.

A second pattern of imagery springs from terms of painting: the paints, the colorings, the varnishes that may either conceal, or, as in the painter's art, reveal. Art in Claudius conceals. "The harlot's cheek," he tells us in his one aside, "beautied with plastering art, Is not more ugly to the thing that helps it Than is my deed to my most painted word." Art in Ophelia, loosed to Hamlet in the episode already noticed to which this speech of the king's is prelude, is more complex. She looks so beautiful— "the celestial, and my soul's idol, the most beautified Ophelia," Hamlet has called her in his love letter. But now, what does beautified mean? Perfected with all the innocent beauties of a lovely woman? Or "beautied" like the harlot's cheek? "I have heard of your paintings too, well enough. God hath given you one face, and you make yourselves another."

Yet art, differently used, may serve the truth. By using an "image" (his own word) of a murder done in Vienna, Hamlet cuts through to the king's guilt; holds "as 'twere, the mirror up to nature," shows "virtue her own feature, scorn her own image, and the very age and body of the time"—which is out of joint—"his form and pressure." Something similar he does again in his mother's bedroom, painting for her in words "the rank sweat of an enseamed bed," making her recoil in horror from his "counterfeit presentment of two brothers," and holding, if we may trust a stage tradition, his father's picture beside his uncle's. Here again the verbal imagery is realized visually on the stage.

The most pervasive of Shakespeare's image patterns in this play, however, is the pattern evolved around the three words, "show," "act," "play."
"Show" seems to be Shakespeare's unifying image in *Hamlet*. Through it
he pulls together and exhibits in a single focus much of the diverse material in his play. The ideas of seeming, assuming, and putting on; the
images of clothing, painting, mirroring; the episode of the dumb show
and the play within the play; the characters of Polonius, Laertes, Ophelia,
Claudius, Gertrude, Rosencrantz and Guildenstern, Hamlet himself—all
these at one time or another, and usually more than once, are drawn into
the range of implications flung round the play by "show."

"Act," on the other hand, I take to be the play's radical metaphor. It
distills the various perplexities about the character of reality into a residual perplexity about the character of an act. What, this play asks again
and again, is an act? What is its relation to the inner act, the intent?
"If I drown myself wittingly," says the clown in the graveyard, "it argues
an act, and an act hath three branches; it is to act, to do, to perform."
Or again, the play asks, how does action relate to passion, that "laps'd in
time and passion" I can let "go by Th' important acting of your dread
command"; and to thought, which can so sickly o'er the native hue of
resolution that "enterprises of great pitch and moment With this regard
their currents turn awry, And lose the name of action"; and to words,
which are not acts, and so we dare not be content to unpack our hearts
with them, and yet are acts of a sort, for we may speak daggers though
we use none. Or still again, how does an act (a deed) relate to an act (a
pretense)? For an action may be nothing but pretense. So Polonius ready-
ing Ophelia for the interview with Hamlet, with "pious action," as he
phrases it, "sugar[s] o'er The devil himself." Or it may not be a pretense,
yet not what it appears. So Hamlet spares the king, finding him in an
act that has some "relish of salvation in 't." Or it may be a pretense that
is also the first foothold of a new reality, as when we assume a virtue
though we have it not. Or it may be a pretense that is actually a mirroring of reality, like the play within the play, or the tragedy of *Hamlet*.

To this network of implications, the third term, "play," adds an additional dimension. "Play" is a more precise word, in Elizabethan par-
lance at least, for all the elements in *Hamlet* that pertain to the art of
the theater; and it extends their field of reference till we see that every
major personage in the tragedy is a player in some sense, and every major
episode a play. The court plays, Hamlet plays, the players play, Rosencrantz and Guildenstern try to play on Hamlet, though they cannot play
on his recorders—here we have an extension to a musical sense. And the
final duel, by a further extension, becomes itself a play, in which everyone but Claudius and Laertes plays his role in ignorance: "The queen
desires you to show some gentle entertainment to Laertes before you fall

to play." "I . . . will this brother's wager frankly play." "Give him the cup."—"I'll play this bout first."

The full extension of this theme is best evidenced in the play within the play itself. Here, in the bodily presence of these traveling players, bringing with them the latest playhouse gossip out of London, we have suddenly a situation that tends to dissolve the normal barriers between the fictive and the real. For here on the stage before us is a play of false appearances in which an actor called the player-king is playing. But there is also on the stage, Claudius, another player-king, who is a spectator of this player. And there is on the stage, besides, a prince who is a spectator of both these player-kings and who plays with great intensity a player's role himself. And around these kings and that prince is a group of courtly spectators—Gertrude, Rosencrantz, Guildenstern, Polonius, and the rest —and they, as we have come to know, are players too. And lastly there are ourselves, an audience watching all these audiences who are also players. Where, it may suddenly occur to us to ask, does the playing end? Which *are* the guilty creatures sitting at a play? When is an act not an "act"?

The mysteriousness of Hamlet's world, while it pervades the tragedy, finds its point of greatest dramatic concentration in the first act, and its symbol in the first scene. The problems of appearance and reality also pervade the play as a whole, but come to a climax in Acts II and III, and possibly their best symbol is the play within the play. Our third attribute, though again it is one that crops out everywhere, reaches its full development in Acts IV and V. It is not easy to find an appropriate name for this attribute, but perhaps "mortality" will serve, if we remember to mean by mortality the heartache and the thousand natural shocks that flesh is heir to, not simply death.

The powerful sense of mortality in *Hamlet* is conveyed to us, I think, in three ways. First, there is the play's emphasis on human weakness, the instability of human purpose, the subjection of humanity to fortune— all that we might call the aspect of failure in man. Hamlet opens this theme in Act I, when he describes how from that single blemish, perhaps not even the victim's fault, a man's whole character may take corruption. Claudius dwells on it again, to an extent that goes far beyond the needs of the occasion, while engaged in seducing Laertes to step behind the arras of a seemer's world and dispose of Hamlet by a trick. Time qualifies everything, Claudius says, including love, including purpose. As for love —it has a "plurisy" in it and dies of its own too much. As for purpose— "That we would do, We should do when we would, for this 'would' changes, And hath abatements and delays as many As there are tongues, are hands, are accidents; And then this 'should' is like a spendthrift's sigh, That hurts by easing." The player-king, in his long speeches to his queen in the play within the play, sets the matter in a still darker light. She means these protestations of undying love, he knows, but our purposes depend on our memory, and our memory fades fast. Or else, he suggests, we propose something to ourselves in a condition of strong feeling, but then the feeling goes, and with it the resolve. Or else our fortunes change, he adds, and with these our loves: "The great man down, you mark his favorite flies." The subjection of human aims to fortune is a reiterated theme in *Hamlet,* as subsequently in *Lear.* Fortune is the harlot goddess in whose secret parts men like Rosencrantz and Guildenstern live and thrive; the strumpet who threw down Troy and Hecuba and Priam; the outrageous foe whose slings and arrows a man of principle must suffer or seek release in suicide. Horatio suffers them with composure: he is one of the blessed few "Whose blood and judgment are so well co-mingled That they are not a pipe for fortune's finger To sound what stop she please." For Hamlet the task is of a greater difficulty.

Next, and intimately related to this matter of infirmity, is the emphasis on infection—the ulcer, the hidden abscess, "th' imposthume of much wealth and peace That inward breaks and shows no cause without Why the man dies." Miss Spurgeon, who was the first to call attention to this aspect of the play, has well remarked that so far as Shakespeare's pictorial imagination is concerned, the problem in *Hamlet* is not a problem of the will and reason, "of a mind too philosophical or a nature temperamentally unfitted to act quickly," nor even a problem of an individual at all. Rather, it is a condition—"a condition for which the individual himself is apparently not responsible, any more than the sick man is to blame for the infection which strikes and devours him, but which, nevertheless, in its course and development, impartially and relentlessly, annihilates him and others, innocent and guilty alike." "That," she adds, "is the tragedy of *Hamlet,* as it is perhaps the chief tragic mystery of life." This is a perceptive comment, for it reminds us that Hamlet's situation is mainly not of his own manufacture, as are the situations of Shakespeare's other tragic heroes. He has inherited it; he is "born to set it right."

We must not, however, neglect to add to this what another student of Shakespeare's imagery has noticed—that the infection in Denmark is presented alternatively as poison. Here, of course, responsibility is implied, for the poisoner of the play is Claudius. The juice he pours into the ear of the elder Hamlet is a combined poison and disease, a "leperous distillment" that curds "the thin and wholesome blood." From this fatal center, unwholesomeness spreads out till there is something rotten in all Denmark. Hamlet tells us that his "wit's diseased," the queen speaks of her "sick soul," the king is troubled by "the hectic" in his blood, Laertes meditates revenge to warm "the sickness in my heart," the people of the kingdom grow "muddied, Thick and unwholesome in their thoughts"; and even Ophelia's madness is said to be "the poison of deep grief." In the end, all save Ophelia die of that poison in a literal as well as figurative sense.

But the chief form in which the theme of mortality reaches us, it seems to me, is as a profound consciousness of loss. Hamlet's father expresses something of the kind when he tells Hamlet how his "[most] seeming-virtuous queen," betraying a love which "was of that dignity That it went hand in hand even with the vow I made to her in marriage," had chosen to "decline Upon a wretch whose natural gifts were poor To those of mine." "O Hamlet, what a falling off was there!" Ophelia expresses it again, on hearing Hamlet's denunciation of love and woman in the nunnery scene, which she takes to be the product of a disordered brain:

> O what a noble mind is here o'erthrown!
> The courtier's, soldier's, scholar's, eye, tongue, sword;
> Th' expectancy and rose of the fair state,
> The glass of fashion and the mold of form,
> Th' observ'd of all observers, quite, quite down!

The passage invites us to remember that we have never actually seen such a Hamlet—that his mother's marriage has brought a falling off in him before we meet him. And then there is that further falling off, if I may call it so, when Ophelia too goes mad—"Divided from herself and her fair judgment, Without the which we are pictures, or mere beasts."

Time was, the play keeps reminding us, when Denmark was a different place. That was before Hamlet's mother took off "the rose From the fair forehead of an innocent love" and set a blister there. Hamlet then was still "Th' expectancy and rose of the fair state"; Ophelia, the "rose of May." For Denmark was a garden then, when his father ruled. There had been something heroic about his father—a king who met the threats to Denmark in open battle, fought with Norway, smote the sledded Polacks on the ice, slew the elder Fortinbras in an honorable trial of strength. There had been something godlike about his father too: "Hyperion's curls, the front of Jove himself, An eye like Mars . . . A station like the herald Mercury." But, the ghost reveals, a serpent was in the garden, and "the serpent that did sting thy father's life Now wears his crown." The martial virtues are put by now. The threats to Denmark are attended to by policy, by agents working deviously for and through an uncle. The moral virtues are put by too. Hyperion's throne is occupied by "a vice of kings," "a king of shreds and patches"; Hyperion's bed, by a satyr, a paddock, a bat, a gib, a bloat king with reechy kisses. The garden is unweeded now, and "grows to seed; things rank and gross in nature Possess it merely." Even in himself he feels the taint, the taint of being his mother's son; and that other taint, from an earlier garden, of which he admonishes Ophelia: "Our virtue cannot so inoculate our old stock but we shall relish of it." "Why wouldst thou be a breeder of sinners?" "What should such fellows as I do crawling between earth and heaven?"

"Hamlet is painfully aware," says Professor Tillyard, "of the baffling human predicament between the angels and the beasts, between the glory of having been made in God's image and the incrimination of being descended from fallen Adam." To this we may add, I think, that Hamlet is more than aware of it; he exemplifies it; and it is for this reason that his problem appeals to us so powerfully as an image of our own.

Hamlet's problem, in its crudest form, is simply the problem of the avenger: he must carry out the injunction of the ghost and kill the king. But this problem, as I ventured to suggest at the outset, is presented in terms of a certain kind of world. The ghost's injunction to act becomes so inextricably bound up for Hamlet with the character of the world in which the action must be taken—its mysteriousness, its baffling appearances, its deep consciousness of infection, frailty, and loss—that he cannot come to terms with either without coming to terms with both.

When we first see him in the play, he is clearly a very young man, sensitive and idealistic, suffering the first shock of growing up. He has taken the garden at face value, we might say, supposing mankind to be only a little lower than the angels. Now in his mother's hasty and incestuous marriage, he discovers evidence of something else, something bestial—though even a beast, he thinks, would have mourned longer. Then comes the revelation of the ghost, bringing a second shock. Not so much because he now knows that his serpent-uncle killed his father; his prophetic soul had almost suspected this. Not entirely, even, because he knows now how far below the angels humanity has fallen in his mother, and how lust—these were the ghost's words—"though to a radiant angel link'd Will sate itself in a celestial bed, And prey on garbage." Rather, because he now sees everywhere, but especially in his own nature, the general taint, taking from life its meaning, from woman her integrity, from the will its strength, turning reason into madness. "Why wouldst thou be a breeder of sinners?" "What should such fellows as I do crawling between earth and heaven?" Hamlet is not the first young man to have felt the heavy and the weary weight of all this unintelligible world; and, like the others, he must come to terms with it.

The ghost's injunction to revenge unfolds a different facet of his problem. The young man growing up is not to be allowed simply to endure a rotten world, he must also act in it. Yet how to begin, among so many enigmatic surfaces? Even Claudius, whom he now knows to be the core of the ulcer, has a plausible exterior. And around Claudius, swathing the evil out of sight, he encounters all those other exteriors, as we have seen. Some of them already deeply infected beneath, like his mother.

Some noble, but marked for infection, like Laertes. Some not particularly corrupt but infinitely corruptible, like Rosencrantz and Guildenstern; some mostly weak and foolish like Polonius and Osric. Some, like Ophelia, innocent, yet in their innocence still serving to "skin and film the ulcerous place."

And this is not all. The act required of him, though retributive justice, is one that necessarily involves the doer in the general guilt. Not only because it involves a killing; but because to get at the world of seeming one sometimes has to use its weapons. He himself, before he finishes, has become a player, has put an antic disposition on, has killed a man— the wrong man—has helped drive Ophelia mad, and has sent two friends of his youth to death, mining below their mines, and hoisting the engineer with his own petard. He had never meant to dirty himself with these things, but from the moment of the ghost's challenge to act, this dirtying was inevitable. It is the condition of living at all in such a world. To quote Polonius, who knew that world so well, men become "a little soil'd i' th' working." Here is another matter with which Hamlet has to come to terms.

Human infirmity—all that I have discussed with reference to instability, infection, loss—supplies the problem with its third phase. Hamlet has not only to accept the mystery of man's condition between the angels and the brutes, and not only to act in a perplexing and soiling world. He has also to act within the human limits—"with shabby equipment always deteriorating," if I may adapt some phrases from Eliot's *East Coker,* "In the general mess of imprecision of feeling, Undisciplined squads of emotion." Hamlet is aware of that fine poise of body and mind, feeling and thought, that suits the action to the word, the word to the action; that acquires and begets a temperance in the very torrent, tempest, and whirlwind of passion; but he cannot at first achieve it in himself. He vacillates between undisciplined squads of emotion and thinking too precisely on the event. He learns to his cost how easily action can be lost in "acting," and loses it there for a time himself. But these again are only the terms of every man's life. As Anatole France reminds us in a now famous apostrophe to Hamlet: "What one of us thinks without contradiction and acts without incoherence? What one of us is not mad? What one of us does not say with a mixture of pity, comradeship, admiration, and horror, Goodnight, sweet Prince!"

In the last act of the play (or so it seems to me, for I know there can be differences on this point), Hamlet accepts his world and we discover a different man. Shakespeare does not outline for us the process of acceptance any more than he had done with Romeo or was to do with Othello. But he leads us strongly to expect an altered Hamlet, and then, in my opinion, provides him. We must recall that at this point Hamlet has been absent from the stage during several scenes, and that such absences in Shakespearean tragedy usually warn us to be on the watch for a new phase in the development of the character. It is so when we leave King Lear in Gloucester's farmhouse and find him again in Dover fields. It is so when we leave Macbeth at the witches' cave and rejoin him at Dunsinane, hearing of the armies that beset it. Furthermore, and this is an important matter in the theater—especially important in a play in which the symbolism of clothing has figured largely—Hamlet now looks different. He is wearing a different dress—probably, as Granville-Barker thinks, his "seagown scarf'd" about him, but in any case no longer the disordered costume of his antic disposition. The effect is not entirely dissimilar to that in *Lear,* when the old king wakes out of his madness to find fresh garments on him.

Still more important, Hamlet displays a considerable change of mood. This is not a matter of the way we take the passage about defying augury, as Mr. Tillyard among others seems to think. It is a matter of Hamlet's whole deportment, in which I feel we may legitimately see the deportment of a man who has been "illuminated" in the tragic sense. Bradley's term for it is fatalism, but if this is what we wish to call it, we must at least acknowledge that it is fatalism of a very distinctive kind—a kind that Shakespeare has been willing to touch with the associations of the saying in St. Matthew about the fall of a sparrow, and with Hamlet's recognition that a divinity shapes our ends. The point is not that Hamlet has suddenly become religious; he has been religious all through the play. The point is that he has now learned, and accepted, the boundaries in which human action, human judgment, are enclosed.

Till his return from the voyage he had been trying to act beyond these, had been encroaching on the role of providence, if I may exaggerate to make a vital point. He had been too quick to take the burden of the whole world and its condition upon his limited and finite self. Faced with a task of sufficent difficulty in its own right, he had dilated it into a cosmic problem—as indeed every task is, but if we think about this too precisely we cannot act at all. The whole time is out of joint, he feels, and in his young man's egocentricity, he will set it right. Hence he misjudges Ophelia, seeing in her only a breeder of sinners. Hence he misjudges himself, seeing himself a vermin crawling between earth and heaven. Hence he takes it upon himself to be his mother's conscience, though the ghost has warned that this is no fit task for him, and returns to repeat the warning: "Leave her to heaven, And to those thorns that in her bosom lodge." Even with the king, Hamlet has sought to play at God. *He* it must be who decides the issue of Claudius's salvation, saving him for a more damnable occasion. Now, he has learned that there are limits to the before and after that human reason can comprehend. Rashness, even, is sometimes good. Through rashness he has saved his life from the commission for his death, "and prais'd be rashness for it." This

happy circumstance and the unexpected arrival of the pirate ship make
it plain that the roles of life are not entirely self-assigned. "There is a
divinity that shapes our ends, Rough-hew them how we will." Hamlet is
ready now for what may happen, seeking neither to foreknow it nor avoid
it. "If it be now, 'tis not to come; if it be not to come, it will be now;
if it be not now, yet it will come: the readiness is all."

The crucial evidence of Hamlet's new frame of mind, as I understand
it, is the graveyard scene. Here, in its ultimate symbol, he confronts, recognizes, and accepts the condition of being man. It is not simply that he
now accepts death, though Shakespeare shows him accepting it in ever
more poignant forms: first, in the imagined persons of the politician, the
courtier, and the lawyer, who laid their little schemes "to circumvent
God," as Hamlet puts it, but now lie here; then in Yorick, whom he knew
and played with as a child; and then in Ophelia. This last death tears
from him a final cry of passion, but the striking contrast between his behavior and Laertes's reveals how deeply he has changed.

Still, it is not the fact of death that invests this scene with its peculiar
power. It is instead the haunting mystery of life itself that Hamlet's
speeches point to, holding in its inscrutable folds those other mysteries
that he has wrestled with so long. These he now knows for what they are,
and lays them by. The mystery of evil is present here—for this is after all
the universal graveyard, where, as the clown says humorously, he holds
up Adam's profession; where the scheming politician, the hollow courtier,
the tricky lawyer, the emperor and the clown and the beautiful young
maiden, all come together in an emblem of the world; where even, Hamlet murmurs, one might expect to stumble on "Cain's jawbone, that did
the first murther." The mystery of reality is here too—for death puts the
question, "What is real?" in its irreducible form, and in the end uncovers
all appearances: "Is this the fine of his fines and the recovery of his re-
coveries, to have his fine pate full of fine dirt?" "Now get you to my
lady's chamber, and tell her, let her paint an inch thick, to this favor she
must come." Or if we need more evidence of this mystery, there is the
anger of Laertes at the lack of ceremonial trappings, and the ambiguous
character of Ophelia's own death. "Is she to be buried in Christian burial
when she willfully seeks her own salvation?" asks the gravedigger. And
last of all, but most pervasive of all, there is the mystery of human limi-
tation. The grotesque nature of man's little joys, his big ambitions. The
fact that the man who used to bear us on his back is now a skull that
smells; that the noble dust of Alexander somewhere plugs a bunghole;
that "Imperious Caesar, dead and turn'd to clay, Might stop a hole to
keep the wind away." Above all, the fact that a pit of clay is "meet" for
such a guest as man, as the gravedigger tells us in his song, and yet that,
despite all frailties and limitations, "That skull had a tongue in it and
could sing once."

After the graveyard and what it indicates has come to pass in him, we know that Hamlet is ready for the final contest of mighty opposites. He accepts the world as it is, the world as a duel, in which, whether we know it or not, evil holds the poisoned rapier and the poisoned chalice waits; and in which, if we win at all, it costs not less than everything. I think we understand by the close of Shakespeare's *Hamlet* why it is that unlike the other tragic heroes he is given a soldier's rites upon the stage. For as William Butler Yeats once said, "Why should we honor those who die on the field of battle? A man may show as reckless a courage in entering into the abyss of himself."

The Historical Approach: *Hamlet*

by Helen Gardner

. . . I am going to consider some questions about *Hamlet*. An example of an unfruitful question because it is too large and too general and leads inevitably to an answer which we ought to have known before we asked it, is the question which some writers seem to feel bound to raise before they approach a play built on the theme of revenge. What did the Elizabethans think of the ethics of private revenge? I have read more than one book in which the author establishes by detailed, indeed relentless, accumulation of statements by preachers and moralists that the Elizabethans thought murder unethical and private revenge sinful. What else should we expect preachers and moralists to say? Questions which lead us to platitudes and foregone conclusions are not worth asking. We might more profitably ponder over the temper of mind which lay behind the Bond of Association of 1584. The councillors who drafted this document, among them the pious Burghley, and the thousands up and down the country who signed it, pledged themselves "in the presence of the eternal and ever-living God," whom they knew to have claimed vengeance as his prerogative, that, in the event of an attack on Elizabeth's person, they would "prosecute to the death" any pretended successor to her throne by whom, or for whom, such an act should be attempted or committed. They swore "to take the uttermost revenge on them . . . by any possible means . . . for their utter overthrow and extirpation." That is, if Elizabeth were assassinated, Mary Stuart should be murdered, whether she were a party to the murder of her cousin or not, and beyond Mary, her son James, as a beneficiary of the crime. "Discarding all scruples," comments Sir John Neale, "they descended to the utter ruthlessness of their enemies." These were law-abiding and God-fearing men. But they believed that the safety of the country and the preservation of the Protestant religion hung on the single life of Elizabeth. They were probably right in believing this. Perhaps if Elizabeth had met the same fate as William the Silent and Henry of Navarre, and England had fallen

"The Historical Approach: *Hamlet*." From *The Business of Criticism* (Oxford: The Clarendon Press, 1959), by Helen Gardner, pp. 35-51. Copyright © 1959 by Oxford University Press. Reprinted by permission of Oxford University Press.

into the chaos of civil and religious wars, the play of *Hamlet,* along with
other precious things, would not exist for us to talk about. We may be
horrified at their forgetting that vengeance was forbidden by their religion, but we must recognize the appalling nature of their dilemma.

As an example of a fruitful question which it did not occur to Bradley
to ask I would cite Professor Dover Wilson's question: "What opinions
were current when Shakespeare was writing about the nature of apparitions?" This is a modest question to which an answer can be found, and
the answer Professor Dover Wilson found—that there was a conflict of
opinion—is an illuminating one. It is consonant with the impression
which the whole play makes upon us and adds to our feeling that Hamlet
is moving in a world where there are no certainties. It casts light on the
relation of Hamlet to Horatio. It gives meaning to a scene which had
puzzled all critics, the cellarage scene. And, lastly, it casts a light upon
the whole development of the play's action. By showing us how serious
and widespread was the debate on the nature of ghosts, it makes us less
ready to accept the notion that Hamlet arranges the play scene as an
excuse for delaying his revenge. The information which Professor Dover
Wilson made available to us strengthens our conception of Hamlet as a
man of intellectual integrity and moral sensibility. To give a parallel
from our own day: two hundred years hence, when, for all I know, modern psychology will seem as outmoded as alchemy or the theory of the
humours, a critic, living in an age of chemical therapy, might fruitfully
inquire what were some of the current opinions on the psychiatrist's role
in society which might help to explain the rather ambiguous treatment of
Reilly in Mr. Eliot's comedy *The Cocktail Party.* Mr. Eliot, as we are
all perfectly aware without considering the matter at all, has been able to
exploit for comic purposes our ambivalent feelings about "mind doctors,"
as Shakespeare exploited for tragic purposes the conflict of opinion in his
day about the reality and reliability of apparitions of departed persons.
We are not asking what Mr. Eliot's own opinions about psychiatrists are,
any more than we are asking whether Shakespeare believed in ghosts.
Nor are we asking what attitude the plays demand that we should assume
to the interference of Reilly or to the moral authority of the Ghost of
Hamlet's father. These are questions which cannot be answered by historical inquiries alone, but historical inquiries can help us to answer
them.

A much more complex and delicate question, which takes us near to
the heart of the play, is raised by the complaint which Johnson makes
about the plot of *Hamlet.* "Hamlet is, through the whole play, rather an
instrument than an agent. After he has, by the stratagem of the play, con-
victed the King, he makes no attempt to punish him, and his death is
at last effected by an incident which Hamlet has no part in producing."
Bradley's celebrated question, which he thinks anyone would ask on

hearing the plot of *Hamlet,* converts Johnson's objection to the conduct of the plot into censure of the conduct of the hero: "But why in the world did not Hamlet obey the ghost at once, and so save seven of those eight lives?" And a highly unsympathetic aside of Mr. Eliot's converts Bradley's complaint at Hamlet's incompetence into a reproach to him for not being aware, as we are, that he "has made a pretty considerable mess of things." Mr. Eliot's rebuke to Hamlet for "dying fairly well pleased with himself" [1] is only logical from a severe moralist if we accept that what the play has shown us is the mess which Hamlet has made of things. Mr. Eliot might, however, have noticed that it is not merely Hamlet who appears to feel at the close that if only the whole truth were known—as we, the audience, know it—the name which he leaves behind him would not be "a wounded name." Horatio's farewell to him and Fortinbras's comment make no suggestion that what we have witnessed is a story of personal failure and inadequacy; and Horatio's summary of what he will tell "the yet unknowing world" does not include any hint that these things have come about through the bungling of the dead Prince. No need of extenuation appears to be felt. On the contrary, the play ends with "the soldiers' music and the rites of war" and a final volley in salute of a dead hero.

The question here, which arises out of the play itself, is how we are to find consistency between the fact of Hamlet's delay, with which he bitterly reproaches himself, the fact, which Johnson pointed out, that the final denouement is not of his making, and the tone of the close of the play, which suggests so strongly that Hamlet has "parted well and paid his score." It hardly seems possible to answer this question, as Mr. Eliot does, by ascribing to Hamlet at the moment of his death, and by implication to his creator, a moral sensibility inferior to our own. When faced with a contradiction of this kind, the critic is bound to ask himself whether he has got the play out of focus. Is there some element in it which he is unaware of, which will, when perceived, make the close seem a full and fitting close? He needs to discover whether there is any means

---

[1] "Even Hamlet, who has made a pretty considerable mess of things, and occasioned the death of at least three innocent people, and two more insignificant ones, dies fairly well pleased with himself" ("Shakespeare and the Stoicism of Seneca," *Selected Essays,* 1932). The odd distinction between the innocent and the insignificant has already been commented on. Mr. Eliot's general complaint about the death-scenes of Elizabethan tragic heroes, whose *apologias* he ascribes to the influence of Seneca, ignores the historical fact that this was an age of public executions in which men were judged by the courage and dignity with which they met public death, and when it was thought proper that at this supreme moment of their lives they should submit their case to the judgement of their fellow-men. The best comment on Othello's last speech and Hamlet's entrusting of his cause to Horatio is provided by Sidneys' Musidorus and Pyrocles in their condemned cell: "In this time, place and fortune, it is lawful for us to speak gloriously."

by which he can decide whether Shakespeare intended his audience to regard Hamlet as having "made a mess of things." And he must ask himself whether what Johnson thought an objection to the conduct of the plot, that the hero does so little to forward it, is a real objection: whether it does actually affect the "satisfaction" which Johnson thought we should feel at the close of the play. The historical fact to which we can turn is that Shakespeare did not invent the plot of *Hamlet*. He chose, presumably because it in some way appealed to his imagination, to remake an older play. And, although this older play no longer exists, there exist other plays on the same kind of subject. A study of these, to see what they have in common with *Hamlet*, may, at the least, suggest to us things which we should take into account in trying to understand the masterpiece which Shakespeare created in this genre. Such a study shows that the answer which Bradley gave to his question "Why in the world did not Hamlet obey the ghost at once?" is only a partial answer. To Bradley's assertion, "The whole story turns upon the peculiar character of the hero," we can object that heroes of very different character also fail to act promptly and also involve themselves and others in the final catastrophe. As for Johnson's comment on the conduct of the plot, we can say that the same complaint can be made to some degree against the plots of other revenge tragedies in the period. What Johnson thought to be a weakness in the plot of *Hamlet* appears to be a feature of the plots of other plays of the same kind and may point us towards a reason for their popularity and even towards what attracted Shakespeare in the old play which he re-made.

The essence of any tragedy of revenge is that its hero has not created the situation in which he finds himself and out of which the tragedy arises. The simplest of all tragic formulas, that a tragedy begins in prosperity and ends in misery, does not fit revenge tragedies. When the action opens the hero is seen in a situation which is horrible, and felt by him and the audience to be intolerable, but for which he has no responsibility. The exposition of such plays does not display the hero taking a fatal step, but the hero confronted with appalling facts. This is as true in Argos as it is in Denmark. But in Elizabethan revenge plays it is not merely the initial situation which is created by the villain. The denouement also comes about through his initiative. It is not the result of a successfully carried out scheme of the revenger. The revenger takes an opportunity unconsciously provided for him by the villain. Given this opportunity, which he seems unable to create for himself, he forms his scheme on the spur of the moment. Thus, in *The Spanish Tragedy*, Lorenzo, believing himself safe and that the secret of Horatio's murder lies buried with Serberine and Pedringano, feigns reconcilement with Hieronymo and invites him to provide a play for the entertainment of the court. By means of this play Hieronymo achieves his vengeance and brings to light the secret crime of Lorenzo. Similarly, in *Titus Andronicus,* which is obviously modelled on *The Spanish Tragedy,* although it exceeds it in horrors, the denouement comes about because Tamora believes she can deal with the old mad Titus and, through him, with his dangerous son Lucius who threatens her and her husband, the Emperor. Confident in her scheme, she delivers herself and her sons into Titus' hands. Up to the point when she calls upon him, disguised as Revenge, Titus has done nothing but indulge in wild gestures of grief and distraction; just as Hieronymo has done nothing to avenge his son before Lorenzo's initiative suggests to him a way of destroying his enemies and revealing their wickedness. Again, in a play written after *Hamlet,* Tourneur's *The Revenger's Tragedy,* the Duke himself asks Vendice, whose mistress he has poisoned because she would not yield to him, to find him a new mistress. He himself arranges the place, a hidden pavilion, and allows his courtiers to believe that he has gone away, so as to ensure secrecy. He thus provides Vendice with the perfect place and time for his vengeance. It seems as if in plays of this kind it was a necessary part of the total effect that the villain should be to some extent the agent of his own destruction. As initiator of the action he must be the initiator of its resolution. The satisfaction of the close included to a less or greater degree the sombre satisfaction which the Psalmist felt at the spectacle of the wicked falling into pits which they had digged for others. Here, obscurely, the hand of heaven could be felt, as Raleigh felt it in the bloody pageant of history:

> Oh by what plots, by what forswearings, betrayings, oppressions, imprisonments, tortures, poysonings, and under what reasons of State, and politique subtlety, have these forenamed Kings, both strangers, and of our owne Nation, pulled the vengeance of God upon themselves, upon theirs, and upon their prudent ministers! and in the end have brought those things to passe for their enemies, and seene an effect so directly contrary to all their owne counsels and cruelties, as the one could never have hoped for themselves, and the other never have succeeded, if no such opposition had ever been made. God hath said it and performed it ever: *Perdam sapientiam sapientium; I will destroy the wisedome of the wise.*[2]

"In the end" the wicked will destroy themselves and "purposes mistook" will fall on "the inventors' heads." The hero waits for his opponent, as if for a signal, and the initiative and activity which Johnson expected from the hero of a play seems not to have been required from heroes in situations of this kind. This conception of a hero who is committed to counter-action, and to response to events rather than to the creation of events, is very powerfully rendered by Tourneur in the exposition of

---

[2] Preface to *The History of the World,* 1614.

The Revenger's Tragedy. The personages of court pass across the stage, while Vendice, holding in his hands the skull of his dead mistress, comments on the parade of vicious power and wealth. He is waiting for "that bald Madam, Opportunity."

When we turn back from reading these plays to *Hamlet* we see that Shakespeare has very greatly developed this basic element in the revenge play of his day. He has developed it to make clear what in them is confused by sensationalism, and by that moral indignation which so easily converts itself to immorality. Great writers perceive what is only half perceived by their lesser contemporaries and express what in them finds only partial or imperfect expression. In other revenge plays, once the signal is given, the revenger produces a scheme of horror by which he destroys his opponent. He becomes an agent, bent on fulfilling the hateful Senecan maxim that crimes are only to be avenged by greater crimes. The irony is only mild. It is ironic that the villain, acting as if all were well, invites his destroyer to destroy him. Once invited, the hero descends with alacrity to the moral level of his opponent. The vengeance when it comes is as hideous as the original crime, or even more hideous, and the moral feelings of the audience are confused between satisfaction and outrage.[3] In the denouement of *Hamlet* the irony is profound. Claudius, who has arranged the whole performance in order to destroy Hamlet, is himself destroyed and destroys his Queen. He is "hoist with his own petard." His tool Laertes acknowledges the justice of his fate as he reveals the plot to which he had consented: "I am justly killed with mine own treachery." Claudius himself makes no such acknowledgement. He dies impenitent; there is "no relish of salvation" in his death. Kyd, with Hieronymo left alive on his hands at the end of the general holocaust, was forced to the weak expedient of making him commit suicide as the only way to preserve any sympathy for him. Hamlet dies as a victim to that constancy to his purposes which has made him "follow the king's pleasure" throughout. The end comes because he has accepted every challenge: "If his fitness speaks, mine is ready." Unlike Hieronymo, Titus, and Vendice, he remains to the last, in his adversary's words, "most generous, and free from all contriving." For there is another point in which an Elizabethan tragedy of revenge differs from the legend of Orestes and from the original Hamlet legend. Everyone in Argos is perfectly well aware that Clytemnestra, with the help of her paramour,

---

[3] It has been suggested by F. T. Bowers (*Elizabethan Revenge Tragedy,* 1940) that we are intended to lose sympathy with Hieronymo when, ignoring the command "Vengeance is mine," he turns to plots himself and undertakes his murderous play. But the final speech of the Ghost makes it quite clear that to Kyd the characters remained to the end divided into sheep and goats. "Good Hieronymo slaine by himselfe" is to be conducted with the innocent Isabella and his accomplice Bel-Imperia to the Elysian fields, while the rest of the cast are to be haled off to Tartarean regions by Revenge.

Aegisthus, murdered her husband, Agamemnon, just as in the old story of Hamlet everyone knows that his uncle Feng is the murderer of his father. In these ancient stories of revenge for blood the criminals are known to be criminals by all their world. They are not "secret men of blood." The secrecy with which Kyd invests the murder of Horatio is carried to such fantastic lengths that at one point in the play it appears that the world in general does not even realize that he is dead. In *Hamlet,* as we know it, whether it was so in the old play or not, only his murderer among living men knows at the beginning of the action that Hamlet the elder was murdered. *The Spanish Tragedy* is built on a powerful moral contrast between the treacherous, subtle, polite Lorenzo and the honest man, Hieronymo, who lives by conscience and the law. At the crisis of the play this contrast is blurred and Hieronymo becomes as crafty as his enemy. In *Hamlet* it is preserved to the end, and Hamlet himself is far more of an instrument and far less of an agent than are his fellow revengers.

The view that the revenger's role was essentially a waiting role, that he was committed by the situation in which he found himself to counteraction, and differentiated from his opponent by lack of guile, does not answer the question "Why does Hamlet delay?" It sets it in a different light. We must still find consistency between his character and his actions, and Bradley's statement that "the whole story turns on the peculiar character of the hero" retains its truth. But to set *Hamlet* against other plays of its time which handle the same kind of subject is to suggest that however much he may reproach himself with his delay, that delay is part of a pattern which is made clear at the close. To ask "Why in the world did not Hamlet act at once?" is to fail to grasp the nature of the dilemma which Kyd crudely adumbrated when he set the man of conscience and duty against the conscienceless and treacherous villain. Hamlet's agony of mind and indecision are precisely the things which differentiate him from that smooth, swift plotter Claudius, and from the coarse, unthinking Laertes, ready to "dare damnation" and cut his enemy's throat in a churchyard. He quickly learns from Claudius how to entrap the unwary and the generous, and betters the instruction. "He will never have a better opportunity," say many critics, when Hamlet, convinced of his uncle's guilt and hot for vengeance, comes on Claudius on his knees. Even Browning's ruthless tyrant, after having long schemed his enemy's destruction, shrank back and "was afraid" when his victim "caught at God's skirts and prayed." Do we really want to see Hamlet stab a defenceless, kneeling man? This "opportunity" is no opportunity at all; the enemy is within touching distance, but out of reach. Hamlet's baffled rage finds an outlet in the speech which shocked Johnson by its depth of hatred. The speech reveals more than its speaker's character. Like many soliloquies, it is proleptic. The moment which Hamlet here declares that he

will wait for, the real opportunity, will come. When Hamlet has gone
and Claudius has risen from his knees, and not before, we know that
Claudius has not found grace. The opportunity which Hamlet awaits
Claudius will now provide. The play has made Hamlet certain of his
uncle's guilt; it has also shown Claudius that his guilt is no longer his
own secret. If he cannot repent, he must, for his own safety, destroy
Hamlet. He will do it in his own characteristic way, by the hand of an
accomplice and by the treacherous man's characteristic weapon, poison.
And Hamlet will destroy Claudius in his own characteristic way also: by
"rashness" and "indiscretion," and not by "deep plots." He will catch
him at the moment when his guilt has been made clear to all the bystand-
ers, so that as he runs the sword through him he will do so not as an
assassin but as an executioner. The dark and devious world in which
Hamlet finds himself, when he accepts the necessity of obeying the command of the Ghost, involves all who enter it in guilt. But Hamlet's most
terrible deed, when he allows himself to be "marshalled to knavery" and
is most contaminated by his world, the sending of the traitors Rosencrantz and Guildenstern to their deaths, is a spontaneous, savage response
to the discovery of their treachery; and his other crime, the killing of
Polonius, with its consequence in the madness and death of Ophelia, is
also unpremeditated.

In *Othello,* Iago, speaking in the role of an honest man, puts crudely to
his master the code of a soldier:

> Though in the trade of war I have slain men,
> Yet do I hold it very stuff o' the conscience
> To do no contriv'd murder.

Hamlet is fittingly borne "like a soldier, to the stage," because in the
secret war which he has waged he has shown a soldier's virtues. Pre-
eminently he has shown the virtue of constancy. He has not laid down
his arms and quitted the field. For Bradley's comment, "Two months
have passed and he has done nothing," we might better say, "Two months
have passed and he is still there, at his post, on guard." The play ends
with a soldier's funeral. It opens with sentries at their watch, being relieved. In his four great tragedies, when his imagination was working at
its highest pitch, Shakespeare relates his beginnings to his ends particularly closely. Granville Barker pointed out how *King Lear* ends as it
began with Lear and his three daughters on the stage and with the
old king hanging on the hope of words from Cordelia's lips. Any writer
dramatizing Cinthio's story of the Moor of Venice would end with the
midnight scenes of the attempted murder of Cassio and the death of
Desdemona. Shakespeare has invented a great midnight opening to balance this close, with brawling in the streets followed by the midnight
scene before the Senate, where, with the approval of Venice, Othello is

united to Desdemona, as in the last scene he is united to her in death before the eyes of the envoys of Venice. *Macbeth* begins and ends with battles. It opens with the epic narrative of the defeat of the thane of Cawdor who had rebelled, and closes with the defeat of the thane of Cawdor who had usurped. And here there is contrast. The first thane confessed his treasons "very freely" and died well, giving up his life, "the dearest thing he owed," "as 'twere a trifle": his successor in the title, Macbeth, fought desperately to the last to preserve a life which had become meaningless to him. The opening and the close of *Hamlet* have the same kind of relation to each other. The soldier on guard, who cannot leave his post until he is relieved or given permission from above, is a metaphor for the soul in this world which comes very easily to Renaissance writers. Its source is Cicero's gloss on the "secret doctrine" which Socrates appealed to in his argument against suicide in the *Phaedo*.[4] The Red Cross Knight uses it against Despair:

> The souldier may not move from watchfull sted
> Nor leave his stand, untill his Captain bed.

And Donne, speaking of this world as "the appointed field," refers to the same commonplace when he chides the "desperate coward" who yields to the foes of him

> who made thee to stand
> Sentinell in his worlds garrison.

The play of *Hamlet* continually recurs to the thought of suicide, and the temptation to give up the battle of life. Hamlet's first soliloquy opens with the lament that the Almighty has "fixed his canon 'gainst self-slaughter," and his last action is to snatch the poisoned cup from the lips of Horatio. Within this frame of soldiers on the watch, being relieved, and of a soldier's laying to rest, I do not believe that the Elizabethans thought that they were witnessing a story of personal failure. Nor do I think that we should do so either, unless we are certain of what, in this situation, would be success.

The tragedy of *Hamlet,* and of plays of its kind, of which it is the supreme example, does not lie in "the unfitness of the hero for his task," or in some "fatal flaw." It is not true that a coarser nature could have cleansed the state of Denmark, some "Hotspur of the North": "he that kills me some six or seven of Scots at a breakfast, washes his hands, and says to his wife, 'Fie upon this quiet life! I want work.'" The tragedy lies in the nature of the task, which only the noble will feel called on to undertake, or rather, in the nature of the world which is exposed to the

---

[4] "Vetat Pythagoras injussu imperatoris, id est dei, de praesidio et statione vitae decedere" (*De Senectute,* 20); cf. *Phaedo,* 62.

hero's contemplation and in his sense of responsibility to the world in which he finds himself. *Hamlet* towers above other plays of its kind through the heroism and nobility of its hero, his superior power of insight into, and reflection upon, his situation, and his capacity to suffer the moral anguish which moral responsibility brings. Hamlet is the quintessence of European man, who holds that man is "ordained to govern the world according to equity and righteousness with an upright heart," and not to renounce the world and leave it to its corruption. By that conception of man's duty and destiny he is involved in those tragic dilemmas with which our own age is so terribly familiar. For how can man secure justice except by committing injustice, and how can he act without outraging the very conscience which demands that he should act?

It will have been apparent for some time that I am coming round to a point where I am demonstrating the historical nature of my own answer to my question. Although I have gone to the Elizabethans to ask how *Hamlet* appeared to audiences which had applauded *The Spanish Tragedy* and *Titus Andronicus,* it is the moral uncertainties and the moral dilemmas of my own age which make me unable to see *Hamlet* in terms of the hero's failure or success in the task which the Ghost lays upon him.

> For this same lord,
> I do repent: but heaven hath pleas'd it so,
> To punish me with this, and this with me,
> That I must be their scourge and minister.

Hamlet, speaking over the body of one of his victims, Polonius, speaks for all those called on to attempt to secure justice, the supporters of "just wars" as well as those who fight in them. In trying to set *Hamlet* back into its own age, I seem to have found in it an image of my own time. The Elizabethan Hamlet assumes the look of the Hamlet of the twentieth century.

That the answers we find are conditioned by our own circumstances does not destroy their value. *Hamlet* is not a problem to which a final solution exists. It is a work of art about which questions can always be asked. Each generation asks its own questions and finds its own answers, and the final test of the validity of those answers can only be time. Johnson, Coleridge, Bradley, all tell us things about *Hamlet* which are consistent with the play as we read it. A critic today cannot hope for more than that his questions and answers will seem relevant, and will continue to seem relevant, to others who read and ponder the play. The reward of the historical approach is not that it leads us to a final and infallible interpretation.

Death in *Hamlet*

by C. S. Lewis

. . . Hamlet for me is no more separable from his ghost than Macbeth from his witches, Una from her lion, or Dick Whittington from his cat. The Hamlet formula, so to speak, is not "a man who has to avenge his father" but "a man who has been given a task by a ghost." Everything else about him is less important than that. If the play did not begin with the cold and darkness and sickening suspense of the ghost scenes it would be a radically different play. If, on the other hand, only the first act had survived, we should have a very tolerable notion of the play's peculiar quality. I put it to you that everyone's imagination here confirms mine. What is against me is the abstract pattern of motives and characters which we build up as critics when the actual flavour or tint of the poetry is already fading from our minds.

This ghost is different from any other ghost in Elizabethan drama—for, to tell the truth, the Elizabethans in general do their ghosts very vilely. It is permanently ambiguous. Indeed the very word "ghost," by putting it into the same class with the "ghosts" of Kyd and Chapman, nay by classifying it at all, puts us on the wrong track. It is "this thing," "this dreaded sight," an "illusion," a "spirit of health or goblin damn'd," liable at any moment to assume "some other horrible form" which reason could not survive the vision of. Critics have disputed whether Hamlet is sincere when he doubts whether the apparition is his father's ghost or not. I take him to be perfectly sincere. He believes while the thing is present: he doubts when it is away. Doubt, uncertainty, bewilderment to almost any degree, is what the ghost creates not only in Hamlet's mind but in the minds of the other characters. Shakespeare does not take the concept of "ghost" for granted, as other dramatists had done. In his play the appearance of the spectre means a breaking down of the walls of the world and the germination of thoughts that cannot really be thought: chaos is come again.

This does not mean that I am going to make the ghost the hero, or the play a ghost story—though I might add that a very good ghost story

"Death in *Hamlet*." From "Hamlet The Prince or The Poem" by C. S. Lewis, Annual Shakespeare Lecture of the British Academy, 1942, *Proceedings of the British Academy* (London: Oxford University Press, 1942), XXVIII, 11-18.

would be, to me, a more interesting thing than a maze of motives. I have started with the ghost because the ghost appears at the beginning of the play not only to give Hamlet necessary information but also, and even more, to strike the note. From the platform we pass to the court scene and so to Hamlet's first long speech. There are ten lines of it before we reach what is necessary to the plot: lines about the melting of flesh into a dew and the divine prohibition of self-slaughter. We have a second ghost scene after which the play itself, rather than the hero, goes mad for some minutes. We have a second soliloquy on the theme "to die . . . to sleep"; and a third on "the witching time of night, when churchyards yawn." We have the King's effort to pray and Hamlet's comment on it. We have the ghost's third appearance. Ophelia goes mad and is drowned. Then comes the comic relief, surely the strangest comic relief ever written—comic relief beside an open grave, with a further discussion of suicide, a detailed inquiry into the rate of decomposition, a few clutches of skulls, and then "Alas, poor Yorick!" On top of this, the hideous fighting in the grave; and then, soon, the catastrophe. . . .

The sense in which death is the subject of *Hamlet* will become apparent if we compare it with other plays. Macbeth has commerce with Hell, but at the very outset of his career dismisses all thought of the life to come. For Brutus and Othello, suicide in the high tragic manner is escape and climax. For Lear death is deliverance. For Romeo and Antony, poignant loss. For all these, as for their author while he writes and the audience while they watch, death is the end: it is almost the frame of the picture. They think of dying: no one thinks, in these plays, of *being dead*. In *Hamlet* we are kept thinking about it all the time, whether in terms of the soul's destiny or of the body's. Purgatory, Hell, Heaven, the wounded name, the rights—or wrongs—of Ophelia's burial, and the staying-power of a tanner's corpse: and beyond this, beyond all Christian and all Pagan maps of the hereafter, comes a curious groping and tapping of thoughts, about "what dreams may come." It is this that gives to the whole play its quality of darkness and of misgiving. Of course there is much else in the play: but nearly always, the same groping. The characters are all watching one another, forming theories about one another, listening, contriving, full of anxiety. The world of *Hamlet* is a world where one has lost one's way. The Prince also has no doubt lost his, and we can tell the precise moment at which he finds it again. "Not a whit. We defy augury. There's a special providence in the fall of a sparrow. If it be now, 'tis not to come: if it be not to come, it will be now: if it be not now, yet it will come: the readiness is all: since no man has aught of what he leaves, what is't to leave betimes?" [1]

---

[1] I think the last clause is best explained by the assumption that Shakespeare had come across Seneca's *Nihil perdis ex tuo tempore, nam quod relinquis alienum est* (Epist. lxix).

If I wanted to make one more addition to the gallery of Hamlet's por-
traits I should trace his hesitation to the fear of death; not to a physical
fear of dying, but a fear of being dead. And I think I should get on quite
comfortably. Any serious attention to the state of being dead, unless it is
limited by some definite religious or anti-religious doctrine, must, I suppose, paralyse the will by introducing infinite uncertainties and rendering
all motives inadequate. Being dead is the unknown x in our sum. Unless
you ignore it or else give it a value, you can get no answer. But this is not
what I am going to do. Shakespeare has not left in the text clear lines of
causation which would enable us to connect Hamlet's hesitations with
this source. I do not believe he has given us data for any portrait of the
kind critics have tried to draw. To that extent I agree with Hanmer,
Rümelin, and Mr. Eliot. But I differ from them in thinking that it is a
fault.

For what, after all, is happening to us when we read any of Hamlet's
great speeches? We see visions of the flesh dissolving into a dew, of the
world like an unweeded garden. We think of memory reeling in its "dis-
tracted globe." We watch him scampering hither and thither like a
maniac to avoid the voices wherewith he is haunted. Someone says "Walk
out of the air," and we hear the words "Into my grave" spontaneously
respond to it. We think of being bounded in a nut-shell and king of
infinite space: but for bad dreams. There's the trouble, for "I am most
dreadfully attended." We see the picture of a dull and muddy-mettled
rascal, a John-a-dreams, somehow unable to move while ultimate dis-
honour is done him. We listen to his fear lest the whole thing may be an
illusion due to melancholy. We get the sense of sweet relief at the words
"shuffled off this mortal coil" but mixed with the bottomless doubt about
what may follow them. We think of bones and skulls, of women breed-
ing sinners, and of how some, to whom all this experience is a sealed
book, can yet dare death and danger "for an egg-shell. . . ."

I believe that we read Hamlet's speeches with interest chiefly because
they describe so well a certain spiritual region through which most of us
have passed and anyone in his circumstances might be expected to pass,
rather than because of our concern to understand how and why this particular man entered it. I foresee an objection on the ground that I am
thus really admitting his "character" in the only sense that matters and
that all characters whatever could be equally well talked away by the
method I have adopted. But I do really find a distinction. When I read
about Mrs. Proudie I am not in the least interested in seeing the world
from her point of view, for her point of view is not interesting; what does
interest me is precisely the sort of person she was. In *Middlemarch* no
reader wants to see Casaubon through Dorothea's eyes; the pathos, the
comedy, the value of the whole thing is to understand Dorothea and see
how such an illusion was inevitable for her. In Shakespeare himself I find

Beatrice to be a character who could not be thus dissolved. We are interested not in some vision seen through her eyes, but precisely in the wonder of her being the girl she is. A comparison of the sayings we remember from her part with those we remember from Hamlet's brings out the contrast. On the one hand, "I wonder that you will still be talking, Signor Benedick," "There was a star danced and under that I was born," "Kill Claudio"; on the other, "The undiscovered country from whose bourne no traveller returns," "Use every man after his desert, and who should 'scape whipping?," "The rest is silence." Particularly noticeable is the passage where Hamlet professes to be describing his own character. "I am myself indifferent honest: but yet I could accuse me of such things that it were better my mother had not borne me. I am very proud, revengeful, ambitious." It is, of course, possible to devise some theory which explains these self-accusations in terms of character. But long before we have done so the real significance of the lines has taken possession of our imagination for ever. "Such fellows as I" does not mean "such fellows as Goethe's Hamlet, or Coleridge's Hamlet, or any Hamlet": it means *men*—creatures shapen in sin and conceived in iniquity—and the vast, empty vision of them "crawling between earth and heaven" is what really counts and really carries the burden of the play. . . .

I feel certain that to many of you the things I have been saying about *Hamlet* will appear intolerably sophisticated, abstract, and modern. And so they sound when we have to put them into words. But I shall have failed completely if I cannot persuade you that my view, for good or ill, has just the opposite characteristics—is naïve and concrete and archaic. I am trying to recall attention from the things an intellectual adult notices to the things a child or a peasant notices—night, ghosts, a castle, a lobby where a man can walk four hours together, a willow-fringed brook and a sad lady drowned, a graveyard and a terrible cliff above the sea, and amidst all these a pale man in black clothes (would that our producers would ever let him appear!) with his stockings coming down, a dishevelled man whose words make us at once think of loneliness and doubt and dread, of waste and dust and emptiness, and from whose hands, or from our own, we feel the richness of heaven and earth and the comfort of human affection slipping away.

Othello: an Introduction

by *Alvin Kernan*

When Shakespeare wrote *Othello,* about 1604, his knowledge of human nature and his ability to dramatize it in language and action were at their height. The play offers, even in its minor characters, a number of unusually full and profound studies of humanity: Brabantio, the sophisticated, civilized Venetian senator, unable to comprehend that his delicate daughter could love and marry a Moor, speaking excitedly of black magic and spells to account for what his mind cannot understand; Cassio, the gentleman-soldier, polished in manners and gracious in bearing, wildly drunk and revealing a deeply rooted pride in his ramblings about senior officers being saved before their juniors; Emilia, the sensible and conventional waiting woman, making small talk about love and suddenly remarking that though she believes adultery to be wrong, still if the price were high enough she would sell—and so, she believes, would most women. The vision of human nature which the play offers is one of ancient terrors and primal drives—fear of the unknown, pride, greed, lust—underlying smooth, civilized surfaces—the noble senator, the competent and well-mannered lieutenant, the conventional gentlewoman.

The contrast between surface manner and inner nature is even more pronounced in two of the major characters. "Honest Iago" conceals beneath his exterior of the plain soldier and blunt, practical man of the world a diabolism so intense as to defy rational explanation—it must be taken like lust or pride as simply a given part of human nature, an antilife spirit which seeks the destruction of everything outside the self. Othello appears in the opening acts as the very personification of self-control, of the man with so secure a sense of his own worth that nothing can ruffle the consequent calmness of mind and manner. But the man who has roamed the wild and savage world unmoved by its terrors, who has not changed countenance when the cannon killed his brother standing beside him, this man is still capable of believing his wife a whore on the slightest of evidence and committing murders to revenge himself. In

"*Othello:* an Introduction." From the Introduction to *Othello,* edited by Alvin Kernan. *The Signet Shakespeare,* Sylvan Barnet, ed. (The New American Library, 1963), pp. xxiii-xxxv. Copyright © 1963 by Sylvan Barnet and Alvin Kernan. Reprinted by permission of The New American Library.

Desdemona alone do the heart and the hand go together: she is what she seems to be. Ironically, she alone is accused of pretending to be what she is not. Her very openness and honesty make her suspect in a world where few men are what they appear, and her chastity is inevitably brought into question in a world where every other major character is in some degree touched with sexual corruption.

Most criticism of *Othello* has concerned itself with exploring the depths of these characters and tracing the intricate, mysterious operations of their minds. I should like, however, to leave this work to the individual reader . . . in order to discuss, briefly, what might be called the "gross mechanics" of the play, the larger patterns in which events and characters are arranged. These patterns are the context within which the individual characters are defined, just as the pattern of a sentence is the context which defines the exact meaning of the individual words within it.

Othello is probably the most neatly, the most formally constructed of Shakespeare's plays. Every character is, for example, balanced by another similar or contrasting character. Desdemona is balanced by her opposite, Iago; love and concern for others at one end of the scale, hatred and concern for self at the other. The true and loyal soldier Cassio balances the false and traitorous soldier Iago. These balances and contrasts throw into relief the essential qualities of the characters. Desdemona's love, for example, shows up a good deal more clearly in contrast to Iago's hate, and vice versa. The values of contrast are increased and the full range of human nature displayed by extending these simple contrasts into developing series. The essential purity of Desdemona stands in contrast to the more "practical" view of chastity held by Emilia, and her view in turn is illuminated by the workaday view of sensuality held by the courtesan Bianca, who treats love, ordinarily, as a commodity. Or, to take another example, Iago's success in fooling Othello is but the culmination of a series of such betrayals that includes the duping of Roderigo, Brabantio, and Cassio. Each duping is the explanatory image of the other, for in every case Iago's method and end are the same: he plays on and teases to life some hitherto controlled and concealed dark passion in his victim. In each case he seeks in some way the same end, the symbolic murder of Desdemona, the destruction in some form of the life principle of which she is the major embodiment.

These various contrasts and parallelisms ultimately blend into a larger, more general pattern that is the central movement of the play. We can begin to see this pattern in the "symbolic geography" of the play. Every play, or work of art, creates its own particular image of space and time, its own symbolic world. The outer limits of the world of *Othello* are defined by the Turks—the infidels, the unbelievers, the "general enemy" as the play calls them—who, just over the horizon, sail back and forth

trying to confuse and trick the Christians in order to invade their do-
minions and destroy them. Out beyond the horizon, reported but unseen,
are also those "anters vast and deserts idle" of which Othello speaks. Out
there is a land of "rough quarries, rocks, and hills whose heads touch
heaven" inhabited by "cannibals that each other eat" and monstrous
forms of men "whose heads grow beneath their shoulders." On the edges
of this land is the raging ocean with its "high seas, and howling winds,"
its "guttered rocks and congregated sands" hidden beneath the waters to
"enclog the guiltless keel."

Within the circle formed by barbarism, monstrosity, sterility, and the
brute power of nature lie the two Christian strongholds of Venice and
Cyprus. Renaissance Venice was known for its wealth acquired by trade,
its political cunning, and its courtesans; but Shakespeare, while reminding us of the tradition of the "supersubtle Venetian," makes Venice over
into a form of *The City,* the ageless image of government, of reason,
of law, and of social concord. Here, when Brabantio's strong passions and
irrational fears threaten to create riot and injustice, his grievances are
examined by a court of law, judged by reason, and the verdict enforced
by civic power. Here, the clear mind of the Senate probes the actions of
the Turks, penetrates through their pretenses to their true purposes,
makes sense of the frantic and fearful contradictory messages which pour
in from the fleet, and arranges the necessary defense. Act I, Scene iii—
the Senate scene—focuses on the magnificent speeches of Othello and
Desdemona as they declare their love and explain it, but the lovers are
surrounded, guarded, by the assembled, ranked governors of Venice, who
control passions that otherwise would have led to a bloody street brawl
and bring justice out of what otherwise would have been riot. The solemn
presence and ordering power of the Senate would be most powerfully
realized in a stage production, where the senators would appear in their
rich robes, with all their symbols of office, seated in ranks around several
excited individuals expressing such primal passions as pride of race, fear
of dark powers, and violent love. In a play where so much of the language
is magnificent, rich, and of heroic proportions, simpler statements come
to seem more forceful; and the meaning of *The City* is perhaps nowhere
more completely realized than in Brabantio's brief, secure answer to the
first fearful cries of theft and talk of copulating animals that Iago and
Roderigo send up from the darkness below his window:

> What tell'st thou me of robbing? This is Venice;
> My house is not a grange.
>
> [I. i. 102-03]

Here then are the major reference points on a map of the world of
Othello: out at the far edge are the Turks, barbarism, disorder, and

amoral destructive powers; closer and more familiar is Venice, *The City,* order, law, and reason. Cyprus, standing on the frontier between barbarism and *The City,* is not the secure fortress of civilization that Venice is. It is rather an outpost, weakly defended and far out in the raging ocean, close to the "general enemy" and the immediate object of his attack. It is a "town of war yet wild" where the "people's hearts [are] brimful of fear." Here passions are more explosive and closer to the surface than in Venice, and here, instead of the ancient order and established government of *The City,* there is only one man to control violence and defend civilization—the Moor Othello, himself of savage origins and a converted Christian.

The movement of the play is from Venice to Cyprus, from *The City* to the outpost, from organized society to a condition much closer to raw nature, and from collective life to the life of the solitary individual. This movement is a characteristic pattern in Shakespeare's plays, both comedies and tragedies: in *A Midsummer Night's Dream* the lovers and players go from the civilized, daylight world of Athens to the irrational, magical wood outside Athens and the primal powers of life represented by the elves and fairies; Lear moves from his palace and secure identity to the savage world of the heath where all values and all identities come into question; and everyone in *The Tempest* is shipwrecked at some time on Prospero's magic island, where life seen from a new perspective assumes strange and fantastic shapes. At the other end of this journey there is always some kind of return to *The City,* to the palace, and to old relationships, but the nature of this return differs widely in Shakespeare's plays. In *Othello* the movement at the end of the play is back toward Venice, the Turk defeated; but Desdemona, Othello, Emilia, and Roderigo do not return. Their deaths are the price paid for the return.

This passage from Venice to Cyprus to fight the Turk and encounter the forces of barbarism is the geographical form of an action that occurs on the social and psychological levels as well. That is, there are social and mental conditions that correspond to Venice and Cyprus, and there are forces at work in society and in man that correspond to the Turks, and raging seas, and "cannibals that each other eat."

The exposure to danger, the breakdown and the ultimate reestablishment of society—the parallel on the social level to the action on the geographical level—is quickly traced. We have already noted that the Venetian Senate embodies order, reason, justice, and concord, the binding forces that hold *The City* together. In Venice the ancient laws and the established customs of society work to control violent men and violent passions to ensure the safety and well-being of the individual and the group. But there are anarchic forces at work in the city, which threaten traditional social forms and relationships, and all these forces center in Iago. His discontent with his own rank and his determination to displace

Cassio endanger the orderly military hierarchy in which the junior serves his senior. He endangers marriage, the traditional form for ordering male and female relationships, by his own unfounded suspicions of his wife and by his efforts to destroy Othello's marriage by fanning to life the darker, anarchic passions of Brabantio and Roderigo. He tries to subvert the operation of law and justice by first stirring up Brabantio to gather his followers and seek revenge in the streets; and then when the two warlike forces are met, Iago begins a quarrel with Roderigo in hopes of starting a brawl. The nature of the antisocial forces that Iago represents are focused in the imagery of his advice to Roderigo on how to call out to her father the news of Desdemona's marriage. Call, he says,

> with like timorous [frightening] accent and dire yell
> As when, by night and negligence, the fire
> Is spied in populous cities.

> [I. i. 72-74]

Fire, panic, darkness, neglect of duty—these are the natural and human forces that destroy great cities and turn their citizens to mobs.

In Venice, Iago's attempts to create civic chaos are frustrated by Othello's calm management of himself and the orderly legal proceedings of the Senate. In Cyprus, however, society is less secure—even as the island is more exposed to the Turks—and Othello alone is responsible for finding truth and maintaining order. Here Iago's poison begins to work, and he succeeds at once in manufacturing the riot that he failed to create in Venice. Seen on stage, the fight on the watch between Cassio and Montano is chaos come again: two drunken officers, charged with the defense of the town, trying to kill each other like savage animals, a bedlam of voices and shouts, broken, disordered furniture, and above all this the discordant clamor of the "dreadful" alarm bell—used to signal attacks and fire. This success is but the prologue for other more serious disruptions of society and of the various human relationships that it fosters. The General is set against his officer, husband against wife, Christian against Christian, servant against master. Justice becomes a travesty of itself as Othello—using legal terms such as "It is the *cause*"—assumes the offices of accuser, judge, jury, and executioner of his wife. Manners disappear as the Moor strikes his wife publicly and treats her maid as a procuress. The brightly lighted Senate chamber is now replaced with a dark Cyprus street where Venetians cut one another down and men are murdered from behind. This anarchy finally gives way in the last scene, when Desdemona's faith is proven, to a restoration of order and an execution of justice on the two major criminals.

What we have followed so far is a movement expressed in geographical and social symbols from Venice to a Cyprus exposed to attack, from *The*

City to barbarism, from Christendom to the domain of the Turks, from
order to riot, from justice to wild revenge and murder, from truth to
falsehood. It now remains to see just what this movement means on the
level of the individual in the heart and mind of man. Of the three major
characters, Desdemona, Othello, and Iago, the first and the last do not
change their natures or their attitudes toward life during the course of
the play. These two are polar opposites, the antitheses of each other. To
speak in the most general terms, Desdemona expresses in her language
and actions an innocent, unselfish love and concern for others. Othello
catches her very essence when he speaks of her miraculous love, which
transcended their differences in age, color, beauty, and culture:

> She loved me for the dangers I had passed,
> And I loved her that she did pity them.
>
> [I. iii. 166-67]

This love in its various forms finds expression not only in her absolute
commitment of herself to Othello, but in her gentleness, her kindness to
others, her innocent trust in all men, her pleas for Cassio's restoration to
Othello's favor; and it endures even past death at her husband's hands,
for she comes back to life for a moment to answer Emilia's question,
"who hath done this deed?" with the unbelievable words.

> Nobody—I myself. Farewell.
> Commend me to my kind lord. O, farewell!
>
> [V. ii. 123-24]

Iago is her opposite in every way. Where she is open and guileless, he
is never what he seems to be; where she thinks the best of everyone, he
thinks the worst, usually turning to imagery of animals and physical functions to express his low opinion of human nature; where she seeks to
serve and love others, he uses others to further his own dark aims and
satisfy his hatred of mankind; where she is emotional and idealistic, he
is icily logical and cynical. Desdemona and Iago are much more complicated than this, but perhaps enough has been said to suggest the
nature of these two moral poles of the play. One is a life force that
strives for order, community, growth, and light. The other is an antilife force that seeks anarchy, death, and darkness. One is the foundation
of all that men have built in the world, including *The City;* the other
leads back toward ancient chaos and barbarism.

Othello, like most men, is a combination of the forces of love and hate,
which are isolated in impossibly pure states in Desdemona and Iago. His
psychic voyage from Venice to Cyprus is a passage of the soul and the
will from the values of one of these characters to those of the other. This

passage is charted by his acceptance and rejection of one or the other. He begins by refusing to have Iago as his lieutenant, choosing the more "theoretical" though less experienced Cassio. He marries Desdemona. Though he is not aware that he does so, he expresses the full meaning of this choice when he speaks of her in such suggestive terms as "my soul's joy" and refers to her even as he is about to kill her, as "Promethean heat," the vital fire that gives life to the world. Similarly, he comes to know that all that is valuable in life depends on her love, and in the magnificent speech beginning, "O now, forever/ Farewell the tranquil mind" (III. iii. 344-45), he details the emptiness of all human activity if Desdemona be proved false. But Iago, taking advantage of latent "Iago-like" feelings and thoughts in Othello, persuades him that Desdemona is only common clay. Othello then gives himself over to Iago at the end of III. iii, where they kneel together to plan the revenge, and Othello says, "Now art thou my lieutenant." To which Iago responds with blood-chilling simplicity, "I am your own forever." The full meaning of this choice is expressed, again unconsciously, by Othello when he says of Desdemona,

> Perdition catch my soul
> But I do love thee! and when I love thee not,
> Chaos is come again.
>
> [III. iii. 90-92]

The murder of Desdemona acts out the final destruction in Othello himself of all the ordering powers of love, of trust, of the bond between human beings.

Desdemona and Iago then represent two states of mind, two understandings of life, and Othello's movement from one to the other is the movement on the level of character and psychology from Venice to Cyprus, from *The City* to anarchy. His return to *The City* and the defeat of the Turk is effected, at the expense of his own life, when he learns *what* he has killed and executes himself as the only fitting judgment on his act. His willingness to speak of what he has done—in contrast to Iago's sullen silence—is a willingness to recognize the meaning of Desdemona's faith and chastity, to acknowledge that innocence and love do exist, and that therefore *The City* can stand, though his life is required to validate the truth and justice on which it is built.

Othello offers a variety of interrelated symbols that locate and define in historical, natural, social, moral, and human terms those qualities of being and universal forces that are forever at war in the universe and between which tragic man is always in movement. On one side there are Turks, cannibals, barbarism, monstrous deformities of nature, the brute force of the sea, riot, mobs, darkness, Iago, hatred, lust, concern for

the self only, and cynicism. On the other side there are Venice, *The City*,
law, senates, amity, hierarchy, Desdemona, love, concern for others, and
innocent trust. As the characters of the play act and speak, they bring
together, by means of parallelism and metaphor, the various forms of
the different ways of life. There is, for example, a meaningful similarity
in the underhanded way Iago works and the ruse by which the Turks try
to fool the Venetians into thinking they are bound for Rhodes when
their object is Cyprus. Or, there is again a flash of identification when
we hear that the reefs and shoals that threaten ships are "ensteeped,"
that is, hidden under the surface of the sea, as Iago is hidden under the
surface of his "honesty." But Shakespeare binds the various levels of
being more closely together by the use of imagery that compares things
on one level of action with things on another. For example, when Iago
swears that his low judgment of all female virtue "is true, or else I am a
Turk" (II. i. 113), logic demands, since one woman, Desdemona, *is* true
and chaste, that we account him "a Turk." He is thus identified with the
unbelievers, the Ottoman Turks, and that Asiatic power, which for
centuries threatened Christendom, is shown to have its social and psychological equivalent in Iago's particular attitude toward life. Similarly,
when Othello sees the drunken brawl on the watchtower, he exclaims,

> Are we turned Turks, and to ourselves do that
> Which heaven hath forbid the Ottomites?
>
> [II. iii. 169-70]

At the very time when the historical enemy has been defeated, his fleet
providentially routed by the great storm, his characteristics—drunken loss
of control, brawling over honor, disorder—begin to conquer the island
only so recently and fortuitously saved. The conquest continues, and the
defender of the island, Othello, convinced of Desdemona's guilt, compares his determination to revenge himself to "the Pontic Sea,/ Whose
icy current and compulsive course/ Nev'r keeps retiring ebb" (III. iii.
450-52). The comparison tells us that in his rage and hatred he has become one with the savage seas and the brute, amoral powers of nature
that are displayed in the storm scene at the beginning of Act II. But
most important is Othello's identification of himself at the end of the
play as the "base Judean" who "threw a pearl away richer than all his
tribe." The more familiar Quarto reading is "base Indian," but both
words point toward the barbarian who fails to recognize value and
beauty when he possesses it—the primitive savage who picks up a pearl
and throws it away not knowing its worth; or the Jews (Judas may be
specifically meant) who denied and crucified another great figure of love,
thinking they were dealing with only a troublesome rabble-rouser. A few
lines further on Othello proceeds to the final and absolute identification

of himself with the infidel. He speaks of a "malignant and a turbaned Turk" who "beat a Venetian and traduced the state," and he then acknowledges that he is that Turk by stabbing himself, even as he once stabbed the other unbeliever. So he ends as both the Turk and the destroyer of the Turk, the infidel and the defender of the faith.

When Iago's schemes are at last exposed, Othello, finding it impossible for a moment to believe that a *man* could have contrived such evil, stares at Iago's feet and then says sadly, "but that's a fable." What he hopes to find when he looks down are the cloven hoofs of the devil, and had they been there he would have been an actor in a morality play, tempted beyond his strength, like many a man before him, by a supernatural power outside himself. In some ways I have schematized *Othello* as just such a morality play, offering an allegorical journey between heaven and hell on a stage filled with purely symbolic figures. This is the kind of abstraction of art toward which criticism inevitably moves, and in this case the allegorical framework is very solidly there. But Othello does not see the cloven hoofs when he looks down; he sees a pair of human feet at the end of a very human body; and he is forced to realize that far from living in some simplified, "fabulous" world where evil is a metaphysical power raiding human life from without, he dwells where evil is somehow inextricably woven with good into man himself. On his stage the good angel does not return to heaven when defeated, but is murdered, and her body remains on the bed, "cold, cold." He lives where good intentions, past services, psychic weaknesses, and an inability to see through evil cannot excuse an act, as they might in some simpler world where more perfect justice existed. In short, Othello is forced to recognize that he lives in a tragic world, and he pays the price for having been great enough to inhabit it.

Here is the essence of Shakespeare's art, an ability to create immediate, full, and total life as men actually live and experience it; and yet at the same time to arrange this reality so that it gives substance to and derives shape from a formal vision of all life that comprehends and reaches back from man and nature through society and history to cosmic powers that operate through all time and space. His plays are both allegorical and realistic at once; his characters both recognizable men and at the same time devils, demigods, and forces in nature. I have discussed only the more allegorical elements in *Othello,* the skeleton of ideas and formal patterns within which the characters must necessarily be understood. But it is equally true that the exact qualities of the abstract moral values and ideas, their full reality, exist only in the characters. It is necessary to know that Desdemona represents one particular human value, love or charity, in order to avoid making such mistakes, as searching for some tragic flaw in her which would justify her death. But at the same time, if we would know what love and charity *are* in all their fullness, then our definition can only be the actions, the language, the emotions of the character Desdemona. She is Shakespeare's word for love. If we wish to know not just the obvious fact that men choose evil over good, but *why* they do so, then we must look both analytically and feelingly at all the evidence that the world offers for believing that Desdemona is false and at all the biases in Othello's mind that predispose him to believe such evidence. Othello's passage from Venice to Cyprus, from absolute love for Desdemona to extinguishing the light in her bedchamber, and to the execution of himself, these are Shakespeare's words for tragic man.

Iago Revisited

by Bernard Spivack

Fie, there is no such man! It is impossible.

IAGO

Long before *Othello* St. Paul addressed the Thessalonians on the *mystery of iniquity*. Applied to the play, the apostle's phrase is a haven of comprehensive explanation compared to all the others that have been advanced to account for Shakespeare's tragedy and for the nature of its agent. Having pursued the meaning of Iago by ingenious and labyrinthine ways, critics and scholars are left, like his greatest victim, "perplex'd in the extreme." It would be ungenerous to the literature on *Othello* not to acknowledge that it affords deep and sensitive insight into the meaning of the play. And in this literature Iago has been rationalized to the last inch of his human similitude. But the hard and literal enigma of Othello's fatal ancient remains intractable. There is still no successful mediation between his terrible vividness, as we *feel* it on the one hand, and the blank he presents to our scrutiny on the other. To his bad eminence above all other figures of evil in the Elizabethan drama he is elevated not only by the shock of his turpitude, the pathos of his victims, and the poetry of his role, but also, and in no small measure, by his mystery. "Qu'est-ce qu'Iago?" asked the Duc de Broglie in a penetrating critique on *Othello* in 1830. The question came after half a century of criticism had already tried to answer it, and the attempts have been legion ever since. But the question abides, and in 1945 Granville-Barker hopelessly threw up his hands at it: "Behind all the mutability there *is,* perhaps, no Iago, only a poisoned and poisonous ganglion of cravings after evil."

What indeed is Iago? In Shakespeare's most compact and painful tragedy he is the artisan of an intrigue that first alienates and then destroys a pair of wedded lovers, in an action fraught with the pathos that

"Iago Revisited." From *Shakespeare and the Allegory of Evil* (New York: Columbia University Press, 1958), by Bernard Spivack, pp. 3-4, 423-30. Copyright © 1958 by Columbia University Press. Reprinted by permission of Columbia University Press. (The work is about the figure of the Vice in early drama and its residual influence on Shakespeare.)

attends the loss of noble love and noble life. He is also the divisive agent of another kind of separation, probably a more tragic theme for the Elizabethans than for us—the divorce of friendship between two generous men. His victims are a beautiful and pure-hearted Venetian woman, a noble and heroic Moorish prince, a loyal and ingenuous fellow soldier, his own honest wife, and a foolish gentleman whose wealth he has drained into his own pocket. He is a soldier, a liar, an adept at dissimulation and intrigue, a cynic, an egotist, a criminal. His crimes, he explains, are motivated by his resentment over the denial of an office to which he aspires and by his desire to recover it, by his suspicion that he is a deceived husband and by his desire for revenge, and by his need ultimately to cover up his previous malefactions. He inflicts unendurable suffering, destroys love and friendship and four lives, and at the end moves off in defiant silence to torture and his own death.

*   *   *

As for that evil itself, it is morally organized beyond almost anything else in the play. Cinthio's ensign was a depraved villain of the blackest stripe—lustful, revengeful, deceitful, cunning, and cowardly. But Shakespeare's figure is something else again—a man of principle, with a subtle coherence between what he believes in general and what he believes in particular. He entertains a comprehensive moral attitude toward the world, society, and the individual; and through that attitude appears the "new man," as he has been called, of the Renaissance, his contours sharp and grim against the orthodox values of the poet's age. To some extent he is a propaganda piece, with just enough exaggeration to send him crashing through the sensibilities of Shakespeare's contemporaries, but with not enough exaggeration to carry his meaning completely home to our own. Today our approval of some of his tenets is hampered only by our mystification that they should be the utterance of a villain: "If the balance of our lives had not one scale of reason to poise another of sensuality, the blood and baseness of our natures would conduct us to most prepost'rous conclusions" (I. iii. 330-34). Where shall we find better doctrine? It was in respect to such a passage that an eminent Shakespearian once offered his students the opinion that Shakespeare's villains express some of the poet's most admirable sentiments. Alas, time devours things, among them the poet's meaning.

Provided we extend the significance of the label beyond Machiavelli, since it embraces concepts of which Tudor England was conscious without the Florentine's instruction, Iago is a Machiavel. Upon the traditional pieties . . . and the system of belief behind them, his derisive assault is fundamental, extending to first principles. When Roderigo whimpers that he is ashamed to be so infatuated but "it is not in my virtue to amend it," the villain's response becomes intelligible only when "virtue" is understood for what it almost certainly does mean: the divine grace flowing into the otherwise helpless nature of man, creating there the power toward good without which salvation is not possible. "Virtue? a fig!" replies Iago, " 'Tis in ourselves that we are thus or thus," demolishing in a phrase the theological foundation beneath the whole system of Christian ethics. He is *homo emancipatus a Deo,* seeing the world and human life as self-sufficient on their own terms, obedient only to natural law, uninhibited and uninspired by any participation in divinity. In addition to his animal nature, man possesses the equipment of will and reason with which to fulfill or regulate his natural appetites. He is the king of beasts, crowned by his superior faculties. And society, by the same token, is the arena of endless competition, more or less organized, between the appetites of one man and another, success attending him who knows "how to love himself" and how to manipulate the natures of other men. Nature is Iago's goddess as well as Edmund's, with the articles of the ancient's faith even more explicit and wider in their application.

Intellect and scorn, suppressing piety and reverence, compose the double-edged instrument with which he lops off life's idealisms. He has looked upon the world for four times seven years and has acutely seen what he has looked upon: the profane world, no more. His credo and conduct shape themselves accordingly. Loyalty in service is the dotage of "honest knaves" who deserve to be whipped for their folly. Candor in human dealings, whereby word and action faithfully mirror the sentiment of the heart, is as grossly inane as wearing the heart upon the sleeve "for daws to peck at." Rich idiots like Roderigo were made to be mulcted without scruple. Generous masters like Othello were made to be cheated. A truly good woman, assuming the doubtful existence of such a creature, is good for nothing except to exhaust herself upon child bearing and petty household accounts. As for love, it is simply physical appetite mediated by will and guided to fulfillment by libertine cunning. A sensible man of the world serves himself and does himself homage, takes his pleasure and profit wherever he finds them, plays to win by any trick, dissembles his intentions, and knows that only fools lament the loss of reputation as if it were a bodily wound. For he knows that the world belongs to the worldling, and that human beings, whatever else they may profess, are in reality moved only by egotism, appetite, and personal advantage. A score of Machiavels on the Elizabethan stage know as much, except that they don't express themselves so effectively. Richard of Gloucester and the Bastard Edmund are past masters of this knowledge, and fragments of it also appear in a number of other Shakespearian characters, Falstaff for one and Antonio of *The Tempest* for another. The Bastard Faulconbridge is enrolled in the same school, but his sympathetic portrait allows him to wear his colors with a difference. Although his "mounting spirit" finds its proper traction in the courses of this world, he is careful, in his first monologue, to announce a pointed reservation:

> . . . though I will not practice to deceive,
> Yet, to avoid deceit, I mean to learn;
> For it shall strew the footsteps of my rising.
>
> [*King John* I. i. 214-16]

The moral distinction in these words is explicit; what is not equally explicit, unless dramatic convention is allowed to assert its own relevant context of meaning, is the reference to the kind of role his is not going to be.

Labels, however, adhere only to surfaces and mock us with superficiality when we try to apply them to Shakespeare's depths. We detect the type with which he begins but lose it in the unique creation with which he ends. Applied to Iago, the Machiavellian label, while supplying some prefatory enlightenment, is too general to carry us very far into the moral meaning of his role. The high art that wrought him into the dense and exclusive design of his own play does not allow him to remain an undifferentiated specimen of villainous humanity according to the commonplace Elizabethan formula of the Machiavel. He is matched and specialized against a theme, and his evil refined into something rare through the ironic felicity of its polarization and the dramatic felicity of its operation within that theme. His cynical naturalism in respect to human motives and relationships is the first principle from which he moves, through a series of narrowing applications, until it creates his opinion of every other person in the play. It also creates something else: his opinion of his own situation. Unless we follow him closely through the descending gyres of his thought, we lose him and soon begin to wonder what he is talking about. Those of his words, however, which apply to the way we are now concerned with him are invariably consistent with the way he is morally organized, and perspicuous in the terms of that organization. He is wonderfully opposed to the theme of the play as its anti-theme, and is, in fact, the most astonishing product of the Shakespearian technique of contrast.

If the play is about anything it is, as we have seen, about love. Its first words concern an elopement and its last the "heavy act" which has brought that elopement's history to its tragic end. Conceivably any sort of villain for any sort of villainous reason might have contrived the intrigue that produces the tragedy, and in Cinthio the motive was frustrated passion. But if one thing more than another can explain Shakespeare's departures from his sources, especially in matters of character and motive, it is his concern with dramaturgic patterns—in this case the pattern of opposites. Creating in Othello and Desdemona romantic love's most splendid votaries, he also creates in Iago its most derisive atheist. To the kind of love existing between hero and heroine, supplying the bright ideal of the play, the ancient is the dark counter-type, the adversary. Although his naturalism is voluble upon a dozen topics, they are all ancillary to its main theme: nothing engrosses him so much as the subject of love or receives from him so mordant a negation. The marriage of true minds, or, for that matter, any level of love above sexual appetite, is exactly what he does not believe in. Nor does he believe that men and women exist in any relationship to each other apart from physical desire. He strikes his proper note in the first scene by the images of animal copulation with which he shocks Brabantio into attention, and descants upon it thereafter through similar images and definitions that are, in fact, consistent deductions from a universal premise: Love, whose imagined mystery bemuses romantic fools like Roderigo, "is merely a lust of the blood and a permission of the will." Before he is through, his nimble logic has roped everyone in the play, including himself, into his sexual syllogism. An Othello in love is merely "an erring barbarian" momentarily enticed but changeable in his appetites. A Desdemona in love is merely "a supersubtle Venetian" who married the Moor for lust and will leave him for youth "When she is sated with his body." Cassio is not handsome and young for nothing:

> He hath a person and a smooth dispose
> To be suspected—fram'd to make women false.
>
> [I. iii. 403-404]

Emilia, being a woman, is faithful to the promiscuous disposition of her sex:

> EMILIA. Do not you chide; I have a thing for you.
> IAGO. A thing for me? It is a common thing—
>
> [III. iii. 301-302]

He himself, being a man, obeys the disposition of his:

> Now I do love her too;
> Not out of absolute lust (though peradventure
> I stand accountant for as great a sin). . . .
>
> [II. i. 300-302]

He thinks like a rigorous geometrician—from his basic proposition straight through to all its corollaries.

Being also a practical man of the world, from corollaries he moves to applications. Since the Moor is what he is and Emilia what she is, it

follows that "I do suspect the lusty Moor hath leap'd into my seat." On
the quay at Cyprus he stands spectator to an exchange of courtesies between Desdemona, who "must change for youth," and Cassio, who is
"handsome, young, and hath all those requisites in him that folly and
green minds look after," and soon imparts to Roderigo what it means:
"Desdemona is directly in love with him." Social kissing between the
sexes, though never quite free from equivocal suggestion, was permissi-
ble in Tudor England (to the astonishment of foreign visitors). Such a
kiss between Cassio and Emilia in his presence suggests the interpretation
natural to him: "For I fear Cassio with my nightcap too." His formulations are progressive, and parts of his second soliloquy (II. i. 294-321)
reach conclusions based on his observations during the reunion of the
voyagers at Cyprus a few moments before. He is even obliged, with the
air of a man of courage taking a calculated risk, to revise one of his previous estimates (for he has just seen and heard Othello's rapt greeting of
Desdemona): "I dare think he'll prove to Desdemona/ A most dear husband." In the same soliloquy he adverts to his discourse with his gull in
order to save us from writing it off as sheer flimflam:

> That Cassio loves her, I do well believe it;
> That she loves him, 'tis apt and of great credit.

In other words, "I really do believe what I have just been saying to
Roderigo." Something else will save us from the same skepticism—a part
of his conversation with Cassio two scenes later:

> IAGO.   Our general cast us thus early for the love of his Desdemona;
>   who let us not therefore blame. He hath not yet made wanton
>   the night with her, and she is sport for Jove.
> CASSIO. She's a most exquisite lady.
> IAGO.   And I'll warrant her full of game.
> CASSIO. Indeed, she's a most fresh and delicate creature.
> IAGO.   What an eye she has! Methinks it sounds a parley to provoca-
>   tion.
> CASSIO. An inviting eye; and yet methinks right modest.
> IAGO.   And when she speaks, is it not an alarum to love?
> CASSIO. She is indeed perfection.
> IAGO.   Well, happiness to their sheets!
>
>   [II. iii. 14-29]

He does not get the confirmation for which he probes, but whether he
changes his mind about Cassio too we shall never know. His separate
suspicions bewilder us less and seem less absurd, at least to our theoretical
consideration of him and them, when we see them for what they actually
are—related local disturbances moving out from the broad weather front

of his sexual doctrine. All of them together, by their mutual reinforce-
ment, exhibit the disposition of his nature, and produce thereby an explanation for the existence of each individually, including the most
prominent of them, his personal jealousy regarding his wife and Othello.
We need also to reckon with the fact that on his own stage he was sup-
ported by a convention of which we are now largely bereft. It would
take more than our fingers and toes to count the dramatized husbands
round about him who jump to similar jealousies about their wives for
no other reason than that they are women and, therefore, in Lear's sufficient phrase, "Down from the waist they are Centaurs"; or imagine a
rival in every male who is not a certified eunuch.

To the extent that the foregoing interpretation is correct, his suspicions, which otherwise swirl like chaff in the wind, subside into an intelligible pattern. He has only two motives, one of them being his cynical
Machiavellianism toward sex, which hovers over everyone in the play and
creates his personal provocation when it lights on his wife and "black
Othello." The other requires only a word. We have no right to believe
that he has a better claim than Cassio's to the lieutenancy, only that he
craves it. And his craving is annexed to a credo of service which, at least
in our own awareness of his moral qualifications, damns his claim. Besides, by every indication, he is intended as a coward, just as he was
featured by Cinthio: "a very great coward, yet his carriage and conversation were so haughty and full of pretension, that you would have taken
him for a Hector or an Achilles." There is no reason to believe that the
play changes this estimate. He is fluent with his dagger, but only in special circumstances: Cassio receives it anonymously in the dark, Roderigo
already wounded and on his back, his wife when he is cornered ("Fie!
your sword upon a woman?"); and he likes to stab and run. Finally, we
can draw conviction on this point from the fact that to Cassio he is "the
bold Iago" and to Lodovico "a very valiant fellow"; for, without excep-
tion, every moral attribute applied to him by anyone in the play is an
ironic finger pointing to the truth of its opposite. As to his contempt for
Cassio's "bookish theoric," it finds its precise equivalent in the feeling
that today's master sergeant might entertain for the young second lieutenant just out of West Point. But unless the case is exceptional, we are
able to assess the potential superiority of the trained, flexible, theoretical
mind against the fossilized know-how of one who has merely slogged
through a dozen years of practical experience. Iago's opinion notwith-
standing, it tells us something of Cassio's qualifications that Othello
should appoint him lieutenant before the beginning of the play and that
the Signoria of Venice should appoint him governor of Cyprus before its
end. But the question of Iago's justification or lack of it is ultimately
meaningless beside the motive fact of his resentment, and his resentment,
like his jealousy, belongs to his bad character. We neglect the intention

within Shakespeare's irony unless we heed Emilia's inadvertent accuracy
in respect to the nature and motives of her husband:

> I will be hang'd if some eternal villain,
> Some busy and insinuating rogue,
> Some cogging, cozening slave, to get some office,
> Have not devis'd this slander. I'll be hang'd else.

> The Moor's abus'd by some most villanous knave,
> Some base notorious knave, some scurvy fellow.

>   Some such squire he was
> That turn'd your wit the seamy side without
> And made you to suspect me with the Moor.

>   [IV. ii. 130-47]

He has every reason for urging her to "Speak within door," for she has
limned him to the life.

Such a portrait, or one reasonably like it, must be accepted because it
exists, but it must also be rejected because it does not exist alone. Com-
promising it by addition and blurring it by invasion is his other life, his
other set of features. They derive from nothing discoverable in Cinthio
or in any naturalistic intention behind the playwright's revision of Cinthio, but have their source in the spectacular image of evil traditional
on the popular stage. We need not expect, however, to find in Iago the
massive dislocation visible in Richard ten years before, and even more
obvious, because even earlier, in Barabas. The contrary elements of the
conflation, no longer layered in broad distinction, are now relatively
merged and granular, with the older image recessive and diminished. For
one thing, the bravura image of multiple deceit, though ramifying upon
as many victims as before, is no longer tandem and episodic, but deftly
organized into a single complex intrigue within a comprehensive dramatic plot. For another, the amoral humor of the moral personification,
having ceased to be explosive, has become pervasive—a mood and a tone
penetrating Iago's role throughout. In the third place, the homiletic dimension of the role, its didactic voice and naked moral display, is relatively subdued and fragmentary, modified by indirection and mainly
limited to sentences and half-sentences that twist in and out of his more
relevant phraseology. Finally, while the stark antinomy of the Psycho-
machia remains, supplying for his aggression an explanation that con-
tradicts his motives, it has suffered attrition, and of the original formula
only part survives: "I hate the Moor." To each of these aspects of the
role we need to address ourselves briefly, allowing the long account already spun to piece out the explication proffered now. . . .

Macbeth

by L. C. Knights

I

Macbeth defines a particular kind of evil—the evil that results from a lust for power. The defining, as in all the tragedies, is in strictly poetic and dramatic terms. It is certainly not an abstract formulation, but lies rather in the drawing out of necessary consequences and implications of that lust both in the external and the spiritual worlds. Its meaning, therefore, is revealed in the expansion and unfolding of what lies within the initial evil, in terms of direct human experience. The logic is not formal but experiential, and demands from us, if we are to test its validity and feel its force, a fulness of imaginative response and a closeness of realization, in which both sensation and feeling become modes of understanding. Only when intellect, emotion, and a kind of direct sensory awareness work together can we enter fully into that exploratory and defining process.

In other words, the essential structure of *Macbeth,* as of the other tragedies, is to be sought in the poetry. That of course is easily said; what it means is something that can only be grasped in relation to specific instances or not grasped at all. We may take as an example Macbeth's "aside" when he has been greeted as Thane of Cawdor.

> This supernatural soliciting
> Cannot be ill; cannot be good:
> If ill, why hath it given me earnest of success,
> Commencing in a truth? I am thane of Cawdor:
> If good, why do I yield to that suggestion
> Whose horrid image doth unfix my hair,
> And make my seated heart knock at my ribs,

"*Macbeth.*" From *Some Shakespearean Themes* (Chatto & Windus, Ltd., 1959; Stanford University Press, 1959), by L. C. Knights. Copyright © 1959 by L. C. Knights. Reprinted by permission of L. C. Knights, Chatto & Windus, Ltd., and Stanford University Press. Illustrative material from works other than *Macbeth* has been omitted from section II, as well as a number of amplifying notes.

> Against the use of nature? Present fears
> Are less than horrible imaginings.
> My thought, whose murder yet is but fantastical,
> Shakes so my single state of man,
> That function is smother'd in surmise,
> And nothing is, but what is not.
>
> [I. iii. 130-42]

This is temptation, presented with concrete force. Even if we attend only to the revelation of Macbeth's spiritual state, our recognition of the body—the very feel—of the experience, is a response to the poetry, to such things as the sickening see-saw rhythm ("Cannot be ill; cannot be good . . .") changing to the rhythm of the pounding heart, the overriding of grammar ("My thought, whose murder yet is but fantastical") as thought is revealed in the very process of formation, and so on. But the poetry makes further claims, and if we attend to them we find that the words do not only point inward to the presumed state of Macbeth's mind but, as it were, outward to the play as a whole. The equivocal nature of temptation, the commerce with phantoms consequent upon false choice, the resulting sense of unreality ("nothing is, but what is not"), which has yet such power to "smother" vital function, the unnaturalness of evil ("against the use of nature"), and the relation between disintegration in the individual ("my single state of man") and disorder in the larger social organism—all these are major themes of the play which are mirrored in the speech under consideration. They emerge as themes because they are what the poetry—reinforced by action and symbolism —again and again insists on. And the interrelations we are forced to make take us outside the speeches of the protagonist to the poetry of the play as a whole. That "smother'd," for example, takes us forward not only to Lady Macbeth's "blanket of the dark" but to such things as Rosse's choric comment after the murder of Duncan:

> by th' clock 'tis day,
> And yet dark night strangles the travelling lamp.
> Is't night's predominance, or the day's shame,
> That darkness does the face of earth entomb,
> When living light should kiss it?
>
> [II. iv. 6-10]

In none of the tragedies is there anything superfluous, but it is perhaps *Macbeth* that gives the keenest impression of economy. The action moves directly and quickly to the crisis, and from the crisis to the full working out of plot and theme. The pattern is far easier to grasp than that of

Lear. The main theme of the reversal of values is given out simply and clearly in the first scene—"Fair is foul, and foul is fair"; and with it are associated premonitions of the conflict, disorder and moral darkness into which Macbeth will plunge himself. Well before the end of the first act we are in possession not only of the positive values against which the Macbeth evil will be defined but of the related aspects of that evil, which is simultaneously felt as a strained and unnatural perversion of the will, an obfuscation of the clear light of reason, a principle of disorder (both in the "single state of man" and in his wider social relations), and a pursuit of illusions. All these impressions, which as the play proceeds assume the status of organizing ideas, are produced by the inter-action of all the resources of poetic drama—action, contrast, statement, implication, imagery and allusion. Thus the sense of the unnaturalness of evil is evoked not only by repeated explicit references ("nature's mischief," "nature seems dead," " 'Tis unnatural, even like the deed that's done," and so on) but by the expression of unnatural sentiments and an unnatural violence of tone in such things as Lady Macbeth's invocation of the "spirits" who will "unsex" her, and her affirmation that she would murder the babe at her breast if she had sworn to do it. So too the theme of the false appearances inseparable from evil, of deceit recoiling on the deceiver, is not only the subject of explicit comment—

> And be these juggling fiends no more believ'd,
> That palter with us in a double sense
>
> [V. viii. 19-20]

—it is embodied in the action, so that Macbeth's despairing recognition of mere "mouth-honour" among his remaining followers (V. iii. 27) echoes ironically his wife's advice to "look like th' innocent flower, But be the serpent under't" (I. v. 64-5) and the hypocritical play of the welcoming of Duncan; and it is reinforced by—or indeed one with—the evoked sense of equivocation and evasiveness associated with the witches, and the cloud of uncertainty that settles on Scotland during Macbeth's despotism. It is fitting that the final movement of the reversal that takes place in the last act should open with the command of Malcolm to the camouflaged soldiers, "Your leavy screens throw down, And show like those you are" (V. vi. 1-2).

II

The assurance of *Macbeth* has behind it, is indeed based on, a deeply imagined resolution of perplexities inherent in any full exposure to life. Freedom from the tyranny of time and illusion is finally related, at the deepest levels of consciousness, to the central affirmations of the spirit; and conversely, the obsessed awareness of time without meaning, like the subjection of mind to appearance, is revealed not simply as consequential on false choice but as intrinsic to it: for "the eye altering alters all." There is a similar assurance in the use of "nature," in that aspect of the play's imaginative structure that impels us to say not merely that Macbeth's crime is unnatural (*i.e.,* inhuman) but that the values against which evil is defined are in some sense grounded in nature. . . .

In Shakespeare's poetic thought we find two apparently contradictory intuitions regarding man's relation to the created world existing independently of human choice and will. Nature and human values are felt as intimately related, and at the same time as antagonistic. . . .

. . . He says—though it takes the whole of *King Lear* to say it adequately—that nature *per se* is something quite other than human nature, and that it cannot properly be conceived in human terms; that its humanly relevant quality only exists in relation to a particular human outlook and standpoint; and that what that quality is depends on the standpoint from which the relation is established. "Nature-as-beneficent" is a concept that only has meaning for the good man—or at all events for the man who admits the imperatives of his own humanity. Perhaps it is easier to grasp this in relation to the world—the given "nature"—of inner experience. The mind ("that ocean, where each kind Does straight its own resemblance find") contains within itself elements corresponding to non-human life—Blake's tiger and lamb. So long as these natural forces are not integrated by the specifically human principle they are, or are likely to become, chaotic and destructive. Given that principle, they may be sublimated and transformed, but they are not disowned: they are freely accepted as the natural sources of life and power.[1] So too with the external world of nature: it is only the man who recognizes his own humanity, and that of others, as something essentially other than a product of the natural world, who is really open to nature; neither fascinated nor afraid, he can respond creatively to its creativeness, and, paradoxically, find in nature a symbol for all that is natural in the other sense—that is, most truly human. It is, I think, some such perception as this, attained in *King Lear,* that lies behind and validates the elaborate and imaginatively powerful analogy between the human order and the order of nature in *Macbeth.*

III

There is no vague "philosophy of nature" in *Macbeth.* The nature against which the "unnaturalness" of the Macbeth evil is defined and

[1] Hobbes, *Leviathan* (Everyman edition), I, 13, p. 65.

judged is human nature; and essential characteristics of that nature—its capacity for and intimate dependence on relationship—are powerfully evoked throughout the play. In Act III, scene iv. Macbeth, overcome by his vision of Banquo's ghost, glances back to a time when murder was common, to what will later be known as the Hobbesian state of nature.

> Blood hath been shed ere now, i' th' olden time,
> Ere humane statute purg'd the gentle weal;
> Ay, and since too, murthers have been perform'd
> Too terrible for the ear: the time has been,
> That, when the brains were out, the man would die,
> And there an end; but now, they rise again,
> With twenty mortal murthers on their crowns,
> And push us from our stools. This is more strange
> Than such a murther is.

> [III. iv. 74-82]

This is a more profound version of the origins of society than is suggested by the notion of contract or expediency. What "purges" the supposed mere multitude and makes it into a "gentle" commonweal is a decree greater than any law in which it may be embodied, for it is what is dictated by the very fact of being human; if you accept your humanity then you can't murder with impunity. Nor is this simply a matter of judicial punishment: the murdered man "rises" again, in you. Killing may be common in wild nature, but it is not natural to man as man; it is a violation of his essential humanity. When Lady Macbeth describes her husbands as "too full o' the milk of human kindness" she intends to be disparaging, as Goneril does when she speaks of Albany's "milky gentleness" or calls him a "milk-liver'd man" (*King Lear,* I. iv. 351; IV. ii. 50). But what the phrase also says is that human kindness is natural to man as man, and, like his mother's milk, nourishes his manhood. When Malcolm accuses himself of imaginary crimes, and in so doing reflects the evil that Macbeth has brought on Scotland, the climax is,

> Nay, had I power, I should
> Pour the sweet milk of concord into Hell,
> Uproar the universal peace, confound
> All unity in earth.

> [IV. iii. 97-100]

"Concord," "peace," "unity"—these are *active* words, signifying not a mere absence of disagreeables, a mere deliverance from "continual fear, and danger of violent death," but the condition of positive human living.

We learn little about a play by making lists of words, but it is a significant fact that *Macbeth* contains a very large number of words expressing the varied relations of life (not only "cousin," "children," "servants," "guest," "host," . . . but "thanks," "payment," "service," "loyalty," "duties" . . .), and that these sometimes, as in Act I. scenes iv. and vi., seem to be dwelt on with a special insistence. At the end of the play, when Macbeth thinks of what he has lost, it is not "honour, wealth and ease in waning age" (*Lucrece,* l. 142) but

> that which should accompany old age,
> As honour, love, obedience, troops of friends
>
> [V. iii. 24-5]

An awareness of those "holy cords" which, though they may be severed, are "too intrince"—too intimately intertwined—"to unloose" (*King Lear,* II. ii. 75-6), is integral to the imaginative structure of *Macbeth.* That the man who breaks the bonds that tie him to other men, who "pours the sweet milk of concord into Hell," is at the same time violating his own nature and thwarting his own deepest needs, is something that the play dwells on with a special insistence.

Now as we have seen in relation to *King Lear,* it is only when the essential needs and characteristics of human nature are given an absolute, unconditional priority that nature in its widest sense can be invoked as an order underlying, invigorating, and in a certain sense offering a pattern for, human nature. So too in *Macbeth.* In Macbeth's apocalyptic soliloquy before the murder, the "Pity" that dominates the chaotic natural forces and rides the whirlwind appears as a new-born babe—an offspring of humanity, naked, vulnerable, and powerful. It is, we may say, because of the symbol of the babe, and all it stands for, that Shakespeare can invoke the powers of nature and associate them, as Professor Wilson Knight shows that he does, with all that is opposed to, and finally victorious over, the powers of destruction.[2]

It is in the scene of Duncan's entry into Macbeth's castle (I. vi.)—"a perfect contrast in microcosm to the Macbeth evil" [3]—that we are most vividly aware of the energies of untaught nature in significant relation to the human order. The scene is set for full dramatic effect between Lady Macbeth's invocation of the powers of darkness ("The raven himself is hoarse, That croaks the fatal entrance . . .") and Macbeth's final resolution, and Duncan's courtesy underlines the irony. But the contrast is not confined to the situation. The suggestion of a sweet fresh air, the pleased

---

[2] See "The Milk of Concord: an Essay on Life Themes in *Macbeth,*" in *The Imperial Theme,* especially pp. 140-1, 144-5, 148-51.

[3] *The Imperial Theme,* p. 142.

contemplation of the birds that build and breed, affect us first as sensory contrasts to the smothering oppression ("Come, thick Night . . .") so recently evoked; but like the images of darkness and disorder the presented scene is inseparable from the values it embodies and defines.

> This guest of summer,
> The temple-haunting martlet, does approve,
> By his lov'd mansionry, that the heaven's breath
> Smells wooingly here: no jutty, frieze,
> Buttress, nor coign of vantage, but this bird
> Hath made his pendent bed, and procreant cradle:
> Where they most breed and haunt, I have observ'd
> The air is delicate.

What we are contemplating here is a natural and wholesome *order,* of which the equivalent in the human sphere is to be found in those mutualities of loyalty, trust and liking that Macbeth proposes to violate. And it is an order that is at one with the life it fosters. The opening lines of the scene, in short, are not only beautiful in themselves, they form an image of life delighting in life. It is in terms of destructive and self-destructive energies that Macbeth's power lust is defined; and it is from the "life" images of the play, which range from the temple-haunting martlets to Macduff's "babes," his "pretty ones," and include all the scattered references to man's natural goods—sleep and food and fellowship—that we take our bearings in the apprehension of evil.

IV

In the great soliloquy of I. vii. Macbeth tries to provide himself with prudential reasons for not committing murder:

> But in these cases,
> We still have judgment here; that we but teach
> Bloody instructions, which, being taught, return
> To plague th'inventor.

But the attempt at a cool calculation of consequences (already at odds with the nervous rhythm and the taut muscular force of the imagery of the opening lines) almost immediately gives way to an appalling vision of judgment.

> Besides, this Duncan
> Hath borne his faculties so meek, hath been

> So clear in his great office, that his virtues
> Will plead like angels, trumpet-tongu'd, against
> The deep damnation of his taking-off . . . .

These lines have of course behind them the traditional conception of the Day of Judgment, and it is nothing less than the nature of judgment that the play reveals. Just as, in Spinoza's words "blessedness is not the reward of virtue but virtue itself," so the deep damnation of this play is revealed in the intrinsic qualities of an evil deliberately willed and persisted in. It is revealed above all as a defection from life and reality.

> So that in vent'ring ill we leave to be
> The things we are for that which we expect;
> And this ambitious foul infirmity,
> In having much, torments us with defect
> Of that we have: so then we do neglect
>   The things we have, and, all for want of wit,
>   Make something nothing by augmenting it.

So Shakespeare had written in *The Rape of Lucrece* (ll. 148-154), where lust—a type sin, "including all foul harms" (l. 199)—was defined as the urge to possess something that in the experience inevitably proves mere loss, an over-reaching into insubstantiality and negation. In *Macbeth* the positives so securely established—the assured intimation of "the things we [*sc.* truly] are"—throw into relief, and so sharply define, the defection that occupies the forefront of the play. It is this that makes the play's irony so deeply significant—the irony of making "something nothing by augmenting it," that is, in Banquo's phrase, "by seeking to augment it" (II. i. 27); and that central irony of losing in gaining—for Macbeth, like Tarquin, is "A captive victor that hath lost in gain" (*Lucrece*, l. 730)—lies behind all the often noted dramatic ironies that multiply as the play proceeds. Fear and disorder erupt into the specious security and apparent order that temporarily succeed the murder of Duncan. "Things bad begun" attempt to "make strong themselves by ill," yet each further step is as "tedious" (Macbeth's word) and self-frustrating as the last. And the concomitant of the outer disorder and inner disintegration (with both of which Macbeth identifies himself in the great invocation of chaos in IV. i.) is something that appears to the observer as the betrayal of life to automatism, and within Macbeth's own consciousness as a deepening sense of the loss of significance. It is a radical failure of the human to inhabit his proper world of creative activity. A brief examination of these two related aspects of that failure will conclude our examination of the play's philosophy.

We touch for the last time on the question of "nature." Early in the play we are told of "the merciless Macdonwald" that he is "worthy to be a rebel,"

> for to that
> The multiplying villainies of nature
> Do swarm upon him.
>
> [I. ii. 9-12]

Now nature, we have seen, is a power that can be invoked in the service of what is essentially right and wholesome on the sole condition that "human kindness" is recognized as an absolute. Nature by itself, however, is clearly a submoral world, and to "Night's black agents" (III. ii. 53) in the outer world correspond, within,

> the cursed thoughts that nature
> Gives way to in repose.
>
> [II. i. 8-9]

Man, the inhabitant of two worlds, is free to choose; but if, disregarding the "compunctious visitings of Nature," he chooses "Nature's mischief" (I. v. 45, 50), his freedom is impaired. He has "untied the winds" (IV. i. 52), and the powers of nature enter the human sphere as autonomous agents: in the language of the play, the "villainies of nature" "swarm upon him" as a more or less passive host.

The explanation of this phrase thus involves us in a consideration of one of the main structural lines of the play, where to the creative energy of good—enlisting and controlling nature's powers—is opposed the automatism of evil. To listen to the witches, it is suggested, is like eating "the insane root, That takes the reason prisoner" (I. iii. 84-5); for Macbeth, in the moment of temptation, "function," or intellectual activity, is "smother'd in surmise"; and everywhere the imagery of darkness suggests not only the absence or withdrawal of light but—"light thickens"—the presence of something positively oppressive and impeding. Both Macbeth and his wife wilfully blind themselves ("Come, thick Night," "Come, seeing Night . . ."), and to the extent that they surrender the characteristically human power of intellectual and moral discernment they themselves become the "prey" of "Night's black agents," of the powers they have deliberately invoked. Automatism is perhaps most obvious in Lady Macbeth's sleep-walking, with its obsessed reliving of the past, but Macbeth also is shown as forfeiting his human freedom and spontaneity. If one ultimate aspect of evil is revealed in Macbeth's invocation of chaos, in his determination to be answered,

> though the treasure
> Of Nature's germens tumble all together,
> Even till destruction sicken

another is suggested by the banal repetitions of the witches' incantations, the almost mechanical beat in which their charms are "wound up." And just as the widespreading confusion (enacted on the "metaphysical" plane) is reflected in the particular action, so Macbeth's terror-stricken advance in evil is tuned to that monotonous beat. "One feels," says W. C. Curry, "that in proportion as the good in him diminishes, his liberty of free choice is determined more and more by evil inclination and that he cannot choose the better course. Hence we speak of destiny or fate, as if it were some external force or moral order, compelling him against his will to certain destruction." [4] Most readers have felt that after the initial crime there is something compulsive in Macbeth's murders; and at the end, for all his "valiant fury," he is certainly not a free agent. He is like a bear tied to a stake, he says; but it is not only the besieging army that hems him in; he is imprisoned in the world he has made.

It is from within that world that, prompted by the news of his wife's suicide, he speaks his last great speech.

> She should have died hereafter:
> There would have been a time for such a word.
> To-morrow, and to-morrow, and to-morrow,
> Creeps in this petty pace from day to day,
> To the last syllable of recorded time;
> And all our yesterdays have lighted fools
> The way to dusty death. Out, out, brief candle!
> Life's but a walking shadow; a poor player,
> That struts and frets his hour upon the stage,
> And then is heard no more: it is a tale
> Told by an idiot, full of sound and fury,
> Signifying nothing.
>
> [V. v. 17-28]

His wife's death, it has often been observed, means nothing to him. Commentators have been exercised to determine the precise meaning of the words with which he greets it—"She should have died hereafter" ("She would have died sometime," or, "Her death should have been deferred to a more peaceable hour"); but the point of the line lies in its

---

[4] Walter Clyde Curry, *Shakespeare's Philosophical Patterns*, p. 105.

ambiguity. Macbeth is groping for meanings, trying to conceive a time when he might have met such a situation with something more than indifference, when death itself might have had a significance it cannot have in the world of mere meaningless repetition that he goes on to evoke. As a final irony this *is* the world where when a thing is done it is merely—"alms for oblivion"—done with, because it is a world devoid of significant relations.

Clearly then we have in this play an answer to Shakespeare's earlier questionings about time's power, as we have also a resolution of his earlier preoccupation with the power of illusion and false appearance. Macbeth *has betrayed himself* to the equivocal and the illusory. So too time appears to him as meaningless repetition because he has turned his back on, has indeed attempted violence on, those values that alone give significance to duration, that in a certain sense make time, for "Without the meaning there is no time".[5] He has directed his will to evil, towards something that of its very nature makes for chaos and the abnegation of meaning. The solid natural goods—ranging from food and sleep to the varied mutualities of friendship, service, love—are witnesses to the central paradox of evil, that however terrible its power it can only lead to "nothing." In the lines,

> . . . it is a tale
> Told by an idiot, full of sound and fury,
> Signifying nothing,

there is combined the apparent force—the sound and fury—and the essential meaninglessness. For Macbeth, now, though in a different sense from when he used the phrase, "nothing is, but what is not."

But the play's last word is not, of course, about evil.

> What's more to do,
> Which would be planted newly with the time,
> As calling home our exil'd friends abroad,
> That fled the snares of watchful tyranny;
> Producing forth the cruel ministers
> Of this dead butcher, and his fiend-like Queen,
> Who, as 'tis thought, by self and violent hands
> Took off her life; this, and what needful else
> That calls upon us, by the grace of Grace,
> We will perform in measure, time, and place.

[5] T. S. Eliot, *The Rock.*

It is a fitting close for a play in which moral law has been made present to us not as convention or command but as the law of life itself, as that which makes for life, and through which alone man can ground himself on, and therefore in his measure know, reality.

Macbeth as the Imitation of an Action

by Francis Fergusson

I propose to attempt to illustrate the view that *Macbeth* may be understood as "the imitation of an action," in approximately Aristotle's sense of this phrase.

The word "action"—*praxis*—as Aristotle uses it in the *Poetics,* does not mean outward deeds or events, but something much more like "purpose" or "aim." Perhaps our word "motive" suggests most of its meaning. Dante (who in this respect is a sophisticated Aristotelian) uses the phrase *moto spiral,* spiritual movement, to indicate *praxis*. In Aristotle's own writings *praxis* is usually rational, a movement of the will in the light of the mind. But Dante's *moto spirale* refers to all modes of the spirit's life, all of its directions, or focuses, or motives, including those of childhood, dream, drunkenness, or passion, which are hardly rationalized at all. When using Aristotle's definition for the analysis of modern drama it is necessary to generalize his notion of action in this way, to include movements of the spirit in response to sensuous or emotionally charged images, as well as consciously willed purpose. But this seems to me a legitimate extension of the basic concept; and I do not think it does real violence to Aristotle's meaning.

Aristotle, in his *Psychology* and his *Ethics,* as well as in the *Poetics,* and Dante, in the *Divine Comedy,* seem to imagine the psyche much as an amoeba looks under the microscope: moving toward what attracts it, continually changing direction or aim, and taking its shape and color from the object to which it is attached at the moment. This movement is "action"; and so we see that while the psyche is alive it always has action; and that this changing action in pursuit of real or imagined objects defines its mode of being moment by moment.

When Aristotle says that a tragedy is the imitation of an action, he is thinking of an action, or motive, which governs the psyche's life for a considerable length of time. Such an action is the quest for Laius's slayer in *Oedipus Rex,* which persists through the changing circumstances of the

"*Macbeth* as the Imitation of an Action" by Francis Fergusson, *English Institute Essays, 1951* (New York: Columbia University Press, 1952). Copyright 1952 by Columbia University Press. Reprinted by permission of Columbia University Press.

play. In this period of time, it has a beginning, a middle, and an end, which comes when the slayer is at last identified.

I remarked that action is not outward deeds or events; but on the other hand, there can be no action without resulting deeds. We guess at a man's action by way of what he does, his outward and visible deeds. We are aware that our own action, or motive, produces deeds of some sort as soon as it exists. Now the plot of a play is the arrangement of outward deeds or incidents, and the dramatist uses it, as Aristotle tells us, as the first means of imitating the action. He arranges a set of incidents which point to the action or motive from which they spring. You may say that the action is the spiritual content of the tragedy—the playwright's inspiration—and the plot defines its existence as an intelligible *play*. Thus, you cannot have a play without both plot and action; yet the distinction between plot and action is as fundamental as that between form and matter. The action is the matter; the plot is the "first form," or, as Aristotle puts it, the "soul," of the tragedy.

The dramatist imitates the action he has in mind, first by means of the plot, then in the characters, and finally in the media of language, music, and spectacle. In a well-written play, if we understood it thoroughly, we should perceive that plot, character, and diction, and the rest spring from the same source, or, in other words, realize the same action or motive in the forms appropriate to their various media.

You will notice that this is a diagrammatic description of the perfect play, perfectly understood. Therefore one cannot hope to illustrate it perfectly, even in the case of a play like *Macbeth*. *Macbeth*, however, does impress most of its readers as having a powerful and unmistakable unity of this kind: the plot, characters, and imagery all seem to spring from the one inspiration. It is that strong and immediately felt unity which I rely on—and upon your familiarity with the play. Not that I am so foolish as to suppose I grasp the play completely or that I could persuade you of my view of it in these few minutes. All I can attempt is to suggest the single action which seems to me to be the spiritual content of the play, and illustrate it, in only a few of its metaphors, plot devices, and characterizations.

The action of the play as a whole is best expressed in a phrase which Macbeth himself uses in Act II, scene 3, the aftermath of the murder. Macbeth is trying to appear innocent, but everything he says betrays his clear sense of his own evil motivation, or action. Trying to excuse his murder of Duncan's grooms, he says,

> The expedition of my violent love [for Duncan, he means]
> Outran the pauser, reason.

It is the phrase "to outrun the pauser, reason," which seems to me to describe the action, or motive, of the play as a whole. Macbeth, of course, literally means that his love for Duncan was so strong and swift that it got ahead of his reason, which would have counseled a pause. But in the same way we have seen his greed and ambition outrun his reason when he committed the murder; and in the same way all of the characters, in the irrational darkness of Scotland's evil hour, are compelled in their action to strive beyond what they can see by reason alone. Even Malcolm and Macduff, as we shall see, are compelled to go beyond reason in the action which destroys Macbeth and ends the play.

But let me consider the phrase itself for a moment. To "outrun" reason suggests an impossible stunt, like lifting oneself by one's own bootstraps. It also suggests a competition or race, like those of nightmare, which cannot be won. As for the word "reason," Shakespeare associates it with nature and nature's order, in the individual soul, in society, and in the cosmos. To outrun reason is thus to violate nature itself, to lose the bearings of common sense and of custom, and to move into a spiritual realm bounded by the irrational darkness of Hell one way, and the superrational grace of faith the other way. As the play develops before us, all the modes of this absurd, or evil, or supernatural, action are attempted, the last being Malcolm's and Macduff's acts of faith.

In the first part of the play Shakespeare, as is his custom, gives us the intimate feel of this paradoxical striving beyond reason in a series of echoing tropes and images. I remind you of some of them, as follows.

From the first Witches' scene:

> When the battle's lost and won. . . .
>
> Fair is foul and foul is fair.

From the "bleeding-sergeant" scene:

> Doubtful it stood;
> As two spent swimmers that do cling together
> And choke their art. . . .
>
> So from that spring whence comfort seem'd to come
> Discomfort swells. . . .
>
> Confronted him with self-comparisons
> Point against point rebellious, arm 'gainst arm. . . .
>
> What he hath lost noble Macbeth hath won.

From the second Witches' scene:

So fair and foul a day. . . .

Lesser than Macbeth, and greater.

His wonders and his praises do contend
Which should be thine or his. . . .

This supernatural soliciting
Cannot be ill, cannot be good. . . .

            . . . nothing is
But what is not.

These are only a few of the figures which suggest the desperate and paradoxical struggle. They are, of course, not identical with each other or with outrunning reason, which seems to me the most general of all. But they all point to the "action" I mean, and I present them as examples of the imitation of action by means of the arts of language.

But notice that though these images themselves suggest the action, they also confirm the actions of the characters as these are shown in the story. The bleeding sergeant, for instance, is striving beyond reason and nature in his effort to report the battle—itself a bewildering mixture of victory and defeat—in spite of his wounds. Even the old King Duncan, mild though he is, is caught in the race and sees his relation to Macbeth competitively. "Thou art so far before," he tells Macbeth in the next scene, "That swiftest wing of recompense is slow/To overtake thee." He then races Macbeth to his castle, whither the Messenger has outrun them both; and when he arrives, he is at once involved in a hollow competition with Lady Macbeth, to outdo her in ceremony.

I do not need to remind you of the great scenes preceding the murder, in which Macbeth and his Lady pull themselves together for their desperate effort. If you think over these scenes, you will notice that the Macbeths understand the action which begins here as a competition and a stunt, against reason and nature. Lady Macbeth fears her husband's human nature, as well as her own female nature, and therefore she fears the light of reason and the common daylight world. As for Macbeth, he knows from the first that he is engaged in an irrational stunt: "I have no spur/To prick the sides of my intent, but only/Vaulting ambition, which o'erleaps itself/And falls on the other." In this sequence there is also the theme of outwitting or transcending time, an aspect of nature's order as we know it: catching up the consequences, jumping the life to come, and the like. But this must suffice to remind you of the Macbeths' actions, which they paradoxically understand so well.

The Porter scene has been less thoroughly studied as a variation on the play's main action. But it is, in fact, a farcical and terrible version of "outrunning reason," a witty and very concentrated epitome of this absurd movement of spirit. The Porter first teases the knockers at the gate with a set of paradoxes, all of which present attempts to outrun reason; and he sees them all as ways into Hell. Henry N. Paul * has explained the contemporary references: the farmer who hanged himself on the expectation of plenty, the equivocator who swore both ways to commit treason for God's sake. When the Porter has admitted the knockers he ironically offers them lewd physical analogies for outrunning reason: drink as tempting lechery into a hopeless action; himself as wrestling with drink. The relation of the Porter to the knockers is like that of the Witches to Macbeth—he tempts them into Hell with ambiguities. And the inebriation of drink and lust, lewd and laughable as it is, is closely analogous to the more terrible and spiritual intoxication of the Macbeths.

Thus, in the first part of the play both the imagery and the actions of the various characters indicate or "imitate" the main action. Aristotle says the characters are imitated "with a view to the action," and the Porter— who has little importance in the story—is presented to reveal the action of the play as a whole in the unexpected light of farcical analogies, con- temporary or lewd and physical.

Before I leave this part of the play I wish to point out that the plot itself—"the arrangement or synthesis of the incidents"—also imitates a desperate race. This is partly a matter of the speed with which the main facts are presented, partly the effect of simultaneous movements like those of a race: Lady Macbeth is reading the letter at the same moment that her husband and Duncan are rushing toward her. And the facts in this part of the play are ambiguous in meaning and even as facts.

These few illustrations must serve to indicate how I understand the imitation of action in language, character, and plot in the first two acts of the play. Macbeth and his Lady are embarked on a race against reason itself; and all Scotland, the "many" whose lives depend upon the monarch, is precipitated into the same darkness and desperate strife. Shakespeare's monarchs do usually color the spiritual life of their realms. And we, who remember Hitlerite Germany, can understand that, I think. Even Hitler's exiles, like the refugees from Russian or Spanish tyranny, brought the shadow to this country with them.

I now wish to consider the action of the play at a later stage, in Act IV, scene 3. This is the moment which I mentioned before, the beginning of Malcolm's and Macduff's act of faith, which will constitute the final variation on "outrunning reason." The scene is laid in England, whither Malcolm and Macduff have fled, and it immediately follows the murder of Macduff's wife and child. Like the exiles we have known in this country, Macduff and Malcolm, though in England, have brought

* See *The Royal Play of Macbeth,* Macmillan, 1950.

Scotland's darkness with them. They have lost all faith in reason, human nature, and common sense, and can therefore trust neither themselves nor each other. They are met in the hope of forming an alliance, in order to get rid of Macbeth; and yet under his shadow everything they do seems unreasonable, paradoxical, improbable.

In the first part of the scene, you remember, Malcolm and Macduff fail to find any basis for mutual trust. Malcolm mistrusts Macduff because he has left his wife and child behind; Macduff quickly learns to mistrust Malcolm, because he first protests that he is unworthy of the crown, to test Macduff, and then suddenly reverses himself. The whole exchange is a tissue of falsity and paradox, and it ends in a sort of nightmarish paralysis.

At this point there is the brief interlude with the Doctor. The king's evil and its cure and the graces which hang about the English throne are briefly described. Paul points out that this interlude may have been introduced to flatter James I; but however that may be, it is appropriate in the build of the scene as a whole. It marks the turning point, and it introduces the notion of the appeal by faith to Divine Grace which will reverse the evil course of the action when Malcolm and Macduff learn to outrun reason in that way, instead of by responding to the Witches' supernatural solicitations as Macbeth has done. Moreover, the Doctor in this scene, in whom religious and medical healing are associated, foreshadows the Doctor who will note Lady Macbeth's sleepwalking and describe it as a perturbation in nature which requires a cure beyond nature.

But to return to the scene. After the Doctor's interlude, Ross joins Malcolm and Macduff, bringing the latest news from Scotland. To greet him, Malcolm clearly states the action, or motive, of the scene as a whole: "Good God, betimes remove/The means that makes us strangers!" he says. Ross's chief news is, of course, Lady Macduff's murder. When he has gradually revealed that, and Macduff and Malcolm have taken it in, accepting some of the guilt, they find that the means that made them strangers has in fact been removed. They recognize themselves and each other once more, in a sober, but not nightmarish, light. And at once they join in faith in their cause and prepare to hazard all upon the ordeal of battle, itself an appeal beyond reason. The scene, which in its opening sections moved very slowly, reflecting the demoralization of Malcolm and Macduff, ends hopefully, with brisk rhythms of speech which prepare the marching scenes to follow.

> This tune goes manly. . . .

> Receive what cheer you may:
> The night is long that never finds the day.

The whole scene is often omitted or drastically cut in production, and many critics have objected to it. They complain of its slowness, of the baroque overelaboration of Malcolm's protests, and of the fact that it is too long for what it tells us about the story. All we learn is that Malcolm and Macduff are joining the English army to attack Macbeth, and this information could have been conveyed much more quickly. In the first part of the play, and again after this scene, everything moves with the speed of a race; and one is tempted to say, at first, that in this scene Shakespeare lost the rhythm of his own play.

Now, one of the reasons I chose this scene to discuss is that it shows, as does the Porter scene, the necessity of distinguishing between plot and action. One cannot understand the function of the scene in the whole plot unless one remembers that the plot itself is there to imitate the action. It is then clear that this scene is the peripeteia, which is brought about by a series of recognitions. It starts with Malcolm and Macduff blind and impotent in Macbeth's shadow and ends when they have gradually learned to recognize themselves and each other even in that situation. "Outrunning reason" looks purely evil in the beginning, and at the end we see how it may be good, an act of faith beyond reason. The scene moves slowly at first because Shakespeare is imitating the action of groping in an atmosphere of the false and unnatural; yet we are aware all the while of continuing speed offstage, where

> each new morn
> New widows howl, new orphans cry, new sorrows
> Strike heaven on the face. . . .

The scene is thus (within the rhythmic scheme of the whole play) like a slow eddy on the edge of a swift current. After this turning, or peripeteia, the actions of Malcolm and Macduff join the rush of the main race, to win. I admit that these effects might be hard to achieve in production, but I believe that good actors could do it.

Shakespeare's tragedies usually have a peripeteia in the fourth act, with scenes of suffering and prophetic or symbolic recognitions and epiphanies. In the fourth act of *Macbeth* the Witches' scene reveals the coming end of the action in symbolic shows; and this scene also, in another way, foretells the end. The last act, then, merely presents the literal facts, the windup of the plot, long felt as inevitable in principle. The fifth act of *Macbeth* shows the expected triumph of Malcolm's and Macduff's superrational faith. The wood does move; Macbeth does meet a man unborn of woman; and the paradoxical race against reason reaches its paradoxical end. The nightmare of Macbeth's evil version of the action is dissolved, and we are free to return to the familiar world, where reason, nature, and common sense still have their validity.

To sum up: my thesis is that *Macbeth* is the imitation of an action (or motive) which may be indicated by the phrase "to outrun the pauser, reason." I have tried to suggest how this action is presented in the metaphors, characters, and plot of the first two acts; and also in the peripeteia, with pathos and recognitions, the great scene between Malcolm, Macduff, and Ross.

I am painfully aware that these few illustrations are not enough to establish my thesis. Only a detailed analysis of the whole play might do that—and such an analysis would take hours of reading and discussion. But I think it would show that Aristotle was essentially right. He had never read *Macbeth*, and I suppose if he could he would find Shakespeare's Christian, or post-Christian, vision of evil hard to understand. But he saw that the art of drama is the art of imitating action; and this insight, confirmed and deepened by some of Aristotle's heirs, can still show us how to seek the unity of a play, even one which shows modes of the spirit's life undreamed of by Aristotle himself.

King Lear: an Introduction

by Alfred Harbage

The play begins with a moment of prose "exposition," an idle conversation about the partition of a kingdom and the bastardy of a son. Its tone is casual, jocular, polite. The son responds decorously to a social introduction. The speakers are wearing familiar masks. It is then as if these murmurs by the portal subsided at the opening of some old but half-remembered ceremony. All is ritual—heralding trumpet, formal procession, symbolic objects in coronet and map, a sequence of arbitrary yet strangely predictable acts. What can be made of it? Why should that patriarch who wishes to yield up his power and possessions require of the receivers declarations of love? Why should that maiden who honestly loves him respond only with declarations of her love of honesty? No logical reasons appear—ritual is ritual, its logic its own. Prose is yielding to poetry, "realism" to reality. *King Lear* is not true. It is an allegory of truth.

That its truths are not literal is the first thing about it discerned by the budding critical faculty. Everything is initially *patterned*—this one making obvious errors which he obviously will rue, these others emerging as the good and the evil in almost geometrical symmetry, with the inevitable sisters-three, the two elder chosen though wicked, the younger rejected though virtuous. Surely these are childish things! A defense has been offered by Tolstoy, in his valedictory judgment that the only truths conveyable in literature can be conveyed in the simplest folk-tale. But *King Lear* is not simple, and Tolstoy himself failed to see its relevance to his doctrine. Freud noticed its primitive features, and compared Goneril, Regan, and Cordelia to the caskets of lead, silver, and gold in *The Merchant of Venice.* He identified Cordelia as the benign, though resisted, call of death. Cordelia as the death-wish—*lovely and soothing death*—how suggestive this is! until we recognize that her identification as the life-wish might be equally suggestive. The value of such reflections lies in

"*King Lear:* an Introduction." From the Introduction to *King Lear,* edited by Alfred Harbage, "The Pelican Shakespeare," Alfred Harbage, ed. (Penguin Books, 1958), pp. 15-29. Copyright © 1958 by Penguin Books Inc. Reprinted by permission of Penguin Books, Inc.

their reminder that the oldest story-patterns have the greatest power to touch off reverberations. No other framework than this parable-myth could have borne so well the weight of what Shakespeare was compelled to say.

The story of Lear and his three daughters was given written form four centuries before Shakespeare's birth. How much older its components may be we do not know. Cordelia in one guise or another, including Cinderella's, has figured in the folklore of most cultures, perhaps originally expressing what Emerson saw as the conviction of every human being of his worthiness to be loved and chosen, if only his *true* self were truly known. The figure of the ruler asking a question, often a riddle, with disastrous consequences to himself is equally old and dispersed. In his *Historia Regum Britanniae* (1136) Geoffrey of Monmouth converted folklore to history and established Lear and his daughters as rulers of ancient Britain, thus bequeathing them to the chronicles. Raphael Holinshed's (1587) declared that "Leir, the sonne of Baldud," came to the throne "in the year of the world 3105, at which time Joas reigned in Juda," but belief in the historicity of such British kings was now beginning to wane, and Shakespeare could deal freely with the record. He read the story also in John Higgins's lamentable verses in *A Mirrour for Magistrates* (1574), and in Edmund Spenser's *Faerie Queene,* II, 10, 27-32. He knew, and may even have acted in, a bland dramatic version, *The True Chronicle History of King Leir,* published anonymously in 1605 but staged at least as early as 1594.

The printing of the old play may mark an effort to capitalize upon the staging of Shakespeare's, performed at court on December 26, 1606, and probably first brought out at the Globe playhouse sometime in 1605, although its allusion to "these late eclipses of the sun and moon" was not necessarily suggested by those of September and October of that year. The only certain anterior limit of date is March 16, 1603, when Samuel Harsnett's *Declaration of Egregious Popishe Impostures* was registered for publication. That this excursion in "pseudo-demonology" was available to Shakespeare is evident in various ways, most clearly in the borrowed inventory of devils imbedded in Edgar's jargon as Tom o' Bedlam. It is of small consequence to fix the date of *King Lear* so far as its relation to the older play is concerned, which must be reckoned as analogue rather than source, but if, as seems certain, it was composed in 1605 or early 1606, it belongs to the same season of the poet's growth as *The Tragedy of Macbeth.*

In its pre-Shakespearean forms, both those mentioned above and others, the Lear story remains rudimentary. The emphasis may vary in various recensions, depending upon whether the author was most interested in the inexpedience of subdividing a kingdom, the mutability of fortune, or, as in the older play, the rewards of Christian virtue; but all are alike in that they end happily for Lear, who is reconciled to Cordelia and restored to his throne. The fact that the story was sometimes followed by a sequel in which Cordelia was finally hounded to suicide by the broodlings of her wicked sisters has little bearing on a remarkable fact: Shakespeare alone and in defiance of precedent conducted Lear to ultimate misery. *Enter Lear with Cordelia in his arms. . . . He dies.* These directions enclose a scene which demonstrates beyond any other in tragic literature the intransigence of poetic art—inventing the inevitable, investing horrifying things with beauty.

Compared with the tragedies of ancient Greece, and it is with these alone that one is tempted to compare it, *King Lear* suggests the Gothic order. Its form is irregular and organic, determined seemingly by a series of upward thrusts of mounting internal energy. There is even a Gothic element of the grotesque, as when mock-beggar, jester, and king, reduced to common condition, hold their mad juridical proceedings in a storm-lashed hovel, or when crazed king and blinded subject exchange lamentations and puns! In the method of Lear's madness there is often a savage humor, more remarkable when all is said than his companioning with a Fool. It was the Fool, however, who seemed to the next age the unpardonable sin against classical decorum. In the 1680 adaptation by Nahum Tate he was expunged from the play, along with the tragic ending. Tate capped the concluding felicities of the pre-Shakespearean versions by huddling up a marriage between Edgar and Cordelia; yet his work held the stage throughout the eighteenth century. It is always ruefully remarked that the greatest critic of the age approved the adaptation, but in fairness we should add that it was not for literary reasons. The pain of Shakespeare's concluding scenes was simply too much for Dr. Johnson; his response is preferable to that of those—fit for treasons, stratagems, and spoils—who can read these scenes unmoved.

The original play, or its approximation, was restored to the stage in the early nineteenth century, after it had begun to receive its critical due from the romantic essayists and poets. It is a poet's play. Keats saw in it the warrant for his conviction that truth and beauty are one, and, more surprisingly, recognized the choral and catalytic function of Lear's jester for the stroke of genius it was. Coleridge, Lamb, and Hazlitt also recorded illuminating judgments, and many critics since, of many different "schools," have said fine things about it.

The question now most frequently debated is whether the play is Christian and affirmative in spirit, or pagan and pessimistic. No work of art could endure the tugs of such a debate without being somewhat torn. "Pessimistic," like "optimistic," is a small word for a small thing, and *King Lear* is not small. It is sad, as all tragedies are sad. It is religious, as all great tragedies are religious. The exclusion of specific Christian reference, more consistent than in any other Shakespearean play of non-

Christian setting, is in harmony with its Old Testament atmosphere
("when Joas ruled in Juda"), but it may reflect nothing more than evasion, in the printed text, of a recent Parliamentary ruling, which in
effect labelled *God* in stage speech as blasphemy, *gods* as mere classical
allusion. Although the play is rather inclusively than exclusively Christian, which can scarcely be deemed a fault, it shows obvious signs of its
genesis in a Christian culture. To cite those involving a single character
(other than Cordelia, who has often been viewed as a Christ-symbol),
there is Edgar's persistence in returning good for evil, his preachments
against the sin of despair, and his reluctance to kill except in trial by
combat with its implied religious sanctions. Great questions are asked of
the unseen powers—"Is there any cause in nature for these hard hearts?"
—and these questions remain unanswered, but the silence which follows
them should be viewed, here as in other contexts, as the substance of
faith. On the human level, the implications of the play are more comforting than the data it abstracts. In our actual world, suffering is not always
ennobling, evil not always self-consuming. In every scene where there is
pain, there is someone who strives to relieve that pain. At the close, the
merciless have all perished; the last sound we hear is the choral voices of
the merciful.

The workers of evil are stylized in a way not quite typical of Shakespeare. He could not love these characters even as characters, except
perhaps Edmund a little. To imitate the dominant animal imagery of the
style, Cornwall is less repellent than Goneril and Regan only as the mad
bull is less repellent than the hyena, they less repellent than Oswald only
as the hyena is less repellent than the jackal. To the latter he failed to
give even that engaging touch of the ludicrous he usually reserved for
assistant villains. It is useless to speak of their "motivation." Like other
aged parents Lear is no gift to good housewifery, and there is something
poignantly familiar about such a one's trudging resentfully to the home of
a second daughter. "Age is unnecessary." But to see a causal relationship
between what he does to Goneril and Regan and what they do to him, or
to interpret their aggression as normal revolt against parental domina-
tion, is simply to be perverse. The play deals directly, and in both its
stories, with one indissoluble bond:

> We'll no more meet, no more see one another.
> But yet thou art my flesh, my blood, my daughter. . . .

Eroded, it leaves no human bond secure. To argue that Edmund's conduct is attributable to humiliating illegitimacy, we must supply him with
an "unconscious" and invoke its spectral evidence; there is no sign of
sensitivity in his lines. Even that curious product of our times, the
liberalism-gone-to-seed which automatically defends anything from

treachery to sadism providing it savors of nonconformity, has found little
to say for this insatiable quintet.

Shakespeare is not normally associated with hatred, but "a fierce hatred
of cruelty and deceitful wickedness" informs *King Lear*—this the opinion
of so pure an aesthetician as Benedetto Croce. Hazlitt has said, "It is
then the best of all Shakespeare's plays, for it is the one in which he was
most in earnest." A non-sequitur may lurk in this assertion, but we
cannot deny its relevance. Our inescapable impression of the play is of its
overwhelming sincerity. It says everything powerfully and everything
twice—and always "what we feel, not what we ought to say." The language varies from the cryptic allusiveness of Lear's "mad" speeches to the
biblical plainness of his pleas for forgiveness; and though it is often difficult, it is never ambiguous. Lamb has been much taken to task for
declaring that "*Lear* is essentially impossible to be represented on a
stage," but more often than not our experiences in the theatre confirm his
view. There have been fine productions, but not very many: one touch of
insincerity can rot everything away.

Those who now "introduce" this play must wish with Hazlitt, and with
much more likelihood of greeting the wish of the reader, that they might
resort to silence, since all that can be said will "fall short of the subject, or
even what we ourselves conceive of it." Yet an effort must be made to state
its theme, and to the present editor there seems no way of doing this
except by focussing the gaze directly and continuously upon Lear himself.

"The King is coming." These words announce the first entrance of the
tragic hero. Let us see him as he is, no preconceptions or critical rumors
spoiling the innocence of our vision. Nothing about him suggests
infirmity or decay. His magnitude and force are far greater than one's
own. He issues commands with the assurance of instinct and lifelong
custom. He holds a map in his hands like a Titan holding a kingdom.
The kingdom spreads before us in his spacious utterance:

> Of all these bounds, even from this line to this,
> With shadowy forests and with champains riched,
> With plenteous rivers and wide-skirted meads,
> We make thee lady.

We make thee lady! Thus he disposes of a sector of the earth, this ring-
giver, this warrior-leader, this chosen one, his only landlord God! Is it
not passing fine . . . ? Here is no soft-brained *Senex*, but the archetypal
King.

As such Lear symbolizes Mankind, and we will say nothing essential
about him by reckoning up his years and growing glib about the symp-
toms of senile dementia. The king-figure surrogate is an understandable
product of the human mind in its early attempts at abstraction, since the

most imposing of single men best lends his image to the difficult concept of Man. His vicissitudes best epitomize the vicissitudes of all, since upon the highest altitude the sun shines brightest and the cold snow lies most deep. Early Renaissance drama was steeped in the tradition of this symbolic figure, sometimes still called *King* as well as *Mankind, Everyman, Genus Humanum,* and the like. He is always identifiable by his centrality in the action, and the mixed company he keeps—vices or flatterers on the one hand, virtues or truth-speakers on the other. And there stands Lear—Goneril and Regan to the left, Kent and Cordelia to the right.

But this is also a family gathering. There is the father, and there the servant, and children of his house. The central figure is, and seems always more so as the play weaves its spell, not only archetypal King, Man, and Father, but particular king, man, and father. No symbol that remained purely symbol could so touch our emotions. To have children of his flesh and blood, the father must be flesh and blood—such as can be old, grow weary, feel cold and wet.

Only a few days of fictional time elapse, only a few hours in the theatre, so that Lear's first words still echo in our ears as we hear his last.

> We make thee lady. . . . Let it be so, thy truth then be thy dower!
> . . . Peace, Kent! Come not between the dragon and his wrath. . . .
> The bow is bent and drawn; make from the shaft. . . . Therefore be
> gone. . . . Let me not stay a jot for dinner; go, get it ready. . . . Call
> the clotpoll back.

Such are Lear's accents at the beginning. And at the close—

> You must bear with me. . . . I am old and foolish. . . . Her voice was
> ever soft, gentle, and low. . . . Pray you undo this button. Thank you,
> sir.

He has learned a new language. We are required to accept this learning as good, but we are forbidden to rejoice.

The play is Lear's gethsemane, its great reality his suffering, which so draws us into itself that our conception of the work as a whole is formed in the crucible of our fear and pity. His anguish is kin with the anguish of Job, Prometheus, Oedipus, and other tragic projections of spirits in agony, but it retains its own peculiar quality. Its cause, its nature, and its meaning will always remain the imperfectly resolved crux of the play; and one can do no more than explain, with such confidence as one is able to muster, how these things appear to him.

To say that Lear gets what he deserves is to share the opinion of Goneril and Regan. (Some have even implied that Cordelia gets what she deserves, anaesthetizing their heads and hearts with obtuse moralisms suggested by the doctrine of "poetic justice.") What does Lear deserve? He is proud and peremptory, and it is better to be humble and temporizing, but there are occupational hazards in being a king, perhaps even in being a father. Is his charge not true that the world has lied to him, telling him he was wise before he was bearded, returning "yea and nay" to everything he said? His guilt is widely shared, and his "flaw" like that of Oedipus seems mysteriously hereditary. And it is linked inextricably with his virtues. We applaud the resurgence of youthful might that cuts down Cordelia's assassin. We admire the valor of his attempts (and they come quite early) to be patient, to compromise, to hold back womanish tears, to cling to his reason. Nothing is more moving than his bewildered attempts to meet "social" obligations as he kneels by Cordelia's body. We love his *manliness*. Pride has its value too.

Lear's errors stem from no corruption of heart. His rejection of Kent and Cordelia is the reflex of his attachment to them. The errors are not the man. The man is one who has valued and been valued by such as they. The things he wants—fidelity and love—are good things. That he should find them in his servant and his child seems to him an aspect of universal order. In his vocabulary, as distinct from Edmund's, such things are *natural*. His inability to distinguish between the false and the true, and his craving for visible displays, are not failings peculiar to him. "How much do you love me?"—few parents suppress this bullying question, spoken or unspoken, however much they may have felt its burden as children. It seems in the nature of some things that they always be learned too late, that as children we might have offered more, as parents demanded less. To punish a thankless child has the appearance of justice, to withdraw in one's age from the cares of state the appearance of wisdom, to dispose of one's goods by gift instead of testament the appearance of generosity. Plain men in their prime have been similarly deceived. Gloucester shakes his head sadly over Lear's injustice, folly, and selfishness as he duplicates his actions.

In the maimed but agile mind of the Fool faithfully dogging Lear's steps, his errors stand as an *idée fixe* and are harped upon with terrible iteration. We should not imitate the example. We may find more meaning in the excess of expiation. The purely physical suffering—denial of rest, exposure to wind and rain—is real, but it strikes the sufferer himself as little more than a metaphor. We may say that his spiritual suffering is in excess of his actual afflictions, that it is selfish and centrifugal, or a mere symptom of aged petulance, but if we do so, we are stopping our ears to the voice of Shakespeare and all his decent spokesmen. Lear's curse of Goneril is still alienating, like his treatment of Cordelia, but when he stands weeping before his cormorant daughters in whom he has put his faith, and they coolly and relentlessly strip him of every vestige of dignity, our hearts turn over. Humility may be good, but this humiliation is evil.

There is no *need* that this man be attended by a hundred knights, that his messenger be deferentially treated, or that his children offer him more than subsistence. His cause rests upon no more rational grounds than our powers of sympathy and imagination. "O reason not the need." As his every expectation is brutally defeated, and he looks in dazed recognition upon the world as it is instead of what he thought it was, of himself as he is instead of what he thought he was, we defer to his past illusions. He had never identified prestige merely as power, had never imagined that the visages of respect, kindliness, and love could contort into the hideous lines of icy contempt and sour indifference.

Lear's anguish now represents for us Man's horror and sense of help-lessness at the discovery of evil—the infiltration of animality in the human world, naked cruelty and appetite. It is a fissure that threatens to widen infinitely, and we see Lear at the center of turbulence as it works its breakage in minds, in families, in nations, in the heavens themselves, interacting in dreadful concatenation.

The significance of Lear's response to his discovery is best seen in the light of Gloucester's. In Sidney's *Arcadia*, II, 10, the "storie of the Paphlagonian unkind King and his kinde sonne" repeats in essence the Lear legend, except that the children, false and true, are sons instead of daughters. By reducing the rank of Sidney's king and interweaving his parallel fate in alternate scenes, Shakespeare is able, amazingly, both further to universalize and further to particularize the experience of Lear. Gloucester also represents Man, but his distinction from Lear suggests the distinction between ordinary and extraordinary men. Gloucester is amiably confused about the tawdriness of his past, of which Edmund is the product, and sentimentally fumbling in the present. What appears in Lear as heroic error appears in him as gullibility. His fine moments are identical with those of a nameless serf of Cornwall's and an ancient tenant of his own—in the presence of cruelty he becomes kind and brave:

> *Gloucester.* I am tied to th' stake, and I must stand the course.
> *Regan.* Wherefore to Dover?
> *Gloucester.* Because I would not see thy cruel nails
>   Pluck out his poor old eyes.

Like Lear he is incorrupt of heart, and he grows in dignity, but his total response to vicious encroachment is something akin to apathy and sur-render; his instinct is to retreat.

Not so with Lear. He batters himself to pieces against the fact of evil. Granted that its disruptive power has been unleashed by his own error, so that error itself partakes of evil, as he is shudderingly aware, yet he remains the great antagonist. Falsity, cruelty, injustice, corruption—their appalling forms swirl about him in phantasmic patterns. His instinct is to rip them from the universe, to annihilate all things if it is the only way to annihilate these things. His charges of universal hypocrisy: "handy-dandy, which is the justice, which is the thief?"—his denial of human responsibility: "None does offend, none—I say none!"—his indictment of life itself:

> Thou know'st, the first time that we smell the air
> We wawl and cry

cancel their own nihilism, because they sound no acquiescence. Lear is the voice of protest. The grandeur of his spirit supplies the impotence of his body as he opposes to evil all that is left him to oppose—his molten indignation, his huge invectives, his capacity for feeling pain.

This quality of Lear seen in retrospect, his hunger after righteousness, gives magnitude to the concluding scenes. His spirit has been doubly lacerated by his own sense of guilt. He has failed "poor naked wretches" no different from himself, and he has wronged Cordelia. His remorse has found expression only in brief occasional utterances, welling up as it were against desperate efforts of containment, but its scalding power is revealed in his acts of abasement when he and Cordelia meet. The final episodes are all vitally linked. When the two are lead in captive, we are made to look back upon their reunion, which he dreams of endlessly reenacting:

> When thou dost ask me blessing, I'll kneel down
> And ask of thee forgiveness;

then forward to their death:

> Upon such sacrifices, my Cordelia,
> The gods themselves throw incense.

The words help to effect that perfect coalescence of particular and general tragic experience achieved as he kneels beside her body. This is a father and his child who will come no more, the father remembering his own unkindness and the child's endearing ways. There is no melioration in his dying delusion that she still lives, no mention of an after-life. It is unspeakably sad. But it merges with a larger yet less devastating sadness. This is also a sacrifice, and although the somber tones of the survivors as they take up the burden of survival give it relevance to the future as well as the past, it is such a sacrifice as obliquely vindicates the gods if upon it they throw incense.

We know, not as an item of faith but of simple demonstrable fact, that we are greatly indebted for such wisdom as we have, that it was bought with "sacrifices." In the struggle of our kind against brutality, the great casualties, spiritual and even physical, have always been among those who have been best and those who have cared most. In the world of this play Cordelia has brought us the truest sense of human goodness, her words "No cause, no cause" the truest sense of moral beauty. She is the perfect offering. And so is Lear. She is best. He cares most for what is best. The play ends as it begins in an allegorical grouping, commemorating humanity's long, agonized, and continuing struggle to be human. The larger meaning gives our tears the dignity of an act of ratification and gratitude: to these still figures we have pitied we owe the gift of feeling pity.

King Lear and the Comedy of the Grotesque

by G. Wilson Knight

It may appear strange to search for any sort of comedy as a primary theme in a play whose abiding gloom is so heavy, whose reading of human destiny and human actions so starkly tragic. Yet it is an error of aesthetic judgment to regard humour as essentially trivial. Though its impact usually appears vastly different from that of tragedy, yet there is a humour that treads the brink of tears, and tragedy which needs but an infinitesimal shift of perspective to disclose the varied riches of comedy. Humour is an evanescent thing, even more difficult of analysis and intellectual location than tragedy. To the coarse mind lacking sympathy an incident may seem comic which to the richer understanding is pitiful and tragic. So, too, one series of facts can be treated by the artist as either comic or tragic, lending itself equivalently to both. Sometimes a great artist may achieve significant effects by a criss-cross of tears and laughter. Chekhov does this, especially in his plays. A shifting flash of comedy across the pain of the purely tragic both increases the tension and suggests, vaguely, a resolution and a purification. The comic and the tragic rest both on the idea of incompatibilities, and are also, themselves, mutually exclusive: therefore to mingle them is to add to the meaning of each; for the result is then but a new sublime incongruity.

King Lear is roughly analogous to Chekhov where Macbeth is analogous to Dostoievsky. The wonder of Shakespearian tragedy is ever a mystery—a vague, yet powerful, tangible, presence; an interlocking of the mind with a profound meaning, a disclosure to the inward eye of vistas undreamed, and but fitfully understood. King Lear is great in the abundance and richness of human delineation, in the level focus of creation that builds a massive oneness, in fact, a universe, of single quality from a multiplicity of differentiated units; and in a positive and purposeful working out of a purgatorial philosophy. But it is still greater in the perfect fusion of psychological realism with the daring flights of a fantastic imagination. The heart of a Shakespearian tragedy is centered

"King Lear and the Comedy of the Grotesque." From The Wheel of Fire (London: Methuen & Co. Ltd., 1949), by G. Wilson Knight, pp. 16-176, 4th ed. revised. Copyright 1949 by Methuen & Co. Ltd. Reprinted by permission of Methuen & Co. Ltd.

in the imaginative, in the unknown; and in *King Lear,* where we touch
the unknown, we touch the fantastic. The peculiar dualism at the root
of this play which wrenches and splits the mind by a sight of incongruities displays in turn realities absurd, hideous, pitiful. This incongruity is Lear's madness; it is also the demonic laughter that echoes in
the *Lear* universe. In pure tragedy the dualism of experience is continually being dissolved in the masterful beauty of passion, merged in
the sunset of emotion. But in comedy it is not so softly resolved—incompatibilities stand out till the sudden relief of laughter or its equivalent
of humour: therefore incongruity is the especial mark of comedy. Now
in *King Lear* there is a dualism continually crying in vain to be resolved
either by tragedy or comedy. Thence arises its peculiar tension of pain:
and the course of the action often comes as near to the resolution of
comedy as to that of tragedy. So I shall notice here the imaginative core
of the play, and, excluding much of the logic of the plot from immediate
attention, analyse the fantastic comedy of *King Lear.*

From the start, the situation has a comic aspect. It has been observed
that Lear has, so to speak, staged an interlude, with himself as chief
actor, in which he grasps expressions of love to his heart, and resigns his
sceptre to a chorus of acclamations. It is childish, foolish—but very human. So, too, is the result. Sincerity forbids play-acting, and Cordelia
cannot subdue her instinct to any judgment advising tact rather than
truth. The incident is profoundly comic and profoundly pathetic. It is,
indeed, curious that so storm-furious a play as *King Lear* should have so
trivial a domestic basis: it is the first of our many incongruities to be
noticed. The absurdity of the old King's anger is clearly indicated by
Kent:

> Kill thy physician, and the fee bestow
> Upon the foul disease.
>
> [I. i. 166]

The result is absurd. Lear's loving daughter Cordelia is struck from his
heart's register, and he is shortly, old and grey-haired and a king, cutting
a cruelly ridiculous figure before the cold sanity of his unloving elder
daughters. Lear is selfish, self-centered. The images he creates of his three
daughters' love are quite false, sentimentalized: he understands the nature
of none of his children, and demanding an unreal and impossible love
from all three, is disillusioned by each in turn. But, though sentimental,
this love is not weak. It is powerful and firm-planted in his mind as a
mountain rock embedded in earth. The tearing out of it is hideous, cata-
clysmic. A tremendous soul is, as it were, incongruously geared to a
puerile intellect. Lear's senses prove his idealized love-figments false, his
intellect snaps, and, as the loosened drive flings limp, the disconnected

engine of madness spins free, and the ungeared revolutions of it are terrible, fantastic. This, then, is the basis of the play: greatness linked to puerility. Lear's instincts are themselves grand, heroic—noble even. His judgment is nothing. He understands neither himself nor his daughters:

> *Regan.* 'Tis the infirmity of his age: yet he hath ever but slenderly known himself.
> *Goneril.* The best and soundest of his time hath been but rash. . . .
>
> [I. i. 296]

Lear starts his own tragedy by foolish misjudgment. Lear's fault is a fault of the mind, a mind unwarrantably, because selfishly, foolish. And he knows it:

> O Lear, Lear, Lear!
> Beat at this gate that let thy folly in,
> And thy dear judgement out.
>
> [I. iv. 294]

His purgatory is to be a purgatory of the mind, of madness. Lear has trained himself to think he cannot be wrong: he finds he is wrong. He has fed his heart on sentimental knowledge of his children's love: he finds their love is not sentimental. There is now a gaping dualism in his mind, thus drawn asunder by incongruities, and he endures madness. Thus the theme of the play is bodied continually into a fantastic incongruity, which is implicit in the beginning—in the very act of Lear's renunciation, retaining the "title and addition" of King, yet giving over a king's authority to his children. As he becomes torturingly aware of the truth, incongruity masters his mind, and fantastic madness ensues; and this peculiar fact of the Lear-theme is reflected in the *Lear* universe:

> *Gloucester.* These late eclipses in the sun and moon portend no good to us: Though the wisdom of nature can reason it thus and thus, yet nature finds itself scourged by the sequent effect: Love cools, friendship falls off, brothers divide: In cities, mutinies; in countries, discord; in palaces, treason; and the bond cracked 'twixt son and father. This villain of mine comes under the prediction; there's son against father: the King falls from bias of nature; there's father against child. We have seen the best of our time: Machinations, hollowness, treachery, and all ruinous disorders, follow us disquietly to our graves.
>
> [I. ii. 115]

Gloucester's words hint a universal incongruity here: the fantastic incongruity of parent and child opposed. And it will be most helpful later to notice the Gloucester-theme in relation to that of Lear.

From the first signs of Goneril's cruelty, the Fool is used as a chorus, pointing us to the absurdity of the situation. He is indeed an admirable chorus, increasing our pain by his emphasis on a humour which yet will not serve to merge the incompatible in a unity of laughter. He is not all wrong when he treats the situation as matter for a joke. Much here that is always regarded as essentially pathetic is not far from comedy. For instance, consider Lear's words:

> I will have such revenges on you both
> That all the world shall—I will do such things—
> What they are, yet I know not; but they shall be
> The terrors of the earth.

[II. iv. 282]

What could be more painfully incongruous, spoken, as it is, by an old man, a king, to his daughter? It is not far from the ridiculous. The very thought seems a sacrilegious cruelty, I know: but ridicule is generally cruel. The speeches of Lear often come near comedy. Again, notice the abrupt contrast in his words:

> But yet thou art my flesh, my blood, my daughter;
> Or rather a disease that's in my flesh,
> Which I must needs call mine: thou art a boil,
> A plague-sore, or embossed carbuncle
> In my corrupted blood. But I'll not chide thee. . . .

[II. iv. 224]

This is not comedy, nor humour. But it is exactly the stuff of which humour is made. Lear is mentally a child; in passion a titan. The absurdity of his every act at the beginning of his tragedy is contrasted with the dynamic fury which intermittently bursts out, flickers—then flames and finally gives us those grand apostrophes lifted from man's stage of earth to heaven's rain and fire and thunder:

> Blow, winds, and crack your cheeks! rage! blow!
> You cataracts and hurricanoes, spout
> Till you have drench'd our steeples, drown'd the cocks!

[III. ii. 1]

Two speeches of this passionate and unrestrained volume of Promethean curses are followed by:

> No, I will be the pattern of all patience;
> I will say nothing.

[III. ii. 37]

Again we are in touch with potential comedy: a slight shift of perspective, and the incident is rich with humour. A sense of self-directed humour would, indeed, have saved Lear. It is a quality he absolutely lacks.

Herein lies the profound insight of the Fool: he sees the potentialities of comedy in Lear's behaviour. This old man, recently a king, and, if his speeches are fair samples, more than a little of a tyrant, now goes from daughter to daughter, furious because Goneril dares criticize his pet knights, kneeling down before Regan, performing, as she says, "unsightly tricks" (II. iv. 159)—the situation is excruciatingly painful, and its painfulness is exactly of that quality which embarrasses in some forms of comedy. In the theatre, one is terrified lest some one laugh: yet, if Lear could laugh—if the Lears of the world could laugh at themselves—there would be no such tragedy. In the early scenes old age and dignity suffer, and seem to deserve, the punishments of childhood:

> Now, by my life,
> Old fools are babes again, and must be used
> With checks as flatteries. . . .
>
> [I. iii. 19]

The situation is summed up by the Fool:

> *Lear.* When were you wont to be so full of songs, sirrah?
> *Fool.* I have used it, nuncle, ever since thou madest thy daughters thy mother: for when thou gavest them the rod, and put'st down thine own breeches. . . .
> [I. iv. 186]

The height of indecency in suggestion, the height of incongruity. Lear is spiritually put to the ludicrous shame endured bodily by Kent in the stocks: and the absurd rant of Kent, and the unreasonable childish temper of Lear, both merit in some measure what they receive. Painful as it may sound, that is, provisionally, a truth we should realize. The Fool realizes it. He is, too, necessary. Here, where the plot turns on the diverging tugs of two assurances in the mind, it is natural that the action be accompanied by some symbol of humour, that mode which is built of unresolved incompatibilities. Lear's torment is a torment of this dualistic kind, since he scarcely believes his senses when his daughters resist him. He repeats the history of Troilus, who cannot understand the faithlessness of Cressid. In *Othello* and *Timon of Athens* the transition is swift from extreme love to revenge or hate. The movement of Lear's mind is less direct: like Troilus, he is suspended between two separate assurances. Therefore Pandarus, in the latter acts of *Troilus and Cressida,* plays a part similar to the Fool in *King Lear*: both attempt to heal the gaping

wound of the mind's incongruous knowledge by the unifying, healing
release of laughter. They make no attempt to divert, but rather to direct
the hero's mind to the present incongruity. The Fool sees, or tries to see,
the humorous potentialities in the most heart-wrenching of incidents:

> *Lear.* O me, my heart, my rising heart! but, down!
> *Fool.* Cry to it, nuncle, as the cockney did to the eels when she put 'em i' the
> paste alive; she knapped 'em o' the coxcombs with a stick, and cried, "Down,
> wantons, down!" 'Twas her brother that, in pure kindness to his horse,
> buttered his hay.
>
> [II. iv. 122]

Except for the last delightful touch—the antithesis of the other—that is
a cruel, ugly sense of humour. It is the sinister humour at the heart of
this play: we are continually aware of the humour of cruelty and the
cruelty of humour. But the Fool's use of it is not aimless. If Lear could
laugh he might yet save his reason.

But there is no relief. Outside, in the wild country, the storm grows
more terrible:

> *Kent.*   . . . Since I was man
> Such sheets of fire, such bursts of horrid thunder,
> Such groans of roaring wind and rain, I never
> Remember to have heard. . . .
>
> [III. ii. 45]

Lear's mind keeps returning to the unreality, the impossibility of what
has happened:

> Your old kind father, whose frank heart gave all—
> O, that way madness lies; let me shun that;
> No more of that.
>
> [III. iv. 20]

He is still self-centred; cannot understand that he has been anything but
a perfect father: cannot understand his daughters' behaviour. It is

> as this mouth should tear this hand
> For lifting food to't? . . .
>
> [III. iv. 15]

It is incongruous, impossible. There is no longer any "rule in unity itself" (*Troilus and Cressida*, IV. ii. 138). Just as Lear's mind begins to

fail, the Fool finds Edgar disguised as "poor Tom." Edgar now succeeds the Fool as the counterpart to the breaking sanity of Lear; and where the humour of the Fool made no contact with Lear's mind, the fantastic appearance and incoherent words of Edgar are immediately assimilated, as glasses correctly focused to the sight of oncoming madness. Edgar turns the balance of Lear's wavering mentality. His fantastic appearance and lunatic irrelevancies, with the storm outside, and the Fool still for occasional chorus, create a scene of wraithlike unreason, a vision of a world gone mad:

> . . . Bless thy five wits! Tom's acold—O, do, de, do, de, do, de. Bless thee from whirlwinds, star-blasting, and taking! Do poor Tom some charity, whom the foul fiend vexes: there could I have him now—and there—and there again, and there.
>
> [III. iv. 57]

To Lear his words are easily explained. His daughters "have brought him to this pass." He cries:

> *Lear.* Is it the fashion that discarded fathers
>   Should have thus little mercy on their flesh?
>   Judicious punishment! 'twas this flesh begot
>   Those pelican daughters.
> *Edgar.* Pillicock sat on Pillicock-Hill.
> *Fool.* Halloo, halloo, loo, loo!
>   This cold night will turn us all to fools and madmen.
>
> [III. iv. 71]

What shall we say of this exquisite movement? Is it comedy? Lear's profound unreason is capped by the blatant irrelevance of Edgar's couplet suggested by the word "pelican"; then the two are swiftly all but unified, for us if not for Lear, in the healing balm of the Fool's conclusion. It is the process of humour, where two incompatibles are resolved in laughter. The Fool does this again. Lear speaks a profound truth as the wild night and Edgar's fantastic impersonation grip his mind and dethrone his conventional sanity:

> *Lear.* Is man no more than this? Consider him well. Thou owest the worm no silk, the beast no hide, the sheep no wool, the cat no perfume. Ha! Here's three on 's are sophisticated! Thou art the thing itself: unaccommodated man is no more but such a poor, bare, forked animal as thou art. Off, off, you lendings! come unbutton here. (*Tearing off his clothes.*)
> *Fool.* Prithee, nuncle, be contented; 'tis a naughty night to swim in.
>
> [III. iv. 105]

This is the furthest flight, not of tragedy, but of philosophic comedy. The autocratic and fiery-fierce old king, symbol of dignity, is confronted with the meanest of men: a naked lunatic beggar. In a flash of vision he attempts to become his opposite, to be naked, "unsophisticated." And then the opposing forces which struck the lightning-flash of vision tail off, resolved into a pefect unity by the Fool's laughter, reverberating, trickling, potent to heal in sanity the hideous unreason of this tempest-shaken night: " 'tis a naughty night to swim in." Again this is the process of humour: its flash of vision first bridges the positive and negative poles of the mind, unifying them, and then expresses itself in laughter.

This scene grows still more grotesque, fantastical, sinister. Gloucester enters, his torch flickering in the beating wind:

> *Fool.* . . . Look, here comes a walking fire.
> > (*Enter* Gloucester, *with a torch*.)
> *Edgar.* This is the foul Flibbertigibbet: he begins at curfew, and walks till the first cock. . . .
>
> > [III. iv. 116]

Lear welcomes Edgar as his "philosopher," since he embodies that philosophy of incongruity and the fantastically-absurd which is Lear's vision in madness. "Noble philosopher," he says (III. iv. 176), and "I will still keep with my philosopher" (III. 4. l. 167). The unresolved dualism that tormented Troilus and was given metaphysical expression by him (*Troilus and Cressida*, V. ii. 134-57) is here more perfectly bodied into the poetic symbol of poor Tom: and since Lear cannot hear the resolving laugh of foolery, his mind is focused only to the "philosopher" mumbling of the foul fiend. Edgar thus serves to lure Lear on: we forget that he is dissimulating. Lear is the centre of our attention, and as the world shakes with tempest and unreason, we endure something of the shaking and the tempest of his mind. The absurd and fantastic reign supreme. Lear does not compass for more than a few speeches the "noble anger" (II. iv. 279) for which he prayed, the anger of Timon. From the start he wavered between affection and disillusionment, love and hate. The heavens in truth "fool" (II. iv. 278) him. He is the "natural fool of fortune" (IV. vi. 196). Now his anger begins to be a lunatic thing, and when it rises to any sort of magnificent fury or power it is toppled over by the ridiculous capping of Edgar's irrelevancies:

> *Lear.* To have a thousand with red burning spits
> Come hissing in upon 'em—
> *Edgar.* The foul fiend bites my back.
>
> > [III. vi. 17]

The mock trial is instituted. Lear's curses were for a short space terrible, majestic, less controlled and purposeful than Timon's but passionate and grand in their tempestuous fury. Now, in madness, he flashes on us the ridiculous basis of his tragedy in words which emphasize the indignity and incongruity of it, and make his madness something nearer the ridiculous than the terrible, something which moves our pity, but does not strike awe:

> Arraign her first. 'Tis Goneril, I here take my oath before this honourable assembly, kicked the poor King her father.
>
> [III. vi. 49]

This stroke of the absurd—so vastly different from the awe we experience in face of Timon's hate—is yet fundamental here. The core of the play is an absurdity, an indignity, an incongruity. In no tragedy of Shakespeare does incident and dialogue so recklessly and miraculously walk the tight-rope of our pity over the depths of bathos and absurdity.

This particular region of the terrible bordering on the fantastic and absurd is exactly the playground of madness. Thus the setting of Lear's madness includes a sub-plot where these same elements are presented with stark nakedness, and no veiling subtleties. The Gloucester-theme is a certain indication of our vision and helps us to understand, and feel, the enduring agony of Lear. As usual, the first scene of this play strikes the dominant note. Gloucester jests at the bastardy of his son Edmund, remarking that, though he is ashamed to acknowledge him, "there was good sport at his making" (I. i. 23). That is, we start with humour in bad taste. The whole tragedy witnesses a sense of humour in "the gods" which is in similar bad taste. Now all the Lear effects are exaggerated in the Gloucester theme. Edmund's plot is a more Iago-like, devilish, inten-tional thing than Goneril's and Regan's icy callousness. Edgar's supposed letter is crude and absurd:

> . . . I begin to find an idle and fond bondage in the oppression of aged tyranny . . .
>
> [I. ii. 53]

But then Edmund, wittiest and most attractive of villains, composed it. One can almost picture his grin as he penned those lines, commending them mentally to the limited intellect of his father. Yes—the Gloucester theme has a beginning even more fantastic than that of Lear's tragedy. And not only are the Lear effects here exaggerated in the directions of villainy and humour: they are even more clearly exaggerated in that of horror. The gouging out of Gloucester's eyes is a thing unnecessary,

crude, disgusting: it is meant to be. It helps to provide an accompany-
ing exaggeration of one element—that of cruelty—in the horror that
makes Lear's madness. And not only horror: there is even again something satanically comic bedded deep in it. The sight of physical torment,
to the uneducated, brings laughter. Shakespeare's England delighted in
watching both physical torment and the comic ravings of actual lunacy.
The dance of madmen in Webster's *Duchess of Malfi* is of the same
ghoulish humour as Regan's plucking Gloucester by the beard: the
groundlings will laugh at both. Moreover, the sacrilege of the human
body in torture must be, to a human mind, incongruous, absurd. This
hideous mockery is consummated in Regan's final witticism after Gloucester's eyes are out:

> Go thrust him out at gates, and let him smell
> His way to Dover.
>
> [III. vii. 93]

The macabre humoresque of this is nauseating: but it is there, and integral to the play. These ghoulish horrors, so popular in Elizabethan
drama, and the very stuff of the *Lear* of Shakespeare's youth, *Titus
Andronicus,* find an exquisitely appropriate place in the tragedy of
Shakespeare's maturity which takes as its especial province this territory
of the grotesque and the fantastic which is Lear's madness. We are, indeed, pointed to this grim fun, this hideous sense of humour, at the back
of tragedy:

> As flies to wanton boys are we to th' gods;
> They kill us for their sport.
>
> [IV. i. 36]

This illustrates the exact quality I wish to emphasize: the humour a
boy—even a nice boy—may see in the wriggles of an impaled insect. So,
too, Gloucester is bound, and tortured, physically; and so the mind of
Lear is impaled, crucified on the cross-beams of love and disillusion.

There follows the grim pilgrimage of Edgar and Gloucester towards
Dover Cliff: an incident typical enough of *King Lear*—

> 'Tis the times' plague when madmen lead the blind.
>
> [IV. i. 59]

They stumble on, madman and blind man, Edgar mumbling:

> . . . five fiends have been in poor Tom at once; of lust, as Obidicut;
> Hobbididance, prince of dumbness; Mahu, of stealing; Modo, of murder;

Flibbertigibbet, of mopping and mowing, who since possesses chambermaids
and waiting-women . . . .

[IV. i. 59]

They are near Dover. Edgar persuades his father that they are climbing
steep ground, though they are on a level field, that the sea can be heard
beneath:

> *Gloucester.* Methinks the ground is even.
> *Edgar.*   Horrible steep.
>   Hark, do you hear the sea?
> *Gloucester.*   No, truly.
> *Edgar.*   Why, then, your other senses grow imperfect
>   By your eyes' anguish.

[IV. vi. 3]

Gloucester notices the changed sanity of Edgar's speech, and remarks
thereon. Edgar hurries his father to the supposed brink, and vividly
describes the dizzy precipice over which Gloucester thinks they stand:

>   How fearful
> And dizzy 'tis to cast one's eyes so low!
> The crows and choughs that wing the midway air
> Show scarce so gross as beetles: Halfway down
> Hangs one that gathers samphire—dreadful trade! . . .

[IV. vi. 12]

Gloucester thanks him, and rewards him; bids him move off; then kneels,
and speaks a prayer of noble resignation—breathing that stoicism which
permeates the suffering philosophy of this play:

>   O you mighty gods!
> This world I do renounce, and, in your sights,
> Shake patiently my great affliction off:
> If I could bear it longer, and not fall
> To quarrel with your great opposeless wills,
> My snuff and loathed part of nature should
> Burn itself out.

[IV. vi. 35]

Gloucester has planned a spectacular end for himself. We are given these
noble descriptive and philosophical speeches to tune our minds to a
noble, tragic sacrifice. And what happens? The old man falls from his

kneeling posture a few inches, flat, face foremost. Instead of the dizzy circling to crash and spill his life on the rocks below—just this. The grotesque merged into the ridiculous reaches a consummation in this bathos of tragedy: it is the furthest, most exaggerated, reach of the poet's towering fantastically. We have a sublimely daring stroke of technique, unjustifiable, like Edgar's emphasized and vigorous madness throughout, on the plane of plot-logic, and even to a superficial view somewhat out of place imaginatively in so dire and stark a limning of human destiny as is *King Lear*; yet this scene is in reality a consummate stroke of art. The Gloucester-theme throughout reflects and emphasizes and exaggerates all the percurrent qualities of the Lear-theme. Here the incongruous and fantastic element of the Lear-theme is boldly reflected into the tragically-absurd. The stroke is audacious, unashamed, and magical of effect. Edgar keeps up the deceit; persuades his father that he has really fallen; points to the empty sky, as to a cliff:

> . . . the shrill-gorged lark so far
> Cannot be seen or heard. . . .
>
> [IV. vi. 59]

and finally paints a fantastic picture of a ridiculously grotesque devil that stood with Gloucester on the edge:

> As I stood here below, methought his eyes
> Were two full moons; he had a thousand noses,
> Horns whelk'd and waved like the enridged sea;
> It was some fiend . . . .
>
> [IV. vi. 70]

Some fiend, indeed.

There is masterful artistry in all this. The Gloucester-theme has throughout run separate from that of Lear, yet parallel, and continually giving us direct villainy where the other shows cold callousness; horrors of physical torment where the other has a subtle mental torment; culminating in this towering stroke of the grotesque and absurd to balance the fantastic incidents and speeches that immediately follow. At this point we suddenly have our first sight of Lear in the full ecstasy of his later madness. Now, when our imaginations are most powerfully quickened to the grotesque and incongruous, the whole surge of the Gloucester-theme, which has just reached its climax, floods as a tributary the main stream of our sympathy with Lear. Our vision has thus been uniquely focused to understand that vision of the grotesque, the incongruous, the fantastically-horrible, which is the agony of Lear's mind:

Enter Lear, *fantastically dressed with wild flowers.*

[IV. vi. 81]

So runs Capell's direction. Lear, late "every inch a king," the supreme pathetic figure of literature, now utters the wild and whirling language of furthest madness. Sometimes his words hold profound meaning. Often they are tuned to the orthodox Shakespearian hate and loathing, especially sex-loathing, of the hate-theme. Or again, they are purely ludicrous, or would be, were it not a Lear who speaks them:

. . . Look, look, a mouse! Peace, peace; this piece of toasted cheese will do't . . . .

[IV. vi. 90]

It is, indeed, well that we are, as it were, prepared by now for the grotesque. Laughter is forbidden us. Consummate art has so forged plot and incident that we may watch with tears rather than laughter the cruelly comic actions of Lear:

> *Lear.* I will die bravely, like a bridegroom. What!
> I will be jovial: come, come; I am a king,
> My masters, know you that?
> *Gentleman.* You are a royal one, and we obey you.
> *Lear.* Then there's life in't. Nay, if you get it, you shall get it with
> running. Sa, sa, sa, sa.
> *Exit running.* Attendants *follow*   [IV. vi. 203].

Lear is a child again in his madness. We are in touch with the exquisitely pathetic, safeguarded only by Shakespeare's masterful technique from the bathos of comedy.

But indeed this recurrent stress on the incongruous and the fantastic is not a subsidiary element in *King Lear*: it is the very heart of the play. We watch humanity grotesquely tormented, cruelly and with mockery impaled: nearly all the persons suffer some form of crude indignity in the course of the play. I have noticed the major themes of Lear and Gloucester: there are others. Kent is banished, undergoes the disguise of a servant, is put to shame in the stocks; Cornwall is killed by his own servant resisting the dastardly mutilation of Gloucester; Oswald, the prime courtier, is done to death by Edgar in the role of an illiterate country yokel—

. . . keep out, che vore ye, or Ise try whether your costard or my ballow be the harder. . . .

[IV. vi. 247]

Edgar himself endures the utmost degradation of his disguise as "poor
Tom," begrimed and naked, and condemned to speak nothing but idiocy.
Edmund alone steers something of an unswerving tragic course, brought
to a fitting, deserved, but spectacular end, slain by his wronged brother,
nobly repentant at the last:

> *Edmund.* What you have charged me with, that have I done;
> And more, much more; the time will bring it out:
> 'Tis past, and so am I. But what art thou
> That hast this fortune on me? If thou'rt noble,
> I do forgive thee.
>   *Edgar.*   Let's exchange charity.
> I am no less in blood than thou art, Edmund;
> If more, the more thou hast wrong'd me.
> My name is Edgar. . . .
>
>   [V. iii. 164]

The note of forgiving chivalry reminds us of the deaths of Hamlet and
Laertes. Edmund's fate is nobly tragic: "The wheel has come full circle;
I am here" (V. iii. 176). And Edmund is the most villainous of all. Again,
we have incongruity; and again, the Gloucester-theme reflects the Lear-
theme. Edmund is given a noble, an essentially tragic, end, and Goneril
and Regan, too, meet their ends with something of tragic fineness in
pursuit of their evil desires. Regan dies by her sister's poison; Goneril
with a knife. They die, at least, in the cause of love—love of Edmund.
Compared with these deaths, the end of Cordelia is horrible, cruel, un-
necessarily cruel—the final grotesque horror in the play. Her villainous
sisters are already dead. Edmund is nearly dead, repentant. It is a matter
of seconds—and rescue comes too late. She is hanged by a common soldier.
The death which Dostoievsky's Stavrogin singled out as of all the least
heroic and picturesque, or rather, shall we say, the most hideous and
degrading: this is the fate that grips the white innocence and resplendent
love-strength of Cordelia. To be hanged, after the death of her enemies,
in the midst of friends. It is the last hideous joke of destiny: this—and
the fact that Lear is still alive, has recovered his sanity for this. The death
of Cordelia is the last and most horrible of all the horrible incongruities
I have noticed:

> Why should a dog, a horse, a rat have life,
> And thou no breath at all?
>
>   [V. ii. 308]

We remember: "Upon such sacrifices, my Cordelia, the gods themselves
throw incense" (V.iii.20). Or do they laugh, and is the *Lear* universe
one ghastly piece of fun?

We do not feel that. The tragedy is most poignant in that it is purposeless, unreasonable. It is the most fearless artistic facing of the ultimate cruelty of things in our literature. That cruelty would be less were there not this element of comedy which I have emphasized, the insistent incongruities, which create and accompany the madness of Lear, which leap to vivid shape in the mockery of Gloucester's suicide, which are intrinsic in the texture of the whole play. Mankind is, as it were, deliberately and comically tormented by "the gods." He is not even allowed to die tragically. Lear is "bound upon a wheel of fire" and only death will end the victim's agony:

> Vex not his ghost. O, let him pass! He hates him
> That would upon the rack of this tough world
> Stretch him out longer.
>
> [V. iii. 315]

King Lear is supreme in that, in this main theme, it faces the very absence of tragic purpose: wherein it is profoundly different from *Timon of Athens*. Yet, as we close the sheets of this play, there is no horror, nor resentment. The tragic purification of the essentially untragic is yet complete.

Now in this essay it will, perhaps, appear that I have unduly emphasized one single element of the play, magnifying it, and leaving the whole distorted. It has been my purpose to emphasize. I have not exaggerated. The pathos has not been minimized: it is redoubled. Nor does the use of the words "comic" and "humour" here imply disrespect to the poet's purpose: rather I have used these words, crudely no doubt, to cut out for analysis the very heart of the play—the thing that man dares scarcely face: the demonic grin of the incongruous and absurd in the most pitiful of human struggles with an iron fate. It is this that wrenches, splits, gashes the mind till it utters the whirling vapourings of lunacy. And, though love and music—twin sisters of salvation—temporarily may heal the racked consciousness of Lear, yet, so deeply planted in the facts of our life is this unknowing ridicule of destiny, that the uttermost tragedy of the incongruous ensues, and there is no hope save in the broken heart and limp body of death. This is the most agonizing of all tragedies to endure: and if we are to feel more than a fraction of this agony, we must have sense of this quality of grimmest humour. We must beware of sentimentalizing the cosmic mockery of the play.

And is there, perhaps, even a deeper and less heart-searing, significance in its humour? Smiles and tears are indeed most curiously interwoven here. Gloucester was saved from his violent and tragic suicide that he might recover his wronged son's love, and that his heart might

'Twixt two extremes of passion, joy and grief,
Burst smilingly.

[V. iii. 200]

Lear dies with the words

Do you see this? Look on her, look, her lips,
Look there, look there!

What smiling destiny is this he sees at the last instant of racked mortality?
Why have we that strangely beautiful account of Cordelia's first hearing
of her father's pain:

. . . patience and sorrow strove
Who should express her goodliest. You have seen
Sunshine and rain at once: her smiles and tears
Were like a better way: those happy smilets,
That play'd on her ripe lip, seem'd not to know
What guests were in her eyes; which parted thence,
As pearls from diamonds dropp'd. In brief,
Sorrow would be a rarity most beloved,
If all could so become it.

[IV. iii. 18]

What do we touch in these passages? Sometimes we know that all human
pain holds beauty, that no tear falls but it dews some flower we cannot
see. Perhaps humour, too, is inwoven in the universal pain, and the
enigmatic silence holds not only an unutterable sympathy, but also the
ripples of an impossible laughter whose flight is not for the wing of
human understanding; and perhaps it is this that casts its darting
shadow of the grotesque across the furrowed pages of *King Lear*.

Character and Society in *King Lear*

by *Arthur Sewell*

King Lear is the play in which Shakespeare returns once again to see man as a human soul, not in opposition to society, not rejecting society, but finding in society the sphere of fulfilment. Order is now seen, for the first time, and perhaps imperfectly, "not merely negative, but creative and liberating." It is a vision of society very different from that discovered in *Othello*. In *Othello* we cannot suppose that society is ever moral or good. Othello and Iago die, but future Othellos will find themselves betrayed in Venice, and future Iagos will still prey upon its profligates. In *King Lear* the conflict is no longer apprehended as a conflict between the individual and society; the conflict is now within society itself. Disorder in the human soul is both the agent and the product of disorder in society. Social order is the condition, as it is the resultant, of sweet and affirmative being, without which man relapses into a beastly and self-destructive individualism.

The play gives an impression of towns and villages and castles, on which the barren moor and the wild marshland are ever ready to encroach. Outside the walls lies the realm of brutishness, of animals and roots, of standing pools and naked madmen. Certain of the characters become exiles from comfort, from decent living, from politeness. Lear, in the wind and the rain and the thunder, and in the hovel, is such an exile. So is Edgar, in the rags of Tom o'Bedlam. So are the fool and, afterwards, the blind Gloucester. The beastly life is very close, near neighbour to civilized man; and man has not much to do to resume the life of the beast.

He has only to cast off his clothes—for in this symbolism Shakespeare dramatically anticipates Carlyle. Clothes alone divide men from the animals:

> Is man no more than this? Consider him well. Thou owest the worm no silk, the beast no hide, the sheep no wool, the cat no perfume. Ha! here's three on's are sophisticated! Thou art the thing itself: unaccommodated man is no more

"Character and Society in *King Lear*." From *Character and Society in Shakespeare* (Oxford: The Clarendon Press, 1951), by Arthur Sewell, pp. 108-21. Copyright 1951 by Oxford University Press. Reprinted by permission of Oxford University Press.

but such a poor, bare, forked animal as thou art: Off, off, you lendings! Come, unbutton here.

And when Lear flings off his clothes we may remember his words to Regan earlier in the play:

> O, reason not the need: our basest beggars
> Are in the poorest thing superfluous:
> Allow not nature more than nature needs,
> Man's life is cheap as beast's: thou art a lady;
> If only to go warm were gorgeous,
> Why, nature needs not what thou gorgeous wear'st,
> Which scarcely keeps thee warm.

Brutish nature is made actual for us in the frequent mention of animals, especially those who prey upon each other. And disorder in humanity is symbolized in rank and wayward weeds which seem ever to encroach on the cultivated field.

The imagery of clothes—and many other things in the play—reinforce the notion that in society "institutions are necessary"; and character in the play is certainly conceived in terms of social rank and function, as well as in terms of the family. We expect trouble, indeed, when at the beginning of the play we learn that Lear intends to continue rank without function, has subscribed his power, and confined it merely to "exhibition," and would manage those "authorities" which he has given away. The bastardy of Edmund ("there was good sport at his making") has such results that we see a "fault," where a woman has "a son for her cradle ere she [has] a husband for her bed." Ironically enough, it is an insistence on the rightness and reasonableness of institutions which gives some point to the sisters' complaint that Lear's hundred retainers are intolerably more than "nature" needs. There is nothing in the play to cast suspicion upon the rightness of external order—there is much in the play to make us feel that without it we are lost, to affirm that not discipline, but indiscipline destroys. But there is also much to support the view that even discipline will destroy where it is not involved in self-discipline and in love.

King Lear—this is a large claim to make—is the only one of Shakespeare's plays in which personal relationship is treated as an end and not as a means; the only play in which personal relationships seem to determine character rather than to have an effect upon character. It is not merely that, say, in *Hamlet* the relationships between Hamlet and his mother and Hamlet and Ophelia are subsidiary in the major vision of the play; it is rather that what these characters are, and especially Hamlet, in his personal relationships, is important and enriches the vision, but the relationship in itself plays no necessary part in that vision and is incidental to it. We may think that Ophelia's kind of love is a betrayal and that Hamlet's spirit is the more embittered: but what concerns us is not that Hamlet should have loved Ophelia but that by love he should be so embittered. In *King Lear,* however, all the characters are conceived—and this is central to the vision—in their relationships with other people, in their relationships with each other, and society is a vital complex of such relationships. In *King Lear,* then, not only is individual character differently conceived, but also living society itself.

The question is one of priority, not psychological but imaginative. In *Hamlet* (to continue the example) the nature of personal relationship is dependent on the nature of the characters: in *King Lear,* in a large measure, the nature of the character is revealed in the personal relationship. In *Hamlet* relationship and character are separable: in *King Lear* they are wholly bound up with each other. So it is that in *King Lear* personal relationships are the field of character-fulfilment.

None other of Shakespeare's plays contains such moving and dramatic references to personal loyalty and love. This play opens with the grand and, perhaps, grotesque announcement of the major theme in Lear's demand that his daughters shall declare their love. I do not find this opening difficult to accept; it is a bold enlargement of that morbidity which can poison affection, when affection gives nothing and asks everything. Lear's need to be told is matched by the two elder daughters' readiness in the telling; and it is seen, not wholly but in part, for what it is, in Cordelia's inability to tell. There follow immediately many variations of the theme; for Burgundy personal relationship is a matter of use, whereas to the King of France it is a matter of value. Kent is loyal, Goneril and Regan whisper together because, for a while, their interests are in common. The King of France finds words for the theme, when he says:

> Love is not love
> When it is mingled with regards that stand
> Aloof from the entire point.

More subtly and more movingly, Cordelia's conduct quickens and illuminates the vision; for her love, which cannot speak, has some regards—she cannot help it—which stands "aloof from the *entire* point." She is to blame, although she can do no other, for keeping herself blameless.

There is no need to rehearse the way in which Shakespeare deepens and develops this vision in the creation of his characters in *King Lear.* One or two of the minor characters catch a vivid if momentary life from it. I think of the servant who bids Cornwall hold his hand:

> I have served you ever since I was a child,
> But better service have I never done you
> Than now to bid you hold.

Or of the old man who brings the blinded Gloucester to Edgar:

> O my good lord!
> I have been your tenant, and your father's tenant,
> These fourscore years.

Such a man sweetens and fortifies institutions with loyalty and service. Loyalty is found in Oswald, too—and in Kent. Lear himself—although this is too large a matter to do more than hint at—insists on his hundred followers, but comes to the moment when he bids the fool go first into the hovel; thinks of "poor naked wretches"; will make a little society of affection in prison with Cordelia; thanks a gentleman for undoing his button. And is not something darker suggested, related to this same vision, when the two sisters both desire Edmund?

> Yet Edmund was belov'd;
> The one the other poison'd for my sake
> And after slew herself.

The weeds, after all, spring from the same soil as the "sustaining corn."

Personal relationships, however, are conceived in two ways—in loyalty and consideration which are owed according merely to the "bond," and in that going out of oneself which makes of love and loyalty something more than is demanded by the bond. So, in the first Act, Lear does a terrible thing to Cordelia; he inhibits in her that love which has no need of a bond. So we apprehend that moral behaviours are inseparably bound up with each other, hers with his, for it is Lear who puts Cordelia in the position of relying merely on the bond. In similar fashion, Kent's honesty shows a loyalty something more than his commitment—and this honesty has in it a bluntness something more than the mere requirement of its occasion. There is, indeed, throughout the play a deep sense of the evil that must mix with goodness—and of the "reason" that may mix with evil; and Shakespeare makes it clear that the admixture of good with evil, of evil with "reason," is both proof and product of the fact that, morally, we are members of each other. There is, indeed, in King Lear, a kind of irony which is not, to any important extent, to be found in any other play: the irony which lies in the contradiction between the rightness of what is said and the wrongness of its being said by that particular character, or in that particular situation, or in that particular manner. Lear is old, and his age is full of changes, but his daughters should not say so. There is no reply—no reply but "Nothing" —to Lear's request that Cordelia should outdo her sisters in protestation of her love; but Cordelia should not make that reply. Kent should warn the king, but loyalty asks for more mannerly phrasing. The vision that is discovered in character in the early part of the play is that vision which sees, in all its complexities, the play in conduct of mere "reason" and "rightness," at odds with that other play of something more than "reason," something more than "rightness." So much is this the theme of the first Act that we may risk the judgment that this is what the play is about. Nature, we are to learn, needs more than reason gives.

Except for the King of France, the first Act shows all the other characters—this is the manner in which they were conceived—determining their conduct and their speech either by self-regarding "reason" or by a sense of "rightness" which has in it something of self-regard. At any rate, conduct in them is determined, in one way or another, according merely to the need or the letter, and, because of this, has in it an admixture of evil and necessary imperfection. Whether the regard for self be "proper" or "improper," at the beginning of the play the impulse in conduct is almost universally self-regarding, or has in it something self-regarding as a presiding element. Something in self, something inhibitory in the conduct of another combining with something in self, prevents a "going out" of the self. Even where the spirit is generous, it is forced to seek refuge in "reason," in the letter, and is thereby frustrated and impoverished. At the end of the play, however, conduct—again in one way or another—becomes something more than "reason" needs. There is, for example, a kind of generosity, a certain "going out" of the self, in Goneril, when she says, "I have been worth the whistle." There is, in this, release from the self, and much more than "reason" needs. So, too, in Edmund's "Yet Edmund was belov'd"; and it is significant that this is followed immediately by something very much like remorse for others. Edmund—and Goneril, too, for that matter—shows himself for a moment as man enough to be damned. When Lear thinks of the "poor naked wretches," there is a most subtle play on all these themes—for such compassion in him has been in the past more than reason has seemed to need and is now a "going out" of himself; and yet in this compassion there is a higher reason, which shows the heavens "more just." Reason and compassion come together at last, when Kent says of the king:

> Vex not his ghost: O! let him pass; he hates him
> That would upon the rack of this rough world
> Stretch him out longer.

And, a little later:

> I have a journey, sir, shortly to go;
> My master calls me, I must not say no.

The movement of the play seems to be from conduct (and character) in which reason is governed by self-regard, to conduct (and character) in which reason is transformed by compassion. In an image, this compassion becomes a healing and medicinal balm. So the third servant says of Gloucester:

> I'll fetch some flax and whites of eggs
> To apply to his bleeding face.

And Cordelia of her father:

> O my dear father! Restoration hang
> Thy medicine on my lips, and let this kiss
> Repair those violent harms that my two sisters
> Have in thy reverence made!

That was one way of representing compassion.

"Institutions are necessary," but they are administered by men, and, necessary though they are, they are no guarantee against viciousness and evil. Lear, in his madness, has a terrible picture of what may lie beneath the façade of social and political institutions, and for a moment we have a vision of all society itself, in its forms and customs, rotten and hypocritical. It is a picture of society in which institutions are all false-seeming, and justice itself is so perverted that it lends itself as a disguise to those very ills on which it passes judgment. The image of clothes is still used by Shakespeare:

> Through tatter'd clothes small vices do appear;
> Robes and furred gowns hide all.

Here is society, as Lear in his madness sees it, without grace, without sweetness. The law conceals what it cannot prevent, and, by stealth, luxury goes to it, pell-mell. As we envisage such a society, we have a physical nausea, which makes us wish, like Lear, "an ounce of civet" to sweeten our imaginations. We have raised the stone and seen the maggots. Shakespeare never gave us a clearer clue—and there is another in that travesty of justice as Lear arraigns the joint-stools in the hovel—to the vision of the play from which the characters draw their identities.

But it is not a merely secular society in which these characters are conceived to have their being. Nor, on the other hand, do I think it can be said (even through allegory) to be a society understood in terms of Christian theology. Nevertheless, to put the matter quite simply, we certainly get the impression in the play that the characters are imagined not only as members of each other but also as members of a Nature which is active both within themselves and throughout the circumambient universe. Man is nowhere so certainly exhibited as a member of all organic creation and of the elemental powers. Man's membership of society is more than legal, is more than political, because it is subtended in a wider membership, in which plants and animals, the wind and the thunder, are also included. And is it too extravagant to suggest that this natural universe is, in the earlier part of the play, peopled not only by men but also by beings of a primitive pagan belief—by Hecate, by Apollo, by Jupiter, by "the gods"; and that the dominion of these beings is, in the action of the play, superseded? Is it, indeed, too extravagant to suggest that in the play we have a veritable change in dispensation? That, at any rate, is the impression given as the imagery changes and one store of images gives way to another. What the final dispensation is, however, it is difficult to determine, for Shakespeare seems not to specify it. The most we can say is that, like the promise of rain in Mr. T. S. Eliot's *The Waste Land,* there are moments and images towards the end of *King Lear* which give promise of grace and benediction.

It is hard, then, to understand how *King Lear* can ever have been taken to be "the most Senecan of all Shakespeare's tragedies." Even Mr. Eliot, while seeking to suggest that there is "much less and much more" than Senecan Stoicism in the play, agrees that "there is [in it] a tone of Senecan fatalism; *fatis agimur.*" I should have thought that of all Shakespeare's tragedies this statement is least true of *King Lear.* It cannot be argued, surely, that we are to take as true for the whole play Gloucester's statement:

> As flies to wanton boys, are we to the gods:
> They kill us for their sport.

The characters seem to me to be self-active and responsible, and even the idea that "ripeness is all" is scarcely resignation as Seneca might have understood it. What might be mistaken for resignation is, indeed, something very different, and not at all Senecan; I mean the humility which manifests itself unmistakably in Lear, in Edgar, in Albany, at the end of the play. Goneril's "I have been worth the whistle" and Edmund's "Yet Edmund was belov'd" have in them something of the element which Mr. Eliot has called "cheering oneself up"; but they are more than that.

Moreover, these utterances come too late, in a moment too desperate, for them to be dismissed merely as the speech of Pride. Not Pride, indeed, but Humility, which is the "reverse" of the stoical attitude, is the most memorable principle at the end of the play; but we could never have known what this Humility was, had we not learned also something about Pride. True humility, moreover, goes hand in hand with compassion, and so it is in the closing scenes of *King Lear*. Does not the play look forward to Dostoievsky, rather than back to Seneca?

In general, the tragic hero is conceived as pursuing a settlement not only with secular society but also with his universe. Settlement with society is not enough; for he must also find for himself an identity which, while giving him mastery over his temporal problems, justifies that mastery with a more than temporal sanction. The nature of his settlement with his universe is determined in the pursuit of settlement itself. In this sense it is true to say that Shakespeare had no "philosophy." It is no prefabricated universe with which the hero seeks to find accommodation; it is no prefabricated universe which at his peril and cost he ignores. The Christian categories never preside over the vision, although, naturally enough, the vision is impregnated with Christian sentiment. Tragedy finds its origin not in a Christian idea of imperfection but in "Renaissance anarchism."

Only through grace, perhaps, if at all, can man find blessedness; and Shakespearian tragedy is tragedy simply because in it Fallen Man seeks to find rehabilitation in "infiniteness"—but without grace. The tragedy is in the failure, and perhaps the failure is general to the case of Man. The tragic character (and in this there is no Senecan "cheering oneself up") will not resign himself to confinement in the secular world; but he has no certitude of status in a world more absolute. We cannot judge the tragic character in terms of our temporal moralities; neither can we schematize those mysteries of redemption which might at last exempt him from such judgments. He believes that he belongs to this world and he believes that he does not. He would jump the life to come—and yet he dare not. He comes to know that "the readiness is all," but that same ripeness, which releases him from the importunities of this world, discovers for him no other. Shakespearian tragedy is the product of the change in men's minds—the Renaissance change—by which men came to feel themselves separate from God; by which, indeed, the idea of God receded from men's habitual certitudes and became no more and often less than an intellectual construction, a merely credible hypothesis, a Being remote and not certainly just or beneficent, perhaps the Enemy. In a world where anarchism was of recent development and men had not yet resigned themselves to a disabling opportunism man's perennial hunger for metaphysical being prompted Shakespeare to create supreme drama out of the question, How shall man find the intersection between that which is in time and that which is out of time? Or, to put the matter simply, and I do not think too simply. What shall we do to be saved?

Timon of Athens

by Mark Van Doren

If Aristotle was right when he called plot the soul of tragedy, "Timon of Athens" has no soul. There are those who claim to know that Shakespeare's soul is in it, exposed at a crisis which experts on the inner lives of authors can read at a glance; but that is an additional way of saying that the play does without complications. Its action is the simplest that can be imagined. Upon the refusal of four friends to lend him money when he needs it Timon passes from the extreme of prodigality to the extreme of misanthropy. "The middle of humanity," whence tragedy no less than comedy derives its strength, he never knows; he knows "but the extremity of both ends." The words are those of Apemantus, who as the churl of the piece is privileged also to say that Timon's transformation is from a madman to a fool, from a flashing phoenix to a naked gull. Apemantus is a harsh critic, but he is a critic. The author's interest is entirely confined to the absolutes of Timon's illusion and disillusion. Not only has he taken no pains to motivate his hero's change of mind, for the episode of the friends' ingratitude is perfunctory; he has taken no pains whatever to put more than lyric force into Timon's utterances before and after. The play is two plays, casually joined at the middle; or rather two poems, two pictures, in swan white and raven black. The contrast is all. This is where the spiritual biographers of Shakespeare come in. The poetry of either half being radical in its intensity and impossible to ignore, they argue that the feeling behind it must be Shakespeare's instead of Timon's, and that the play was never anything but an excuse to rid the poet's bosom of its perilous stuff— granted, to be sure, that he is responsible for all of it as it stands. Assuming that he is, we can agree that the play as written leaves him open to the charge of having expressed himself rather than his theme. But the field of conjecture is so wide that any step taken across it may be in the right direction, and we may wish to escape into an alternative theory which starts from the supposition that "Timon of Athens" is Shake-

"*Timon of Athens.*" From *Shakespeare* (New York: Holt, Rinehart and Winston, Inc., 1939), by Mark Van Doren, pp. 249-53. Copyright 1939 by Mark Van Doren. Reprinted by permission of Holt, Rinehart and Winston, Inc.

speare's last tragedy and that it was never finished. If this was the case, then he may have been tired of tragedy—through with it as an artist and exhausted by its tensions. This alone could account for his relapse into the lyric mode, for the concentration of his interest upon the things his hero says rather than upon the meaning of the fact that he says them. It may not matter to criticism what theory we hold, so long as we recognize the limits of the play before us.

No play of Shakespeare's confesses its limits more frankly. It is content to be abstract, to leave unclothed the symbols of which its poetry is made. The hall in Timon's house where he dispenses bounty is allegorical in its splendor, a chamber prepared for the performance of generous miracles, not an inhabitable portion of one man's dwelling. Timon as its host, moving gracefully to music while servants bear in urns of fruit and caskets of jewels, bowing to friends as though they were gods and receiving gifts from them—two brace of greyhounds, four milk-white horses trapped in silver—as blissfully as he bestows his own gifts in return, clapping his hands to summon a masque of ladies dressed as Amazons so that the lords his guests may dance with them to the strains of lutes and hautboys, and now and then giving golden voice to his inexpressible love:

> I could deal kingdoms to my friends,
> And ne'er be weary
>
> [I. ii. 226-27]

—this Timon is not so much a man as a figure representing Munificence, an abstraction in whom madness may not matter. For we see some meaning in Apemantus's epithet when we overhear the steward's attempts to convince Timon that he is bankrupt, and when we realize that he is giving away borrowed wealth. But he is already fantastic, and our fears for him are not real. Neither is our pity for him real when later on we listen to his rages as he stands in the middle of an empty plain outside of Athens and digs in the bare ground for symbols barer still—"one poor root" and "yellow, glittering, precious gold."

> This yellow slave
> Will knit and break religions, bless the accurs'd,
> Make the hoar leprosy ador'd, place thieves
> And give them title, knee, and approbation
> With senators on the bench. This is it
> That makes the wappen'd widow wed again;
> She, whom the spital-house and ulcerous sores
> Would cast the gorge at, this embalms and spices
> To the April day again. Come, damn'd earth,

> Thou common whore of mankind, that puts odds
> Among the rout of nations, I will make thee
> Do thy right nature.
>
> [IV. iii. 33-44]

Such a speech has its terrors, and with many another speech in the play it belongs somewhere near the top of Shakespeare's poetry. But it is not terrible that Timon should be saying such things as it was terrible that Lear should say the things he said. Gold has been a symbol wherewith Timon could express his love. Now it is a symbol wherewith he can express his hate. That is all. It is as naked a piece of poetic property as the hole he stands in, as the root he throws up, as the cave he enters and leaves, and as the sea by which he is to die. Nakedness itself becomes a symbol in this play—nakedness as something which Timon's extremity desires and as something which he has in death, for he makes his everlasting mansion where the light foam of the sea may beat his grave-stone daily (IV. iii. 379-80), and where the only tears will be those of vast Neptune (V. iv. 78). The scene is not populated as Lear's Britain was, nor does what happens to its hero concern us so much. The parallel is suggested not only by the action as a whole but by a particular speech of Apemantus:

> Call the creatures
> Whose naked natures live in all the spite
> Of wreakful heaven, whose bare unhoused trunks,
> To the conflicting elements expos'd,
> Answer mere nature; bid them flatter thee.
>
> [IV. iii. 227-31]

Here might be the king who in his own extremity discovered the existence of poor naked wretches with houseless heads and unfed sides. But Timon, though he goes farther in speech than Lear ever went, moves us not half so deeply, and in fact does not move us at all. Lear's obscenity was innocence to this:

> Hold up, you sluts,
> Your aprons mountant. . . . Be whores still;
> And he whose pious breath seeks to convert you,
> Be strong in whore, allure him, burn him up;
> Let your close fire predominate his smoke,
> And be no turncoats. . . . Whore still;
> Paint till a horse may mire upon your face;
> A pox of wrinkles!
>
> [IV. iii. 134-48]

But it was heart-breaking to hear, as this is not because there is no heart in Timon to break, or any other organ. He is pure mouth-piece, even when his poetry is best:

> Go, live rich and happy;
> But thus condition'd: thou shalt build from men;
> Hate all, curse all, show charity to none,
> But let the famish'd flesh slide from the bone,
> Ere thou relieve the beggar.
>
> [IV. iii. 532-36]

He himself is pure symbol, a misanthrope and not a man.

The play confesses as much in the conduct of such action as it has. Schematism is everywhere apparent. There are three malcontents: Timon, Apemantus, and Alcibiades. Three servants enter Timon's hall bearing gifts (I. ii). Three friends refuse money to Timon in three consecutive scenes (III. i. ii. iii), and three strangers comment upon the triple outrage (III. ii). In his solitude Timon is visited by three significant individuals: Alcibiades, Apemantus, Flavius. And the banditti who come are three in number. This is obviously the work of a playwright who does not care how much his machinery shows, just as the poetry is the work of a man who does not mind announcing this themes—in the first half they are friendship, music, love, praise, and summer tears, in the second half they are hate, rage, roots, gold, bleak earth and sky, unvesseled sea, and winters too hard for weeping.

If the spiritual experts are right and "Timon of Athens" is a personal play, its interest, over and above the intrinsic interest of its poetry, is in the limit of pessimism it reaches. There could scarcely be more railing and cursing in five acts than we have here, and indeed there is to be no more of these commodities in Shakespeare. One is free to conjecture that in Timon's tomb Shakespeare buried his own bitterness—in a bleak, open, timeless place where the only tears are Neptune's, and where a "sea of air" broods in its vast empty arc above another sea whose waves are without memory. It is not necessary to conjecture thus, and if one wishes to do so, it is well to remember that on the subject of Shakespeare's inner life there can be no authority. The great dead deserve whatever peace is possible. The temptation, however, is real in view of the mood which dominates four comedies still to come. Whatever the truth about Shakespeare was, "Timon of Athens" is some kind of transition between his last tragedies and his last comedies—or, as the term goes, his romances. It looks both ways: backward through "Lear" to the pestilent congregation of vapors in which Hamlet was befouled, and forward with "Antony and Cleopatra" to thick amber air and the rich difficult sunset of reconciliation.

Antony and Cleopatra

by S. L. Bethell

Antony and Cleopatra has been treated the least kindly of Shake-speare's great tragedies, with the possible exceptions of *Coriolanus* and *Timon of Athens*. The general outcry has been against its loose construc-tion: Dr. Johnson, admitting the play's "variety," thought that the events were "produced without any art of connection or care of disposition." [1] Professor Schücking also deplores "a decided falling off" in the handling of the plot. He instances the scene on Pompey's galley, where the drink-ing song (he believes) "completely *isolates the scene*,[2] detaching it from the context of the whole in a manner which is unequalled even in Shake-speare." [3] These charges, both general and particular, have been ade-quately rebutted in Mr. Granville-Barker's *Preface*,[4] where the tight and balanced construction is closely analysed, and the blame transferred from Shakespeare to those editors who, thinking in terms of localised scenes, produced an incredible number of them out of Shakespeare's properly indivisible text. The play is now seen to be a careful pattern of inter-woven and contrasting episodes, all duly subordinate to the main design: the presentation of Antony and Cleopatra in the broad context of the Roman Empire.

A more serious problem is presented to the critics by apparent incon-sistencies in psychology, and a general failure to adhere to Aristotelian precepts. Even the revolutionary critics are troubled. Professor Schück-ing[5] feels a sharp discontinuity in the presentation of Cleopatra, between the royal courtezan of the earlier scenes, and the tragic queen who in the

"*Antony and Cleopatra.*" From *Shakespeare and the Popular Dramatic Tradition* (London: Staples Press, 1944), by S. L. Bethell, pp. 116-31. Copyright 1944 by Staples Press. Reprinted by permission of Staples Press.

[1] *v. Johnson on Shakespeare*, ed. Raleigh (Henry Frowde, 1908), p. 180.

[2] Professor Schücking's italics.

[3] Schücking, *op. cit.*, p. 135.

[4] Harley Granville-Barker: *Prefaces to Shakespeare*, Second Series (Sidgwick & Jackson, 1930); *v.* especially p. 121. In this chapter I have derived much valuable help from Mr. Granville-Barker's Preface, though my conclusions are very different from his.

[5] *op. cit.*, pp. 119 *et seq.*

end chooses death rather than to be the victim of a Roman triumph. Professor Stoll [6] finds the characters nobler than their deeds, or their love "greater than their natures," and ascribes this, somewhat vaguely, to poetic and dramatic factors; whilst Mr. Granville-Barker[7] suggests that we are concerned with great action rather than psychology. Professor Stoll and Mr. Granville-Barker are thus in direct contradiction, one finding greatness in character rather than action, the other in action rather than character. None of these modern critics supplies an answer to their predecessors' problem; indeed they share the traditional attitudes, and their attempt to isolate character and action is a precarious and inadequate solution. It remains true that, regarding the play psychologically, one cannot reconcile the vicious, the vulgar, and the commonplace in Antony and Cleopatra, with the sublimity with which they are invested, especially as they face defeat and death. With a naturalistic approach to character, one might well regard Antony as a licentious old ruffian whose political and military talents are forfeited through lust; and Cleopatra as the Egyptian harlot, shameless, selfish, cowardly and sex-obsessed. Their transformation in the end would then appear psychologically inconsistent, an unworthy dramatic trick to dodge the moral issue—implying a sort of conversion without repentance, or perhaps the glorification of splendid vice.

In any event, it is quite clear that we are not intended to think of Antony and Cleopatra as a lecher and a strumpet—or only in a strictly qualified sense. To do justice to Shakespeare, we must radically alter our critical approach, and begin—and end—with the poetry itself. What everybody has noticed in the verse of *Antony and Cleopatra* is its Brobdingnagian imagery: objects of tremendous size and power are constantly utilised to illustrate some quality of character or situation. The employment of such imagery is not limited to one or two personages in the play, but is characteristic of them all. There is, in fact, no attempt to differentiate characters by the verse they speak, except to some extent with Octavius Caesar, whose verse is normally dull and flat and impersonal, or else staccato as he issues orders. But when he speaks of Antony, or Cleopatra, or the Empire, his verse too takes on the grandeur and dignity met with in the others: e.g. his description of Antony's military asceticism:

> . . . on the Alps
> It is reported thou didst eat strange flesh,
> Which some did die to look on;

> [*A.a.C.* I. iv. 66]

---

[6] *Art and Artifice in Shakespeare,* pp. 146-47.
[7] *op. cit.,* pp. 111-12.

and his speech on Antony's death is in the same high strain. This pervading suggestion of size and strength and importance, conveys the imperial theme[8] and the dignity of the persons involved. But it is more precisely informative than this. In the first scene, for example, the Romans watch in disgust as Antony, Cleopatra, and their Egyptian train, pass by. Philo, thinking of the old Antony, remembers

> . . . those his goodly eyes,
> That o'er the files and musters of the war
> Have glow'd like plated Mars. . . .
>
> [I. i. 2]

Antony has since become false to his position in the Empire:

> Take but good note, and you shall see in him
> The triple pillar of the world transform'd
> Into a strumpet's fool.
>
> [I. i. 11]

And then we hear Antony and Cleopatra:

> *Ant.:* There's beggary in the love that can be reckon'd.
> *Cleo.:* I'll set a bourn how far to be beloved.
> *Ant.:* Then must thou needs find out new heaven, new earth.
>
> [I. i. 15]

The lovers speak of their love in the same large way in which Philo speaks of Antony the general, or Antony the triumvir. If he is "the triple pillar of the world," their love is even greater, for this world cannot contain it: the new heaven and new earth of apocalyptic vision are alone adequate to circumscribe it. This speech in the first minute of the play looks forward to the "husband, I come" (V. ii. 290) of Cleopatra in her triumphant death—an instance of the close unity of Shakespeare's poetic conception. What I must immediately note, however, is the application, here and throughout the play, of the same colossal imagery—the world, the heavenly bodies, the gods, etc.—to the theme of empire and the theme of love. It is a deliberate equation, for these themes are conjoined too frequently for accident. Even Scarus, after the sea-fight, exclaims:

---

[8] *The Imperial Theme* is the title of a book by Professor Wilson Knight, which, however, I have not consulted.

> The greater cantle of the world is lost
> With very ignorance; we have kiss'd away
> Kingdoms and provinces—

[III. x. 6]

"kiss'd" as the verb; "kingdoms and provinces," the object of the verb: in this way, by purely literary means, we are compelled to feel Cleopatra's love as quite commensurable with the honours of war and statecraft against which it must be weighed. The lovers' ceremoniousness with one another—always "my queen" and "my lord"—strengthens the dignity of their love. There is no disguising its sensuality: "The beds i' the east are soft," says Antony (II. vi. 51); and Cleopatra can "take no pleasure in aught an eunuch has" (I. v. 9)—but it is expressed in the poetry only. There is no attempt to show Cleopatra's sensual nature upon the stage— out of regard for the boy actor, says Mr. Granville-Barker.[9] How would the old Hollywood have rejoiced in Egyptian orgies, and a semi-nude Cleopatra strutting with the "sword Philippan" (II. v. 23) about an impossible palace bedroom! Such events in Shakespeare are off-stage, and, as revealed in the verse, can be delicately attuned to a tone of loving reminiscence. When Cleopatra does appear with her lover, it is her wit we admire, and her changing moods which claim our attention. She is no stage "vamp," but her sensual qualities have been translated into the medium of words. It is not primarily to spare the boy actor's blushes, or to avoid his incompetent rendering of female passion, that Shakespeare adopts this method; for any degree of naturalism would have nullified the suggestion of the verse, and we should be back in good earnest with the problem of the naturalistic critic unsolved. But the poetic building-up process is continuous. Even the lovers' oaths bring the theme of world empire into the context of passionate love.

> Let Rome in Tiber melt, and the wide arch
> Of the ranged empire fall!

[I. i. 33]

> Melt Egypt into Nile!

[II. v. 78]

> Sink Rome, and their tongues rot
> That speak against us!

[III. vii. 16]

While the two themes of love and empire are thus paralleled in power and grandeur, they are at the same time sharply contrasted as conflicting

---

[9] *op. cit.,* p. 204.

alternatives presented to Antony's choice. The contrast is geographically
expressed, as between East and West, or Egypt and Rome. "Cleopatra"
and "Egypt" are almost synonymous: as "Egypt" (III. xi. 51) she is up-
braided for her desertion, and she is addressed as "Egypt" in passionate
reconciliation later:

> I am dying, Egypt, dying. . . .
>
> [IV. xv. 18]

Octavius Caesar stands for the Roman qualities, as Cleopatra does for
the Egyptian. Octavia is the translation of Rome into woman: on the
level of character as well as plot, she is a projection of the theme of
empire into the theme of love:

> Octavia is of a holy, cold, and still conversation.
>
> [II. vi. 130]

In stagecraft also, the contrast between Egypt and Rome is insisted upon,
as Mr. Granville-Barker has shown.[10] It is evident in the very first scene,
when the Roman soldiers watch grimly as Antony and Cleopatra move
across the stage with their Egyptian train. Later, Antony has just agreed
to marry Octavia when, in Enobarbus' great speech, we are given the
poetic essence of what Egypt and Cleopatra stand for:

> The barge she sat in, like a burnish'd throne,
> Burn'd on the water—
>
> [II. ii. 196]

it is more vividly Egyptian than any pageant furnished out of properties.
Again, in the next scene, Antony promises fidelity to Octavia:

> I have not kept my square; but that to come
> Shall all be done by the rule;
>
> [II. iii. 6]

and at once *Enter* Soothsayer, whom we have last seen in Egypt. The
scene ends with Antony again under the Egyptian spell:

> I will to Egypt:
> And though I make this marriage for my peace,
> I' the east my pleasure lies.
>
> [II. iii. 38]

---

[10] *op. cit.,* pp. 117 *et seq.*

Even adjectivally the contrast is preserved. Cleopatra jeers:

> He was disposed to mirth; but on the sudden
> A Roman thought hath struck him;
>
> [I. ii. 86]

and Enobarbus:

> He will to his Egyptian dish again.
>
> [II. vi. 134]

Egypt and its attractions are insisted on throughout the play, and not least in the Roman scenes where they are intruded piquantly—or even farcically with Lepidus' drunken enquiries concerning "your crocodile" (II. vii. 46). Act III, Scene vi, is interesting for its presentation of Rome in contrast. We hear first of the activities of Antony, and an impressive list is given of kings who have assembled to his standard:

> Bocchus, the king of Libya; Archelaus,
> Of Cappadocia; Philadelphos, king
> Of Paphlagonia; the Thracian king, Adallas;
> King Malchus of Arabia; King of Pont;
> Herod of Jewry; Mithridates, king
> Of Comagene; Polemon and Amyntas,
> The kings of Mede and Lycaonia,
> With a more larger list of sceptres.
>
> [III. vi. 69]

Caesar, however, is undismayed:

> But let determined things to destiny
> Hold unbewail'd their way,
>
> [III. vi. 84]

he says, enunciating the Stoic, Roman philosophy; and the name of Rome rings out once and again with an assurance of stability and security:

> Let Rome be thus
> Inform'd. . . .
>
> [III. vi. 19]
>
> . . . but you are come
> A market-maid to Rome;
>
> [III. vi. 50]

Welcome to Rome;

[III. vi. 85]

Each heart in Rome does love and pity you—

[III. vi. 92]

as Octavia, deserted by Antony for Egypt, returns to her brother and her natural Rome-ward allegiance.

Egypt and Rome are thus opposed throughout the play: they represent contradictory schemes of value, contradictory attitudes to, and interpretations of, the universe. It is difficult to isolate these opposed systems in a brief space without appearing to dogmatise, and the reader must understand that a great many supporting quotations have been omitted in order to reduce the argument into a reasonable compass. The whole play should be read with the opposition of Egyptian and Roman values in mind. First, then, Egypt and Rome stand respectively for love and duty, or for pleasure and duty, or even love-pleasure and duty. Supporting quotations are hardly necessary here: Cleopatra embodies the love-pleasure principle, of which the "Roman thought" (I. ii. 87), the call to duty, is the negation. Closely related to this is the opposition of indulgence and restraint: in Egypt "Epicurean cooks" (II. i. 24) provided breakfasts as horrifying to Mecaenas as to the modern mind. Caesar is not at home in carousals:

> . . . our graver business
> Frowns at this levity,

[II. vii. 127]

he says. Antony's men must drink deep before the battle:

> . . . to-night I'll force
> The wine peep through their scars—

[III. xiii. 190]

but Caesar allows a feast after due consideration of supplies:

> And feast the army; we have store to do't,
> And they have earn'd the waste.

[IV. i. 15]

"Waste" is a significant word here, and the contrast is forced home by wedging this brief scene in Caesar's camp between two larger scenes with the forces of Antony.

More generally—and more philosophically—we have in the contrast

between Egypt and Rome, the old opposition with which Shakespeare
was concerned in the comedies and in *Troilus and Cressida*, between
"intuition" and "reason"; on the one hand the final authority of the
spontaneous affections, on the other the authority of worldly wisdom or
practical common sense (Caesar is very like Ulysses in general outline).
Antony had made, says Enobarbus,

> . . . his will
> Lord of his reason.

[III. xiii. 3]

He clings to Cleopatra against all sober judgment (Act III, Scene xiii);
he is familiar and a little sentimental with his faithful followers (Act
IV, Scene ii); and heaps coals of fire upon Enobarbus (Act IV, Scenes v·
and vi); he is prepared to meet Caesar in single combat (III. xiii. 25).
Caesar is cold and calculating: for reasons of state he will give up his·
apparently beloved sister to the lecherous old Antony, and in full and
disapproving knowledge of Antony's mode of life:

> Let us grant, it is not
> Amiss to tumble on the bed of Ptolemy;
> To give a kingdom for a mirth; to sit
> And keep the turn of tippling with a slave;
> To reel the streets at noon, and stand the buffet
> With knaves that smell of sweat.

[I. iv. 16]

He has a low opinion of the people:

> This common body,
> Like to a vagabond flag upon the stream,
> Goes to and back, lackeying the varying tide,
> To rot itself with motion.[11]

Caesar would never be betrayed into Antony's abandonment of the solid
benefits of the triumvirate. He will not be tempted into bravado by
Antony's challenge:

[11] It is interesting to note how "vagabond," "lackeying," "varying," build up the un-
certain rhythm; also how image and object interfuse. "Vagabond" and "lackeying" apply metaphorically to the flag image and literally to the crowd of which the flag is an
image; "varying," goes equally with "tide" and "crowd."

[I. iv. 44]

> . . . let the old ruffian know
> I have many other ways to die; meantime
> Laugh at his challenge.
>
> [IV. i. 4]

Faced with the dead Cleopatra he is either moved for a moment, or speaks out of character:

> . . . she looks like sleep,
> As she would catch another Antony
> In her strong toil of grace;
>
> [V. ii. 349]

but he has just become interested medically:

> If they had swallow'd poison, 'twould appear
> By external swelling;
>
> [V. ii. 348]

and it is this point that he dwells on:

> Most probable
> That so she died;
>
> [V. ii. 356]

for his last words are merely a ceremonious close to the play, with little significance for character.

Caesar incarnates the practical reason, or worldly wisdom, with which are closely linked the notions of restrictive morality and political order (Stoicism and the Roman law). Antony has a foot in both worlds: I have already contrasted him with Caesar, but there are also points of comparison. He is a Roman and has his share of Roman fortitude; he has mortified the flesh for military glory; and if Caesar will sacrifice his sister for political ends, Antony will sacrifice her, Cleopatra, and himself in the same cause, at least until the lure of Egypt proves too strong. Antony's position is central, for the choice between Egypt and Rome is for him to make. It is Cleopatra who stands opposite Caesar, incarnating "intuition," the life of the spontaneous affections, with which are linked the notions of expansive morality and æsthetic order (it is the positive affections which transcend her "baser life" [V. ii. 293]; while the dignity of sense-experience is vindicated poetically in Enobarbus' great description of the barge incident).

Justice is done to Rome, but the tendency is to depreciate the Roman

values. There is a machine-like inevitability in Caesar, accompanied by
a certain calculating meanness. When he speaks for himself, his verse is
deflated:

> Let our best heads
> Know, that to-morrow the last of many battles
> We mean to fight. . . .

[IV. i. 10]

Imperial corruption subdues the note of Roman virtue. The banquet
scene, with Menas whispering insidious suggestions into Pompey's ear,
attains a political *reductio ad absurdum* when the drunken Lepidus is
carried out:

> A' bears the third part of the world, man.

[II. vii. 96]

The next scene, which should certainly follow at once, as Mr. Granville-
Barker says,[12] and not be separated by an act division, shows the Roman
soldier at work, efficient and triumphant, but suspicious:

> Who does i' the wars more than his captain can
> Becomes his captain's captain: and ambition,
> The soldier's virtue, rather makes choice of loss,
> Than gain which darkens him.

[III. i. 21]

With Shakespeare, the new Renaissance virtue of ambition is usually
treated as a vice: so in *Julius Caesar* Antony tries to clear Caesar's memory of the imputation. That ambition is the soldier's virtue implies
Shakespeare's judgment upon the soldier (cf. Othello's "big wars, That
make ambition virtue!" [*Oth.* III. iii. 349]). Cleopatra's is the final verdict:

> . . . 'tis paltry to be Caesar:
> Not being Fortune, he's but Fortune's knave,
> A minister of her will.

[*A.a.C.* V. ii. 2]

The Egyptian qualities crystallised in Cleopatra, are correspondingly
raised in our esteem by subtle poetic means. The materials are not very
promising. This is the Cleopatra who will

---

[12] *op. cit.*, pp. 121-22.

> . . . wander through the streets and note
> The qualities of people,
>
> [I. i. 53]

or

> Hop forty paces through the public street,
>
> [II. ii. 234]

or even play a practical joke with "a salt-fish on his hook" (II. v. 17), and, as she recalls

> . . . next morn,
> Ere the ninth hour, I drunk him to his bed;
> Then put my tires and mantles on him, whilst
> I wore his sword Philippan.
>
> [II. v. 20]

It is easy to remember her as that certain queen who, in her "salad days" (I. v. 73), was carried "to Caesar in a mattress" (II. vi. 71): a mixture of hoyden and strumpet, with a strong flavour of Nell Gwynne. But Shakespeare, taking boldly for thesis that "everything becomes" her (I. i. 49), transmutes these qualities by poetic paradox. No wonder Cleopatra's character worries the psychologist; it is not so much a character as an extended metaphysical conceit:

> I saw her once
> Hop forty paces through the public street;
> And having lost her breath, she spoke, and panted,
> That she did make *defect perfection*,
> And, *breathless*, power *breathe* forth.
>
> [II. ii. 233]

The conceit is brought out by the resemblance of form in words of opposite meaning, the opposites in Cleopatra being resolved as the word-sounds are assimilated. Again:

> . . . other women cloy
> The appetites they feed; but she makes hungry
> Where most she satisfies: for vilest things
> Become themselves in her; that the holy priests
> Bless her when she is riggish.
>
> [II. ii. 241]

Here again is paradox, and the fusion of opposites: there is a benediction upon her sensuality. Similarly of the love of Antony and Cleopatra:

> Eternity was in our lips and eyes,
> Bliss in our brows' bent; none our parts so poor,
> But was a race of heaven.[13]

[I. iii. 35]

Their love being heavenly, Cleopatra is herself a goddess. Enobarbus' description has a ritual flavour; and in the barge Cleopatra was actually dressed as Venus:

> O'er-picturing that Venus where we see
> The fancy outwork nature—

[II. ii. 205]

a characteristic hyperbole, for it is claimed that she excels Apelles' picture, which itself excelled nature. She habitually dressed as a deity:

> . . . she
> In the habiliments of the goddess Isis
> That day appear'd; and oft before gave audience,
> As 'tis reported, so,

[III. vi. 16]

says Caesar, who seems shocked. She has the mystery of divinity:

---

[13] As I have already spoken of metaphysical conceits in this connection, it is interesting to note the rhythm of the second line here with its careful pointing by alliteration. It resembles very closely certain passages in Donne's Satires, including the famous

> On a huge hill,
> Cragged, and steep, Truth stands—

and, so far as I know, reappears only in Benlowes and Gerald Manley Hopkins before the present century. Commentators have been worried by "a race of heaven": Malone's paraphrase "of heavenly origin" is preferable to Warburton's "smack of flavour of heaven." I should like to suggest, very tentatively, that we may have here a metaphorical use of the "race" derived from *radix:* cf. "a race or two of ginger" (*W.T.* IV. iii. 50)—or at least a fusion of this meaning with that suggested by Malone. In any event the general meaning is clear and of far-reaching significance. The lovers' poorest or least honourable parts (presumably the sexual organs) were the root from which the "heavenly" experience of their love had grown—or (according to Malone's interpretation) had proved themselves of heavenly origin, in the physical expression of their love. Both interpretations associate sensual love with religious experience and doctrine—an association which is continued throughout the play.

> She is cunning past man's thought;
>
> > [I. ii. 150]

her nod, like Jove's, will be obeyed:

> Cleopatra
> Hath nodded him to her;
>
> > [III. vi. 65]

she has the same sort of immortality as Keats' nightingale, in virtue of her symbolic function:

> Age cannot wither her, nor custom stale
> Her infinite variety.
>
> > [II. ii. 240]

Her age is insisted on, that we may know her beauty and attraction to be perennial: she remembers her "salad days" (I. v. 73) when old Julius Caesar was in Egypt, and she is unchanged in beauty when she meets his son. Yet she describes herself as being

> . . . with Phoebus' amorous pinches black,
> And wrinkled deep in time.
>
> > [I. v. 28]

This is perhaps the most significant phrase applied to Cleopatra. In blunt prose she is described as being sunburnt, old, and wrinkled. Taken literally this would contradict all descriptions of her beauty: wrinkles were no more admired in Shakespeare's day than now; and sunburn, strangely enough, was regarded as a serious blemish:

> The Grecian dames are sunburnt and not worth
> The splinter of a lance.
>
> > [T.a.C. I. iii. 282]

In Cleopatra's remarkable conceit, however, the common attributes of age and ugliness are taken as the material of immortal beauty. The passage is fully intelligible only if symbolically interpreted—if we allow the poetry to do its work. For poetically the "deep in time" gives her an infinite age: it does not suggest an old woman, but an immortal; and "Phoebus' amorous pinches" thus become more than a metonymy for sunburn—she is an immortal lover of the sun-god, of Phoebus-Apollo, the god of poetry and song, the paragon of male beauty, and therefore a worthy mate for such as Cleopatra.

The choice which Antony has to make between Rome and Egypt is thus heavily weighted by Shakespeare on the Egyptian side. Antony is a lordly man, a natural Egyptian. In his Roman days he was prodigal of pains (as an ascetic differs from a careful man):

> . . . thou didst drink
> The stale of horses, and the gilded puddle
> Which beasts would cough at: thy palate then did deign
> The roughest berry on the rudest hedge;
> Yea, like the stag, when snow the pasture sheets,
> The barks of trees thou browsed'st; on the Alps
> It is reported thou didst eat strange flesh,
> Which some did die to look on.
>
> [*A.a.C.* I. iv. 61]

He was as magnificent in his Egyptian pleasures:

> . . . his delights
> Were dolphin-like.
>
> [V. ii. 88]

His generosity and *bonhomie* have been mentioned: it was his generosity that killed Enobarbus, a natural Egyptian with a deceptively Roman exterior. For Enobarbus tried time-serving—prudence, Caesar would have called it—and died in consequence, "by moonlight, of a broken heart." [14]

Antony's love can measure up to Cleopatra:

> Fall not a tear, I say; one of them rates
> All that is won and lost—
>
> [III. xi. 69]

and the goddess immortalises her mortal lover as he dies:

> O, wither'd is the garland of the war,
> The soldiers' pole is fall'n: young boys and girls
> Are level now with men; the odds is gone,
> And there is nothing left remarkable
> Beneath the visiting moon.
>
> [IV. xv. 64]

---

[14] Granville-Barker, *op. cit.*, p. 226.

Antony chose Egypt, intuition, the life of the spontaneous affections, with its moral and æsthetic corollaries; of all which Cleopatra is the focus and symbol. Shakespeare does not satisfy the psychologists with his character of Cleopatra; but he does not attempt a character in the sense of Trollope, or George Eliot, or even Dickens. In Cleopatra he presents the mystery of woman, the mystery of sensuality, an exploration of the hidden energies of life, and a suggestion of its goal. Intuition or spontaneous feeling is opposed to practical wisdom, generosity to prudence, love to duty, the private affections to public service; and the former in each instance is preferred. Not that the Roman values are entirely repudiated: there is a case for Caesar, "Fortune's knave" (V. ii. 3) though he be. But the Egyptian values are affirmative; the Roman, negative or restrictive: the good life may be built upon the Egyptian, but not upon the Roman. It is a way of saying that the strong sinner may enter heaven before the prudential legislator. In *Antony and Cleopatra* the strong sinners meet their purgatory here. They do not desire or seek it; it is forced upon them from without—grace which visits them in the guise of defeat. Changes of character inexplicable by psychological determinism are readily explained if we perceive that Shakespeare is applying theological categories. Earthly defeat is the providential instrument of eternal triumph: it comes undesired, but when it comes, is freely accepted, and so converted into a process of necessary cleansing. Antony's purgatory lies in military failure and a bungled suicide prompted by the false report of Cleopatra's death; Cleopatra's in surviving Antony, and in the thought of a Roman triumph. In the end the better Roman qualities are needed to transmute the Egyptian into eternal validity. Antony dies,

> . . . a Roman by a Roman
> Valiantly vanquish'd;

> [IV. xv. 57]

and Cleopatra, too, would emulate the Roman virtue:

> Let's do it after the high Roman fashion,
> And make death proud to take us.

> [IV. xv. 87]

Shakespeare nowhere approves suicide outside the Roman plays, but in them he seems to accept it, along with the pantheon, as data. It would be wrong, then, to condemn these suicides as from a Christian point of view. Antony's and Cleopatra's view of the hereafter is hardly Christian either, but their assurance is emphatically not pagan. Antony says:

> Where souls do couch on flowers, we'll hand in hand,
> And with our sprightly port make the ghosts gaze:
> Dido and her Aeneas shall want troops,
> And all the haunt be ours—
>
> [IV. xiv. 51]

this is not the shadow world of *Aeneid VI*. Cleopatra's death is more studied, as she symbolises the affirmation of life. She, too, must go by the Roman way of negation:

> My desolation does begin to make
> A better life.
>
> [V. ii. 1]

In desolation she realises her inalienable possessions, that she is above Fortune, whereas Caesar is "Fortune's knave." Deprived of earthly love, she is denuded also of her earthly glory, and sees herself

> No more, but e'en a woman, and commanded
> By such poor passion as the maid that milks
> And does the meanest chares.
>
> [IV. xv. 73]

She must realise her common humanity for her symbolic function to be of general validity. It is by deprivation and denial that she attains re-affirmation, on a higher plane, of her essential nature; so that she faces death and the hereafter in the fullest confidence, claiming Antony for the first time by the name of husband:

> . . . husband, I come:
> Now to that name my courage prove my title!
> I am fire and air; my other elements
> I give to baser life.
>
> [V. ii. 290]

Her death-speeches are as fully sensual as any before: even

> The stroke of death is as a lover's pinch,
> Which hurts, and is desired;
>
> [V. ii. 298]

and she hastens to meet first her "curled Antony" (V. ii. 304) in heaven.

In *Lear*, Shakespeare struggled with the problem of evil; in *Macbeth*, with the problem of sin in a Christian universe. In *Antony and Cleopatra*, he returns to the old problem: what are the positive bases of the good life? He finds them in the affections, and the affections as rooted deep in the sensual nature. Of these Cleopatra is the symbol, sensual even in death; for, paradoxically, it is these Egyptian values which must survive death. Caesar, the worldly wise, is "ass unpolicied!" (V. ii. 310). However shocking to the Nordic man, this position is theologically orthodox. Caesar's sins are deeper-seated and more deliberate than the sins of Antony and Cleopatra, and his heart is entirely set on the passing world. There is significance in Cleopatra's greeting to Antony after his short-lived victory:

> Lord of lords!
> O infinite virtue, comest thou smiling from
> The world's great snare uncaught?
>
> [IV. viii. 16]

She is his good, and not his evil genius, rescuing him from an undue preoccupation with the world, which is a snare and a delusion (cf. the Psalmist's frequent use of the "snare" metaphor, e.g. Ps. CXLI. 10). Nevertheless the Egyptian values need a Roman purgatory to fit them for survival; they are cleansed, through adversity, of the taint of selfishness. Antony kills himself in order to rejoin Cleopatra whom he believes to be dead; Cleopatra looks forward in the same way to their future reunion. Purged of selfish fear, the element of self-giving inherent in the sensual nature is revealed in its eternal significance, while Caesar, on the other hand, has no such selfless hold upon eternity. This is one way of poetically stating the resurrection of the body:

> . . . she looks like sleep,
> As she would catch another Antony
> In her strong toil of grace.
>
> [V. ii. 349]

Perhaps here, as elsewhere,[15] the word "grace" may have a tinge of theological significance.

[15] cf. Ch. V, Section IV, p. 106 and *The Winter's Tale*, I. ii. 99.

Coriolanus: an Introduction

by Harry Levin

This play, which must have seen its first performance in 1608 or thereabouts, may be the last of Shakespeare's tragedies as we define them today. Criticism has tended to range it beside his greatest for its power, its amplitude, and its craftsmanship. But it has never been so popular as the others; and that is by no means surprising, since it so expressly calls into question the equivocal values of popularity. On an elementary human basis, Shakespeare's appeal has always been exerted through his characters, and through the bonds of sympathy that ally them with the spectator or the reader. From the outset of *Coriolanus*, however, such an identification is harshly repelled; and modern ideology, which disposes us to sympathize less readily with the hero than with the viewpoint of his antagonists, has slanted and colored our understanding of both. Yet recent history, by grimly reviving the very issues that Shakespeare dramatized, has greatly increased the importance and the impressiveness of his dramatization. *Coriolanus* has been found, on revival, to be more fraught with significance for our time than any other drama in the Shakespearean repertory. Max Reinhardt's production in Germany was turbulently prophetic. French crowds rioted when, in the years between the wars, it was performed at the Comédie Française.

Shakespeare's audiences, on occasion, could be quite as explosive. His England must often have seemed to be rifted internally, as well as externally menaced. Even while he was writing *Coriolanus*, outcries over the scarcity of grain were daily reaching London from the Midlands. A Stuart monarch, recently enthroned, claimed more authority and wielded less than his Tudor predecessors had done. Strong-willed men could make spectacular bids for power; Sir Walter Raleigh was being held in the Tower on charges of conspiracy; the Earl of Essex had incited Londoners to fight in the streets a few years before; and for that insurrection *Richard II* had been utilized as propaganda. Such, of course, had not been

"*Coriolanus:* an Introduction." From the Introduction to *Coriolanus*, edited by Harry Levin, "The Pelican Shakespeare," Alfred Harbage, ed. (Penguin Books Inc., 1956), Copyright © 1956 by Penguin Books Inc. Reprinted by permission of Penguin Books Inc.

Shakespeare's purpose. His mounting sequence of histories had made England's coming-of-age coincide with his own, and had subsumed—along with the English past—the most triumphant decade of the first Elizabeth's reign. Therefore his chronicle plays had been somewhat controlled by considerations of patriotism, royal prerogative, and the relative familiarity of the facts. Seeking a freer field of political observation, pushing toward profounder formulations of statecraft, shifting his concern from the ruler's duties and rights to those of the citizen, Shakespeare was inevitably led to a point where more distant roads converge: the archetype of city-states, the keystone of western traditions, Rome.

At the beginning of his tragic period—the opening years of the seventeenth century—he essayed this republican theme in *Julius Caesar.* He resumed it with an even grander sequel, *Antony and Cleopatra,* but not until after completing his exhaustive explorations of personality in *Hamlet, Othello, Macbeth,* and *King Lear.* Thus *Coriolanus* rounds out a trilogy, though it stands somewhat apart from the other two Roman plays, possibly nearer to *Antony and Cleopatra* in scope and to *Julius Caesar* in subject. All three, taken together, constitute a great debate on ethics, in which the statement of private interests is balanced against the counterstatement of public responsibilities. *Julius Caesar* lays the dialectical groundwork by showing a group of individuals in conflict over the state. *Antony and Cleopatra* shows its individualistic hero and heroine rejecting their obligations to their respective states and behaving as if they were laws unto themselves. *Coriolanus* explores the extreme situation of the individual who pits himself against the state. Here Julius Caesar might have proved a monumental counterpart; but Shakespeare's portrait was brief and enigmatic, registering the impact of Caesarism on others, notably on the conscience of Marcus Brutus; and Brutus, acting "in the general common good," presented the obverse of the Roman coin whereon Coriolanus is stamped incisively.

The historical Caius Marcius Coriolanus, figuring in the earliest annals of the Republic, had won his victory at Corioli in 493 B.C. He may indeed have been a half-legendary embodiment of patrician resistance to the increasing demands of the plebeians and especially their newly appointed spokesmen, the tribunes. Hence, instead of being elected to the consulate, he was banished, and went over to the enemy as the hero does in the play. In the end, as the historian Mommsen sums it up, "he expiated his first treason by a second, and both by death." Poetic justice was better served than either side. Shakespeare drew his version of these episodes from Plutarch's *Lives,* the source that inspired him most, that treasury of ancient biography which comprises a series of comparative studies in heroic citizenship. Plutarch, the Greek moralist, saw Coriolanus as an outstanding example of the peculiarly Roman conception of virtue: *virtus,* which is translated "valiantness." The vice that attended and finally defeated this salient quality was "willfulness." Plutarch's contrasting parallel is the career of Alcibiades, whose ingratiating suppleness —like Antony's—throws the intransigent arrogance of Coriolanus into bold relief. That the latter was brought up by his widowed mother, and was chiefly animated by the desire to please her, Plutarch is at pains to emphasize.

Shakespeare follows Plutarch so very closely that he often echoes the phraseology of the magnificent Elizabethan translation by Sir Thomas North. Volumnia's plea to her son in Act V, eloquently massive as it is, is scarcely more than a metrical adaptation of North's prose. On the other hand, her appeal to him in Act III is Shakespeare's interpolation; he has reserved his right to modify and augment his material in the interests of psychological motivation and dramatic equilibrium; and those two interventions of Volumnia, in each case changing the mind of Coriolanus, are the turning-points of the plot. Rhetoric, the art of persuasion, determined not only the style but also the structure of *Julius Caesar:* Cassius persuades Brutus, Brutus persuades the people, Mark Antony persuades them otherwise. *Coriolanus* is not less Roman in its recourse to public speech; and speech-making triumphs ironically over war-mongering; but now the forensic mode is that of dissuasion. The candidate actually dissuades the people from voting for him; the general at length is dissuaded from pursuing his revenge. His vein is negation: curses, threats, and invectives from first to last. Once he rallies his men; many times he scolds them. When he girds the gods, his rant sounds more like the misanthropic Timon than the iconoclastic Tamburlaine. Yet how narrowly it misses the tone of Hotspur!

Coriolanus to the contrary, the word is not "mildly." The language of the play reverberates with the dissonance of its subject-matter and the thunder-like percussion of its protagonist. The words are so tensely involved in the situation that they do not lend themselves much to purple passages or quotations out of context. Reflecting a stylistic transition, they seem to combine the serried diction of Shakespeare's middle period with the flowing rhythm of his later plays. The speeches frequently begin and break off in the middle of a line; but the cadence of the blank verse persists through occasional setbacks; and sometimes the overlapping pentameters are more evident to the ear than on the page. This has been a problem for editors, many of whom have regarded the difficulties of the text as invitations to change it. The present edition assumes that the unique redaction of *Coriolanus,* which has come down to us through the folios, is more or less authoritative; and that, except for some obvious readjustments and a few unavoidable emendations, it simply needs to be modernized in spelling and punctuation. The original stage directions, which are unusually explicit, convey a suggestion of pageantry commanding the full resources of the resplendent Globe. And from a contemporary sketch of *Titus Andronicus,* we know that the Elizabethans could approximate Roman dress.

Though the scenes march by in swift continuity, moving from camp to camp and faction to faction, the acts are sharply divided, as if to stress the division among the characters. Act I presents the hero in his proper field of action, the battlefield, where heroism can be demonstrated in its simplest terms as valiantness. Act II brings him reluctantly home to his triumph, and even more grudgingly into the electoral campaign. This goes against him in Act III and leads, after another disastrous attempt at propitiation, to the decree of banishment. Act IV pursues the exiled Coriolanus traversing the distance between Rome and Antium, and betraying himself and his fellow Romans to the Volscian general, Aufidius. Act V witnesses his capitulation and consummates his tragedy: military commitment, resisting civic pressure, yields to domestic. Throughout these vicissitudes he sustains his predominating role, the central figure when he is on stage, the topic of discussion when he is not. His monolithic character is measured by no single foil of comparable stature— least of all by his rival, Aufidius, who has failed to square accounts with him honorably, and vowed to do so through dishonorable means if necessary—but by his dynamic relations with all the others, on the diverging levels of family, city, and enemy.

The one is accordingly weighted against the many; and the tendency toward monodrama is counterpoised by an unusual number of choric roles—citizens, officers, soldiers, servants, other ranks of society. The scales tip during the roadside interview between a Roman and a Volscian, with its implication that Coriolanus is taking the same road to espionage and betrayal. As for the populace, the tribunes can hardly speak for it because it is so vocal on its own behalf; the mistake of Coriolanus is to believe that its "voices" are merely votes. Generalization soon breaks down into Hob and Dick, and the types are individualized, loudly insisting upon their individuality. There are some ugly mob-scenes and one violent outbreak of street-fighting, but mother-wit is the characteristic weapon. The humorous mediator, Menenius Agrippa, can handle this pithy prose idiom. The crowd in turn can rise to the pitch of blank verse, while their shrewd heckling enlivens his tale of the belly and the members. The First Citizen, great toe though he may be, accepts the question-begging metaphor that identifies the organ of digestion with the deliberation of the Senate. But, logically enough, he presses the claims of the other parts, including the soldierly arm. The parable will apply to the choleric hero as much as to the angry mob.

In a subsequent argument, when Coriolanus is compared to a disease, Menenius retorts that he is rather a diseased limb which can be cured. By this time many sores and wounds have been metaphorically and literally probed, thereby revealing other aspects of the body politic. The

age-old fable expounded by Menenius, appeasing the uproar of the intro-
ductory scene, has served to establish an ideal of social order—the concept of commonweal, *res publica*—more honored in the breach than the
observance. It has also concretely grounded the imagery of the play in
the matter at hand, the dearth of corn, the fundamental problem of nour-
ishment. The struggling classes seek to feed on each other; Menenius is
a self-confessed epicure; the poor justify themselves by hungry proverbs;
and Coriolanus finds himself in their desperate position when he appears
at the feast of Aufidius. In close association with these images of food, battle is described as if it were harvest, with the swords of destruction figu-
ratively turning into the ploughshares of fertility. Another associated
train of thought runs to animals, always an inspiration for name-calling.
The hero is introduced as a dog to the people, who are curs to him then
and crucially later. The prevailing code is dog-eat-dog.

Menenius points the moral succinctly when he demands: "On both
sides more respect." Since both sides indulge in such embittered polemics,
interpretation has varied between the extremes of left and right, now un-
derlining the dangers of dictatorship and now the weaknesses of democ-
racy, according to the political adherence of the interpreters. Nothing
could better attest what Coleridge, in this connection, called "the won-
derful philosophic impartiality in Shakespeare's politics." His portrayal
of the multitude, whose sedition he arms with a grievance, is anti-dema-
gogic rather than anti-democratic. The demagogues are the tribunes,
portrayed in unequivocal cynicism, dissuading the plebs from the suf-
frage they have already pledged to Coriolanus. Coriolanus, on his side,
is no friend of the people; and it is to the credit of his integrity that he
cannot act a part he does not feel. He earns, with an authoritarian vengeance, the title that Ibsen would bestow in irony upon his humanitarian
Dr. Stockmann—*An Enemy of the People*. All men are enemies, rivals
if not foes, to Coriolanus. His aggressive temperament could never be
happy until it had lurched all other swords of the garland. His fight
against the world is not for booty nor praise nor office, but for acknowl-
edged superiority; he does not want to dominate but to excel; and he
cannot bear the thought of subordination.

We need not look far afield for the school that nurtured that spirit of
single-minded competitiveness. The Roman matron, the masculine dow-
ager, the statuesque Volumnia, is both father and mother to her son; and
she has taught him aristocratic scorn along with martial courage. His
wife, the gracious Virgilia, in contrast is sheer femininity; and her main
attribute, like Cordelia's, is silence. His young son chases butterflies with
congenital resolution; subsequently Coriolanus commands a Volscian
army as eager as boys chasing butterflies. No man can withstand him
and only one woman can plead with him. In yielding to her, in feeling
this ultimate modicum of feminine tenderness, the strong man becomes

again—as it were—a child. Thence the sting in the last taunt of Aufidius. Under the epithet "traitor" Coriolanus has slightly flinched. But "boy!" "Thou boy of tears!" In significant contradistinction, we are reminded continually that the tribunes are elderly men. Leadership, as Volumnia's boy had learned it in the wars, was largely an individual matter of athletic prowess, having little to do with the sort of maturity that peaceful civilian government requires. Perhaps the trouble, as analyzed by Aufidius, lay in a soldier's inability to move "from th' casque to th' cushion." The virtues of war may well be the vices of peace; the man on horseback, dismounted, a sorry creature.

T. S. Eliot's modernized *Coriolan* consists of two poems: "Triumphal March" and "Difficulties of a Statesman." These headings suggest the dilemma of Shakespeare's protagonist. His is not an internal struggle; so far as his two short soliloquies indicate, the treason causes him less mental anguish than the election; and, what is even worse, at Antium he employs the flatteries he has despised at Rome. Rather it is the external manifestation of his colossal pride that exalts him, all but deifies him, and renders the slippery turns of fortune more precipitous than the Tarpeian Rock. "Rome or I! One or the other must fall!" Such is the climax, verbalized by Wagner, to Beethoven's orchestration of this theme. "The note of banishment," the note that James Joyce kept hearing in Shakespeare's plays, is never more plangently sounded than in the parting denunciation of Coriolanus to the Romans: "I banish you!" Never was man more alienated than he, as the gates of Rome close behind him and he is forced to seek "a world elsewhere." The scene reverses his initial triumph, when the gates of Corioli shut him in alone of all the Romans. The ironic pattern is completed, on his return to the hostile town, by his fatal words to its citizens. And note the emphatic position of the first personal pronoun:

> If you have writ your annals true, 'tis there
> That, like an eagle in a dovecote, I
> Fluttered your Volscians in Corioles.
> Alone I did it.

Othello, at a similar moment, had the satisfaction of recalling his services to the state. Caius Marcius—Coriolanus no longer—can only glory in his isolation. The word "alone" is repeated more than in any other Shakespearean work; and, from the welter of similes, the most memorable is "a lonely dragon." We end by realizing the ambiguity of the foreign name this Roman has proudly flaunted. How can he expect it to be anything but a target of hatred for the orphans and widows and comrades-in-arms of men he has killed? After the combat in which he gained it, he had generously tried to befriend a certain Volscian, and had characteristically forgotten the poor man's name—a touch which Shakespeare added to Plutarch's anecdote. Shakespeare's insight, detailed as it is, confirms an observation cited from Plato by Plutarch: that such overriding egoism can only terminate in "desolation." This must be that desolation of solitude which the American imagination has paralleled in the career of another tragic captain, Melville's Ahab.

Chronology of Important Dates

1564 (April 26)	William Shakespeare baptized in Stratford.
1582 (November)	Married to Anne Hathaway.
1583 (May 26)	Baptism of daughter Susanna.
1585 (February 2)	Baptism of twins Hamnet and Judith.
1589-1594	*Titus Andronicus.*
1592	Attacked and defended as actor and playwright in London.
1593-1594	*Venus and Adonis* and *The Rape of Lucrece* dedicated to Southampton.
1594	Joins in forming Lord Chamberlain's company of actors.
c.1595	*Romeo and Juliet.*
1596	Hamnet Shakespeare dies.
1597	New Place in Stratford purchased.
1598	Praised by Francis Meres as leading English playwright.
1599	Applies for right to quarter Arden coat of arms with Shakespeare coat of arms (drawn up for his father in 1596).
c.1599	*Julius Caesar.*
1599	The Globe Playhouse built.
c.1601	*Hamlet.*
1601	John Shakespeare, his father, dies.
1603	Lord Chamberlain's company becomes the King's Men.
c.1604	*Othello.*
c.1605-1606	*Macbeth* and *King Lear.*
c.1607	*Timon of Athens.*
c.1608	*Antony and Cleopatra* and *Coriolanus.*
1609	King's Men acquire the Blackfriars Playhouse.
c.1611-1612	Shakespeare retires to Stratford.
1616 (April 23)	Shakespeare dies.
1623	Collected plays published in Folio.

Notes on the Editor and Authors

ALFRED HARBAGE, the editor, is Cabot Professor of English at Harvard University. He is the General Editor of the *Pelican Shakespeare* and the author of a number of books on Shakespeare and the drama, of which the most recent is *William Shakespeare: A Reader's Guide.*

H. B. CHARLTON was Professor of English at the University of Manchester. His *Shakespearian Comedy,* like his *Shakespearian Tragedy,* enjoys the status of a "standard work."

WILLARD FARNHAM is Professor Emeritus of the University of California at Berkeley and is still active as an editor and visiting lecturer. He is the author of *Shakespeare's Tragic Frontier,* as well as *The Medieval Heritage of Elizabethan Tragedy.*

HEREWARD T. PRICE is Professor Emeritus of Michigan State University and a Fellow of the The Folger Shakespeare Library. He is a lexicographical expert as well as a Renaissance scholar.

DONALD A. STAUFFER was, before his death in 1952, Professor of English and Chairman of the Department at Princeton University. He wrote both historical and critical works of great value.

BRENTS STIRLING is Professor of English at the University of Washington. He is the author of *The Populace in Shakespeare* and *Unity in Shakespearian Tragedy.*

MAYNARD MACK is Professor of English at Yale University. He is the General Editor of *Twentieth Century Views* and the author and editor of other works, including *Essays on Shakespeare and the Elizabethan Drama.*

HELEN GARDNER is a Fellow of St. Hilda's College and Reader in Renaissance English Literature at Oxford University. The author of *The Art of T. S. Eliot* and of works on Donne and the Metaphysical Poets, she has edited the volume on Donne in the Twentieth Century Views Series.

C. S. LEWIS was Professor of Medieval and Renaissance English Literature at Cambridge University and an author and critic of great versatility. He died in 1963.

ALVIN KERNAN is Associate Professor of English at Yale University and the author of a work on Renaissance satire, *The Cankered Muse.*

BERNARD SPIVACK is Professor of English at the University of Massachusetts and the author of a study of English Renaissance drama focused upon the character of the Vice, *Shakespeare and the Allegory of Evil.*

L. C. KNIGHTS is Professor of English at Bristol University. He is the author of *Drama and Society in the Age of Jonson* and a number of other critical works.

FRANCIS FERGUSSON is University Professor of English at Rutgers University. He is the author of *The Idea of a Theatre, Dante's Dream of the Mind,* and other works.

G. WILSON KNIGHT is Professor of English at Leeds University. He is the author of many well-known works on Shakespeare and other literary topics.

ARTHUR SEWELL is Byron Professor of English at the University of Athens. He is the author of *Literature and Society in Shakespeare* and other works.

MARK VAN DOREN is former Professor of English at Columbia University and one of America's most distinguished poets and men of letters.

S. L. BETHELL, poet as well as critic, was until his death Lecturer in English Language and Literature in the University College of South Wales and Monmouthshire.

HARRY LEVIN is Babbit Professor of Comparative Literature at Harvard University. He is the author of *The Overreacher: A Study of Marlowe* and of works on a wide range of literary subjects, most recently *The Gates of Horn,* an analysis of realism in the French novel.

Selected Bibliography

(As with most Shakespearean topics, the literature on the tragedies is copious. The following list includes books only, and with a few exceptions only those which have appeared since the first quarter of the present century. It should be supplemented by the books mentioned in the footnotes and text references of the present anthology.)

I. WORKS TREATING SHAKESPEAREAN TRAGEDY IN GENERAL, OR MORE THAN ONE OF THE MAJOR TRAGEDIES:

Baker, Howard. *Induction to Tragedy.* Baton Rouge: Louisiana State University Press, 1939.

Bradley, A. C. *Shakespearean Tragedy.* London: Macmillan, 1904; reprint, 1950.

Bush, Geoffrey. *Shakespeare and the Natural Condition.* Cambridge: Harvard University Press, 1956.

Campbell, Lily B. *Shakespeare's Tragic Heroes: Slaves of Passion.* New York: Cambridge University Press, 1930.

Chambers, E. K. *Shakespeare, a Survey.* London: Macmillan, 1925.

Cunningham, J. V. *Woe or Wonder: The Emotional Effect of Shakesperean Tragedy.* Denver: University of Denver Press, 1951.

Farnham, Willard. *Shakespeare's Tragic Frontier: The World of His Final Tragedies.* Berkeley: University of California Press, 1950.

Granville-Barker, Harley. *Prefaces to Shakespeare.* 2 vols. Princeton: Princeton University Press, 1946-47.

Harbage, Alfred. *Shakespeare: A Reader's Guide.* New York: Farrar, Straus and Co., 1963.

Harrison, G. B. *Shakespeare's Tragedies.* London: Routledge and Kegan Paul, 1951.

Holloway, John. *The Story of the Night.* London: Routledge and Kegan Paul, 1961.

James, D. G. *The Dream of Learning.* Oxford: The Clarendon Press, 1951.

Knight, G. Wilson. *The Imperial Theme.* 3rd ed. London: Methuen, 1951.

Lawlor, John. *The Tragic Sense in Shakespeare.* London: Chatto and Windus, 1960.

Leech, Clifford. *Shakespeare's Tragedies.* London: Chatto and Windus, 1950.

Ribner, Irving. *Patterns in Shakespearian Tragedy.* London: Methuen, 1960.

Rosen, William. *Shakespeare and the Craft of Tragedy*. Cambridge: Harvard University Press, 1960.

Siegel, Paul N. *Shakespearean Tragedy and the Elizabethan Compromise*. New York: New York University Press, 1957.

Spencer, Theodore. *Shakespeare and the Nature of Man*. New York: Macmillan, 1942.

Stoll, Elmer Edgar. *Art and Artifice in Shakespeare*. New York: Cambridge University Press, 1933.

————. *Shakespearean Studies, Historical and Comparative in Method*. New York: G. E. Stechert and Co., 1942.

Traversi, Derek. *An Approach to Shakespeare*. New York: Doubleday, 1956.

Weisinger, Herbert. *Tragedy and the Paradox of the Fortunate Fall*. Michigan State College Press, 1953.

Whitaker, Virgil K. *Shakespeare's Use of Learning*. San Marino, Calif.: The Huntington Library, 1953.

Wilson, Harold S. *On the Design of Shakespearean Tragedy*. Toronto: University of Toronto Press, 1957.

II. THE ROMAN PLAYS:

Bradley, A. C. *Oxford Lectures on Poetry*. London: Macmillan, 1909; reprint, 1950.

Charney, Maurice. *Shakespeare's Roman Plays*. Cambridge: Harvard University Press, 1955.

MacCallum, M. W. *Shakespeare's Roman Plays and Their Background*. London: Macmillan, 1910.

Palmer, John. *Political Characters of Shakespeare*. New York: St. Martin's Press, 1945.

Phillips, James E. *The State in Shakespeare's Greek and Roman Plays*. New York: Columbia University Press, 1940.

Schanzer, Ernest. *The Problem Plays of Shakespeare*. New York: Shocken Books, 1963.

Stirling, Brents. *The Populace in Shakespeare*. New York: Columbia University Press, 1949.

III. HAMLET:

Alexander, Peter. *Hamlet: Father and Son*. Oxford: The Clarendon Press, 1955.

Bowers, Fredson T. *Elizabethan Revenge Tragedy*. Princeton: Princeton University Press, 1940.

Fergusson, Francis. *The Idea of a Theatre*. Princeton: Princeton University Press, 1949.

Grebanier, Bernard D. *The Heart of Hamlet*. New York: W. W. Norton, 1949.

Jones, Ernest. *Hamlet and Oedipus*. New York: W. W. Norton, 1910, 1949.

Knights, L. C. *An Approach to Hamlet*. London: Chatto and Windus, 1960.

Levin, Harry. *The Question of Hamlet*. New York: Oxford University Press, 1959.

Madariaga, Salvador de. *On Hamlet*. London: Hollis and Carter, 1948.

Tillyard, E. M. W. *Shakespeare's Problem Plays*. London: Chatto and Windus, 1951.

Walker, Roy. *The Time Is Out of Joint*. London: A. Dakers, 1948.

Wilson, J. Dover. *What Happens in Hamlet*. New York: Macmillan, 1940.

IV. OTHELLO:

Elliott, G. R. *Flaming Minister*. Durham: Duke University Press, 1953.

Heilman, Robert B. *Magic in the Web: Action and Language in Othello*. Lexington: University of Kentucky Press, 1956.

Rosenberg, Marvin. *The Masks of Othello*. Berkeley: University of California Press, 1961.

V. MACBETH:

Curry, Walter C. *Shakespeare's Philosophical Patterns*. Baton Rouge: Louisiana State University Press, 1937.

Elliott, G. R. *Dramatic Providence in Macbeth*. Princeton: Princeton University Press, 1958.

Paul, Henry N. *The Royal Play of Macbeth*. New York: Macmillan, 1950.

Walker, Roy. *The Time Is Free*. New York: Macmillan, 1949.

VI. KING LEAR:

Danby, John F. *Shakespeare's Doctrine of Nature: A Study of King Lear*. London: Faber and Faber, 1949.

Heilman, Robert B. *This Great Stage: Image and Structure in King Lear*. Baton Rouge: Louisiana State University Press, 1948.

Sewell, Richard B. *The Vision of Tragedy*. New Haven: Yale University Press, 1959.

TWENTIETH CENTURY VIEWS

Forthcoming Titles